Indian Breads

Dr G. Padma Vijay has been a regular freelance writer for the Diet File column in *Femina* as well as the *Times of India* (New Bombay) supplement. She was a nutrition consultant for *Femina's* cookery section for eight years and conducted workshops on diet and nutrition for various ailments. She was also a nutrition counsellor at the Diet Mantra Centre in Mumbai.

She is the author of fourteen books on subjects like cooking, diet, nutrition and quizzing. *A Perfect Cookbook for Pregnant Women and Nursing Mothers* won the 2011 Gourmand International Cookbook Award, in the diet and nutrition category at the country level. *101 Dishes that Enhance Mood & Reduce Stress* was among the three books nominated for the World Best Book Gourmand International Cookbook Award in 2019 and won second place in the World Cookbook Award in the dietary section at Macau.

Indian Breads won the Gourmand India Cookbook Award in the Best Bread Cookbook category, 2015, and was nominated in the same category for the Gourmand World International Cookbook Awards, 2016, Yantai, China.

G. PADMA VIJAY

Indian Breads

A Comprehensive Guide to Traditional
and Innovative Indian Breads

First published by westland ltd in 2015

Published by Westland Books, a division of Nasadiya Technologies Private Limited, in 2023

No. 269/2B, First Floor, 'Irai Arul', Vimalraj Street, Nethaji Nagar, Alapakkam Main Road, Maduravoyal, Chennai 600095

Westland and the Westland logo are the trademarks of Nasadiya Technologies Private Limited, or its affiliates.

ISBN: 9789357769280

10 9 8 7 6 5 4 3 2 1

Design: Seema Sethi

Photographs by: Raveesh

Photographs edited by: Ravi Srinivasan

Printed at HT Media Ltd, Greater Noida

CONTENTS

Introduction	1
Indian Breads	3
Different Types of Indian Breads	7
Guidelines for Indian Breads	17
Nutritional Values of Breads Made with Whole Grain Cereals and Millets	19

VEGETARIAN FLATBREADS — 21

Paratha | Sada Paratha	22
Tava Paratha | Shallow Fried Paratha	23

PAN-FRIED AND TOASTED PARATHAS WITH LEAFY GREENS

Palak Paratha	24
Band Gobi Paratha | Methi Paratha	25
Chini Band Gobi Paratha | Bathua Paratha	26
Sarson Ka Saag Paratha | Gongura Paratha	27

PAN-FRIED AND TOASTED PARATHAS WITH ROOT VEGETABLES

Muli Paratha	28
Gajar Paratha | Chukandar Paratha	29
Shalgam Paratha | Shakharkand Paratha	30

PAN-FRIED AND TOASTED PARATHAS WITH STEM VEGETABLES

Aloo Paratha | Suran Paratha	31
Ganth Gobi Paratha	32

PAN-FRIED AND TOASTED PARATHAS WITH BULBS AND RHIZOMES

Hara Pyaz Paratha | Adrak Paratha | Koki Roti	33
Lassoon Paratha | Hara Lassoon Paratha	34

PAN-FRIED AND TOASTED PARATHAS WITH OTHER VEGETABLES

Phool Gobi Paratha | Mattar Paratha	35
Kela Paratha | Shimla Mirch Paratha	36
Lauki Paratha | Petha Paratha	37
Shahi Sabji Paratha | Kacha Aam Paratha	38

PAN-FRIED AND TOASTED PARATHAS WITH HERBS

Hara Dhania Paratha	39
Pudina Paratha | Parsley Paratha | Celery Paratha	40

PAN-FRIED AND TOASTED PARATHAS WITH DAIRY PRODUCTS

Makhan Paratha	41
Cheese Paratha | Cheese-Paneer-Lal Mirch Paratha	42
Paneer Paratha | Kashmiri Paratha	43
Hara Sabji-Paneer Paratha	44

PAN-FRIED AND TOASTED PARATHAS WITH SEEDS AND SPICES

Til Paratha | Kalonji Paratha | Ajwain Paratha	46
Bhopla Paratha | Alsi Paratha | Khas-Khas Paratha | Saunf Paratha	47
Masala Paratha	48

PAN-FRIED AND TOASTED PARATHAS WITH NUTS

Badam Paratha | Mungphali Paratha | Kaju Paratha | Akhrot Paratha | Pista Paratha ... 49

OTHER PAN-FRIED AND TOASTED PARATHAS

Tofu-Hara Pyaz Paratha ... 50

Soya-Hara Mattar Paratha | Khumb Paratha ... 51

Teekha, Meetha and Khatta Paratha | Sabji Paratha ... 52

Palak-Paneer Paratha | Methi-Aloo Paratha ... 53

Makkai-Pudina Paratha | Kopra Paratha ... 54

Nariyal Paratha | Fruit Paratha ... 55

LACHHA PARATHAS (MULTILAYERED FLATBREADS)

Sada Lachha Paratha ... 56

Makhan Lachha Paratha | Hara Bhaji Lachha Paratha ... 57

Amritsari Lachha Paratha | Paneer Lachha Paratha ... 58

Kasoori Methi Lachha Paratha | Masala Tikadia ... 59

Satpuro Phulko ... 60

TANDOORI & TAVA ROTIS (BAKED & TOASTED FLATBREADS)

Makhan Tandoori Roti | Malai Tandoori Roti ... 62

Khamiri Roti ... 63

Khooba Roti | Kashmiri Roti ... 64

CHAPATTIS (PAN-FRIED FLATBREADS)

Dough for Chapattis | Ghee Chapatti ... 65

Sada Chapatti | Lassoon Chutney Chapatti ... 66

Butter Chapatti | Adrak Chutney Chapatti ... 67

Madakku Chapatti ... 68

PHULKAS (FIRE-ROASTED PUFFED FLATBREADS)

Dough for Phulkas | Phulka ... 69

Pad Roti ... 70

THEPLAS (THIN FLATBREADS)

Sada Thepla | Methi Thepla | Doodhi Thepla | Muli Thepla ... 71

BHAKRIS (SMALL FLATBREADS)

Methi Bhakri | Sada Bhakri ... 72

PURI (FRIED PUFED FLATBREAD)

Dough for Puris | Sada Puri ... 73

Pudina Puri | Tomato Puri | Methi Puri | Masala Puri ... 74

Palak Puri | Pakwan ... 75

Bedmi Puri ... 76

Mung Dal Puri ... 77

Besan Puri ... 78

FLATBREADS MADE WITH REFINED WHEAT FLOUR

NAAN (BAKED FLATBREAD)

Cheese Naan | Dough for Naans | Butter Naan ... 80

Sada Naan | Cheese-Lal Mirch Naan | Lassoon Naan | Til Naan ... 81

Amritsari Naan | Kashmiri Naan ... 82

Sheermal ... 83

KULCHAS (BAKED ROUND FLATBREADS)

Dough for Kulchas | Sada Kulcha ... 84

Butter Kulcha | Pyaz Kulcha | Hara Dhania Khulcha | Kasoori Methi Kulcha ... 85

Masala Kulcha | Paneer Kulcha |
Cheese-Lal Mirch Kulcha　86

PAROTTAS (FLAKY, FLUFFY FLATBREADS)

Dough for Parottas　87

Malabar Parotta | Veechu Parotta　88

OTHER FLATBREADS MADE WITH REFINED FLOUR

Tandoori Roti | Roomali Roti　90

Sada Mughlai Lachha Paratha |
Reshmi Paratha　91

FRIED FLATBREADS MADE WITH REFINED WHEAT FLOUR

Bhatura　92

Luchi | Matarshutir Kachori　93

Aloo Kachori | Radhaballabhi　94

FLATBREADS MADE WITH REFINED WHEAT FLOUR AND SEMOLINA

Khasta Roti　95

Khasta Puri　96

FLATBREDS MADE WITH RICE FLOUR

Malabar Ari Pathiri | Coconut Pathiri　97

Ney Pathiri | Masala Orotti | Orotti　98

Tandlachi Bhakri | Rice Puri　99

Biyyamu Roti | Brown Rice Roti　100

Akki Otti　101

FLATBREADS MADE WITH MAIZE FLOUR

Makkai Ki Roti | Masala Makkai Roti |
Methi Makkai Roti　102

Stuffed Corn Roti　103

Tikkar　104

FLATBREADS MADE WITH BARLEY FLOUR

Jau Roti | Herby Barley-Pearl Millet Roti |
Jau Paratha　105

FLATBREADS MADE WITH OAT FLOUR

Oats Roti | Oats Missi Roti | Veggie Oats-
Barley Roti　106

FLATBREADS MADE WITH RYE FLOUR

Rye Roti | Rye Paratha　107

FLATBREADS MADE WITH PEARL MILLET (BAJRA) FLOUR

Sada Bajra Roti　108

Bajra-Aloo Roti | Soya-Paneer-Bajra Roti　109

FLATBREADS MADE WITH SORGHUM (JOWAR) FLOUR

Jowar Roti | Jowar-Bajra Roti |
Hara Jowar-Oats Roti　110

FLATBREADS MADE WITH FINGER MILLET (RAGI/MANDUA) FLOUR

Ragi/Mandua Roti | Mandua Ki Roti　111

Tofu-Ragi/Mandua Roti | Gahat Dal Bhara
Mandua Roti　112

FLATBREADS MADE WITH LESSER KNOWN MILLET FLOURS

Korralu Roti | Kangini-Aloo Roti　113

Sama Roti | Kutti-Aloo Roti | Varagulu Roti | Barri-
Aloo Roti　114

Shama/Jhangora Roti | Shama/Jhangora-Aloo
Roti | Arikalu Roti | Kodra-Aloo Roti　115

FLATBREADS MADE WITH MULTIGRAIN FLOUR (WHEAT, RICE, SORGHUM, MILLETS, OATS, PULSES AND SOYA BEAN)

Multigrain Rotlo — 116

Masala Multigrain Roti | Multigrain Rotli/Phulka | Multigrain Stuffed Paratha — 117

Mixed Hara Bhaji Paratha | Chota Bhuta Paratha | Aloo-Cheese Paratha — 118

Aloo-Gobi Paratha | Aloo-Palak Paratha | Tomato-Pyaz Paratha | Aloo-Paneer Paratha — 119

Thalipeeth | Dhapate — 120

Vada — 121

FLATBREADS MADE WITH WHEAT FLOUR AND LEGUME/PULSE FLOUR

Missi Roti — 122

Rajma Roti | Kabuli Chana Paratha — 123

Sattu Paratha — 124

Chana Dal Paratha — 125

Mung Dal Paratha — 126

Choori Ka Paratha | Urad Dal Paratha — 127

Dal Dhokli — 128

Paneer-Cheese Paratha | Herb Paratha — 129

Mixed Root Vegetable Paratha | Mixed Stem Vegetable Paratha — 130

NON-VEGETARIAN FLATBREADS — 131

EGG FLATBREADS

Anda Paratha — 132

Anda Naan | Anda Roll | Egg Cone — 133

Egg Wraps — 134

Bihari Kabab Roll | Mughlai Anda Lachha Paratha — 135

Sada Baida Roti — 136

Cheese Baida Roti | Paneer Baida Roti — 137

SEAFOOD FLATBREADS

Chemeen Paratha — 138

Meen Pathiri — 139

Meen Orotti — 140

CHICKEN FLATBREADS

Shahi Murgh Paratha — 141

Murgh Baida Roti — 142

Chicken Orotti — 143

MUTTON FLATBREADS

Kheema Naan — 144

Mughlai Kheema Paratha — 145

Punjabi Kheema Paratha — 146

Mutton Baida Roti — 147

Erachi Pathiri | Erachi Orotti — 148

SWEET FLATBREADS — 149

SWEET FLATBREADS MADE WITH WHOLEWHEAT FLOUR

Meethi Roti — 150

Vedmi — 151

Sweet Biscuit Bhakri | Mixed Dal Poli — 152

Mung Dal Halwa Poli | Gajar Halwa Poli — 153

Masoor Dal Halwa Poli | Chukandar Halwa Poli — 154

Shakharkand Halwa Poli | Corn Halwa Poli — 155

Sooji Halwa Poli | Gud Poli | Chini Paratha | Meetha Nut Paratha — 156

Meetha Beej Paratha | Meetha Paneer Paratha | Meetha Narial Paratha | Til-Gud Ki Roti — 157

Sada Gud Ki Roti | Kutti | Chapatti Cone with Chopped Fruits — 158

Mitho Loli | Chapatti Cone with Fruit Yogurt — 159

Churma | Sweet Egg Toast — 160

SWEET FLATBREADS MADE WITH REFINED WHEAT FLOUR

Puran Poli 161

Puran Puri 162

Sweet Mattiri 163

Shahi Meetha Paratha 164

Bakar Khani 165

Mawa Kachori 166

Malpuas 167

Khajoor Ni Ghari 168

Sweet Puris 169

SWEET FLATBREADS MADE WITH RICE FLOUR

Taftan 170

Chatti Pathiri 171

Churuttu 172

Ellada 173

Ariselu | Kemenya Roti 174

Meetha Pitha 175

FLATBREADS AS SNACKS 176

FLATBREAD SNACKS MADE WITH WHOLEWHEAT FLOUR

KHAKRA (CRISP, THIN FLATBREAD)

Sada Khakra 177

Masala Khakra | Kasoori Methi Khakra | Methi Khakra | Pudina Khakra 178

SAVOURY BISCUIT BHAKRIS (THICK, SMALL BISCUITS)

Jeera Biscuit Bhakri 179

Jeera Biscuit Bhakri Open Sandwich | Kasoori Methi Biscuit Bhakri | Kasoori Methi Biscuit Bhakri Open Sandwich 180

Kalonji Biscuit Bhakri | Kalonji Biscuit Bhakri Open Sandwich | Paratha Sandwich 181

Paratha Pizza with Mixed Sprouts 182

Soya Cutlet Chapatti Wrap | Paratha Pizza with Mixed Vegetables 183

Corn and Chickpea Roll | Chapatti Cone with Spicy Capsicum 184

Chapatti Cone with Teekha Paneer | Chapatti Cone with Brown Rice, Mixed Sprouts and Vegetables 185

Namkeen Pitha 186

Littis 187

Baati 188

Mattar Baati | Bafla 189

FLATBREAD SNACKS MADE WITH REFINED WHEAT FLOUR

Jeera Mattiri 190

Khasta Kachori 191

Masala Mattiri | Kasoori Methi Mattiri 192

FLATBREAD SNACKS MADE WITH OTHER FLOURS

Bajra Khakra 192

Makkai Mathri | Soya Khakra | Ragi/Mandua Khakra 193

Multigrain Khakra | Jowar Baati | Besan Mathri 194

Soya-Paneer Paratha 195

Parsi Bhakra 196

FLATBREAD SNACKS MADE WITH SEMOLINA AND REFINED WHEAT FLOUR

Dahi Batata Puri | Flat Puris 197

Farsi Puri | Sev Puri | Sev Batata Puri 198

Puris with Sprouts or Spicy Vegetables | Dahi Batata Puri 199

Small Puffed Puris | Sprout Puri | Pani Puri 200

FLATBREAD SNACKS MADE WITH RICE FLOUR

Kuzhalappam — 201

Odappalu — 202

FLATBREADS AS FASTING FOODS — 203

FASTING FLATBREADS MADE WITH BUCKWHEAT (KUTTU) FLOUR

Kuttu Paratha — 204

Kuttu Puri — 205

FASTING FLATBREADS MADE WITH AMARANTH (RAJGIRA) FLOUR

Rajgira Paratha | Rajgira Puri — 206

FASTING FLATBREADS MADE WITH SAGO (SABUDANA) FLOUR

Sabudana Puri | Sabudana Thalipeeth — 207

FASTING FLATBREADS MADE WITH WATER CHESTNUT (SINGHADA) FLOUR

Singhada Roti | Singhada Puri — 208

PAV (SOFT BREAD)

Pav — 209

Brown Pav | Buttered Pav | Cheese Pav | Paneer Pav — 210

Pav Bhaji — 211

Paneer Pav Bhaji | Cheese Pav Bhaji | Pav with Mixed Sprouts | Usal Pav — 212

Vada Pav — 213

Misal Pav | Cheese Vada Pav | Vegetable Patty Pav | Batata Bhajjia Pav — 214

Samosa Pav — 215

Pyaz Bhajjia Pav | Pav Sandwich — 216

Dabeli with Potato Patty | Dabeli with Vegetable Patty — 217

DISHES SERVED WITH INDIAN BREADS — 218

Sooji Halwa — 218

Tava Bhaji | Sweet, Sour and Pungent Chutney | Tomato Chutney — 219

Mughlai Baingan Masala — 220

Navratan Korma — 221

Shimla Mirch Ka Salan — 222

Kadhai Sabji — 223

Bhindi Masala — 224

Kolhapuri Sabji — 225

Hara Soya-Paneer Masala — 226

Mixed Sprouts — 227

Gahat Ki Dal — 228

Sindhi Dal to Serve with Pakwan — 229

Usal — 230

Dal Makhani — 231

Dal Tadka — 232

Panchmel Dal — 233

Anda Curry — 234

Makhani Murgh — 235

Mutton Masala — 236

GLOSSARY OF INGREDIENTS — 237

INTRODUCTION

ndia is a land of several regions, religions, castes, culture, languages and cuisines. The cuisines of India are influenced by physical locations, such as proximity to the sea, mountains or deserts, the seasons and the availability of ingredients. They are tongue-tickling, providing contrasts in colour, flavour and textures. Traditional foods prepared in the different parts of the country are diverse and this holds true for Indian breads, which are an important part of an Indian meal.

Indian flatbreads differ from Western bread loaves. A flatbread is made with a mixture of flour, salt and water which is kneaded thoroughly to form a pliable dough. A little fat is often added to the dough to make the bread softer. The dough is divided into portions, rolled out on a lightly floured board into circles or triangles and are toasted on a hot pan, baked in a tandoor (clay oven) or even fried. Most flatbreads are unleavened and can be sweet or savoury.

The soil and climate in north India are suitable for wheat. It is the staple diet there, and flatbreads are made with wholewheat and refined flour. Flatbreads made with wheat flour are also popular in western and central India.

Those made with millet flours, such as pearl millet (bajra), sorghum (jowar) and finger millet (ragi/mandua), are consumed in the west, as the land and climate are suitable for growing that crop. They are called by different names in different parts of India — rotis in Rajasthan, north India and south India; bhakris in Maharashtra; rotlos in Gujarat.

Maize grows in Punjab and Rajasthan and maize flour flatbread are made here.

Rice is the staple diet for several Indians, particularly in south, east and northeast India. It is served with many dishes and is prepared in various forms, including flatbreads. Short-grained rice (colam) is preferred in south India and is ground into flour for flatbreads as well.

The north Indian parathas, rotis and naans differ considerably from south Indian pathiris and orottis, while the similarities in the flatbreads in different regions clearly showcase the unity in diversity of Indian culture and food. For example, the north Indian lachha paratha is similar to the south Indian parotta, while the Marathi phulka is like the Gujarati rotli.

While writing this book, I have retained the original recipes for the traditional Indian breads. I was offered several recipes for the same breads by my friends and I have balanced the ingredients of the different versions. Since the book contains traditional recipes, health tips are given for those items that are high in fat and calories. These can change eating habits. I have also included some innovative, nutritious and wholesome Indian breads in the book.

G. Padma Vijay

INDIAN BREADS

reads and rice contribute to the carbohydrate intake in the Indian diet and are consumed with dishes rich in other macronutrients (fats and protein) and micronutrients (vitamins and minerals).

Flours Used to Make Flatbreads

Flatbreads are made with whole and refined wheat flours, rice flour, millet flours, multigrain flours and flour from pulses. Multigrain flours include different cereals, millets, pulses and legumes.

Plain and Stuffed Flatbreads

Flatbreads are served plain or stuffed with a variety of fillings such as vegetables, dairy products, nuts, seeds, pulses, chutneys, eggs and meat. Hyderabad (Andhra Pradesh), Lucknow (Uttar Pradesh), Awadh (Uttar Pradesh), Jaipur (Rajasthan), Udaipur (Rajasthan) and Kashmir (Jammu and Kashmir) are influenced by Mughlai cuisine which is reflected in their flatbreads stuffed with meats. Stuffed flatbreads, in fact, are one-dish meals.

Dough to Make Flatbreads

The dough can be prepared in 5 mins using a food processor or manually. Cold water is used for doughs made with wheat flour, whereas hot water is required for rice and millet flours to increase binding as they lack gluten. Most flatbreads, such as parathas, chapattis and phulkas, are made with unleavened dough where no leavening agents — yeast, baking soda, baking powder — are used. Some — naan and Mughlai lachha paratha — need a leavening agent.

The dough should be kneaded thoroughly to make soft flatbreads. Unleavened dough must be left to rest for 20-30 mins. Leavened dough needs to rise for an hour or more. In both cases, knead the dough once again before rolling it out.

Most Indian flatbreads are cooked just before serving. The dough can be prepared in advance and refrigerated. Bring it out 30 mins before cooking so that it comes to room temperature. A little fat is often kneaded into the dough to make it softer.

Rolling the Dough

Most flatbreads made with wheat and rice flour are rolled with a rolling pin on a lightly floured board, whereas millet flour breads are flattened between the palms of the hands or pressed on a greased baking sheet with the fingertips. This is because dough made with millet flours has a tendency to break owing to lack of gluten and a high fibre content. If millet flours are mixed with wholewheat flour in equal quantities, the dough can be rolled.

Cooking Techniques

Most flatbreads, such as parathas, chapattis and theplas, are toasted on a hot griddle with a little oil, ghee or white butter. Parathas are also shallow-fried. Others like rotis and naans are baked in a tandoor (clay oven). Some, like puris, luchis and bhaturas are deep-fried in oil. Phulkas are first cooked on a hot griddle and then put directly on an open flame so they puff up. Today, flatbreads are toasted in non-stick pans without oil, and electric tandoors or regular ovens are used.

Shape, Size, Texture and Taste

Flatbreads in north Indian and Mughlai cuisines are large and thick, whereas those in west India are small or medium-sized and thin. Flatbreads in south India are medium-sized and of medium thickness.

The shape, size and texture of a flatbread depend on the amount of dough used, patience in making the bread and the cooking techniques employed. They can be circular, oval, triangular and even square shaped. Lachha parathas, tava parathas, parottas and bhaturas are 8" to 12" in diameter, while sada or stuffed parathas, phulkas, chapattis, theplas and breads made with millet flours are 5" to

6″ wide. Puris, luchis and the bhakris of Gujarati cuisine are 2½″ to 3″, while the puris used in chaat (street food) are 1″ to 1½″ in diameter.

Flatbreads are thin or thick, soft or crisp and flaky or firm, depending on the cooking technique used. Phulkas and theplas are soft and thin, while khakras are very thin and crisp. Flatbreads used for chaat are also crisp. Lachha parathas and parottas are flaky, fluffy; also, like bhaturas, they are thick. Some flatbreads such as phulkas and chapattis are single-layered, while parathas have a few layers and lachha parathas and parottas are multilayered depending on the number of times the dough is folded while rolling it.

Serving Flatbreads

Flatbreads are served at breakfast, lunch and dinner, particularly where wheat and millets form the staple diet. Khakras and puris for chaat are served as snacks with tea.

They are usually served with a pickle, onion rings, lime wedges and plain curd or raita; or with gravied pulses and legumes or vegetarian or non-vegetarian curries.

DIFFERENT TYPES OF INDIAN BREADS

Breads Made with Wholewheat Flour

Paratha: Pan-fried, unleavened flatbreads, parathas have a few layers and are slightly thick. They are toasted on a hot pan with a little oil or ghee or are shallow-fried. Parathas are consumed in the north Indian states, especially Punjab. They are often smeared with home-made white butter or cream before serving.

Lachha Paratha: Lachha parathas or lachedhar parathas are unleavened, round, multilayered flatbreads that are cooked on a hot pan and are popular in Punjabi cuisine.

Chapatti: Unleavened flatbreads with 1-2 layers, chapattis are thicker than phulkas and thinner than parathas. They are toasted on a hot pan with a little oil. Chapattis are served in western India, especially in Maharashtra.

Tandoori Roti: Tandoori rotis are prepared with an unleavened dough. They are smaller and thicker than chapattis and are cooked in a clay oven. They are popular in north India, especially Punjab.

Khamiri Roti: These are leavened, thick, spongy flatbreads from Mughlai cuisine.

Phulka: Unleavened, single-layered flatbreads, phulkas are thinner than chapattis and parathas and are eaten in Maharashtra. The rotlis of Gujarat are similar to phulkas.

Thepla: Theplas are unleavened flatbreads, toasted on a hot pan with oil. They are thinner than phulkas and are popular in Gujarat. They are also called dhebras.

Bhakri: Toasted, puffed, unleavened flatbreads, bhakris are thin and small and served in Gujarati cuisine.

Biscuit Bhakri: Sweet or savoury biscuit bhakris from Gujarat and Rajasthan are unleavened, thick, crisp flatbreads.

Puri: Deep-fried, puffed, unleavened, small and round, puris can be plain or stuffed and are served in most Indian cuisines.

Khakra: Khakras are unleavened, thin, crisp flatbreads, toasted, till all the water content evaporates. They are served in Gujarati cuisine as a breakfast dish or an evening snack with spiced tea.

Hard or Soft Bread Balls Served in Dal or Vegetable Gravies: Hard bread balls, such as littis and baatis, and soft ones, like baflas, are unleavened breads. Littis (stuffed with roasted gram flour) are served in Bihar, while baatis and baflas are popular in Rajasthani cuisine and are served with a dal.

Sweet Flatbreads: Several sweet flatbreads in the form of rotis, parathas (plain or stuffed with sweetened pulses, vegetables, dried fruits, semolina or dairy products) are made with wholewheat flour. These include meethi roti, vedmi, poli, mitho loli, kutti and gud roti.

Breads Made with Refined Wheat Flour

Naan: Naans are leavened flatbreads, popular in north India, especially Punjab, and are served with curries. They can be oval or triangular. Rolled out with a rolling pin, they are thinner than kulchas and are cooked in a tandoor.

Kulcha: Leavened flatbreads, kulchas, are consumed in north India, especially Punjab. Kulcha chana is a famous dish in this part of India, where any type of kulcha is served with chickpea curry. Kulchas are round, pressed or patted with the palms and are thicker than naans. They are also cooked in a tandoor.

Tandoori Roti: Tandoori rotis served in restaurants are leavened flatbreads made with refined wheat flour, cooked in a tandoor.

Roomali Roti: Served in Mughlai cuisine, roomali rotis are very thin and large, leavened flatbreads folded like a handkerchief. At home, they are stretched with the fingers and toasted on the reverse side of a tava or wok. In restaurants, the partially rolled out dough is rotated and thrown up in the air to increase the size.

Lachha Paratha: Lachha parathas served in restaurants are leavened flatbreads made with refined wheat flour. Leavened or unleavened lachha parathas are popular in Mughlai cuisine. They are triangular shaped in eastern India.

Parottas: Soft, layered, unleavened flatbreads, parottas are served in the south Indian states of Kerala, Tamil Nadu and Karnataka and the east Indian state of West Bengal. They are made with plenty of ghee. Parottas, especially egg parottas (muttai parottas), are a familiar street food in all these states of south India. They are also served at marriages and festive occasions. Parottas are usually served with a spicy curry and onion slices. South Indian parottas are similar to north Indian lachha parathas.

Mughlai Paratha: Mughlai parathas are leavened flatbreads stuffed with a vegetarian or non-vegetarian filling and deep-fried.

Luchi: Luchis are unleavened small, round fried flatbreads served in Bengal.

Kachori: Stuffed luchis are called kachoris in Bengal.

Bhatura: Bhaturas are leavened, large, soft, fried flatbreads. They are served with spicy chickpeas (chana bhatura) in north India — a great favourite.

Mattiri: Leavened, fried, crisp flatbreads flavoured with spices such as cumin seeds, mattiris are consumed as snacks during festivals in Punjab and are similar to the Rajasthani mathris.

Sweet Flatbreads: Sweet flatbreads, similar to those made with wholewheat flour are also made with refined flour. These include puran poli, puran puri, mattiri, sheermal, malpua and bhakar khani.

Breads Made with Refined Wheat Flour and Semolina

Several flatbreads are made with a combination of wheat flour and semolina.

Khasta Roti: Khasta rotis are leavened flatbreads cooked in a tandoor and popular in Rajasthani cuisine.

Khasta Puri: These are unleavened, small, round flatbreads, deep-fried in oil and consumed in Rajasthani cuisine.

Small Flat Puris: Unleavened flatbreads, these puris are used in the preparation of chaat items, such as sev puri, dahi batata puri, etc.

Small Puffed Puris: Small, puffed puris are unleavened flatbreads used in the preparation of chaat items such as pani puri.

Farsi Puri: These are crisp, thick, fried flatbreads, served as a snack in Gujarat.

Bhakra: Bhakras are fried flatbreads served as a snack in Parsi cuisine.

Breads Made with Rice Flour

Pathiri: Unleavened, thin, soft flatbreads, pathiris are popular in Kerala, especially when coconut is added to the flour. They are toasted on a pan but can also be fried. They are served with non-vegetarian curries.

Orotti: Orottis are unleavened flatbreads consumed in Kerala. They are thicker than pathiris as they are flattened with the hand. They are stuffed with fish, chicken and minced meat.

Chaval Bhakri or Roti: These are unleavened flatbreads in Marathi cuisine. Biyyamu rotis, made with rice flour in Andhra Pradesh, are similar.

Puris: Puris are also made with rice flour.

Odappalu: These are unleavened, deep-fried flatbreads from Andhra Pradesh.

Khuzaalappam: These are unleavened, deep-fried flatbreads served in Kerala.

Sweet Flatbreads: Several sweet flatbreads are made with rice flour, including taftan, chatty pathiri, churuttu, ellada, ariselu and pitha.

Breads Made with Other Grains

Several flatbreads are made with other whole grain cereals such as maize (corn), barley, oats and rye. These contain less gluten than wheat and are slightly crisp.

They also do not puff up as easily. However, their texture improves when they are made with equal parts of wholewheat flour.

While making the dough from these grains, it is not necessary to use warm or hot water when it is kneaded. Nor is it necessary to sprinkle water on the surface of the breads while toasting them, as they contain some gluten.

Makkai ki Roti: Makkai ki roti is an unleavened flatbread made with maize flour. It is served in Punjab in the winter with sarson ka saag (mustard greens).

Barley Roti: These unleavened flatbreads are not popular but are good for diabetics.

Oats Roti: Oats rotis are unleavened flatbreads. White or rolled oats comprise only the seed coat and have no free flour, so they are made with an equal portion of wheat flour. Again, this flatbread is not popular, but is good for diabetics.

Rye Roti: Unleavened flatbreads, rye rotis have a high fibre content. Awareness about this grain is increasing in India and its importance is rising. Rye breads are popular in Europe.

Tikkar: Tikkars are unleavened flatbreads made with a combination of maize and wheat flours in Rajasthan.

Breads Made with Millet Flours

Flatbreads made with millet flours — pearl millet (bajra), sorghum (jowar), finger millet (ragi/mandua) — are served plain or stuffed with vegetables and dairy products. Lesser known millets such as foxtail millet (kangni), little millet (kutti), Indian barnyard millet (jhangora), kodo millet (kodra) and white or proso millet (barri) are also used. Millet flour breads are popular in the rural areas of India.

While kneading a millet flour dough, warm salted water is added to the flour. While toasting the flatbread on the pan, the upper surface is evenly sprinkled with 1 tbsp of water and flipped over only after the water evaporates.

Bajra Roti or Bhakri: These unleavened flatbreads are made with pearl millet flour in Maharashtra, Gujarat, Rajasthan and Karnataka. The rotis are toasted on a hot pan without any fat, but smeared with ghee just before serving. It is a staple diet during the winter months. Khakra, the Gujarati crisp flatbread, is also made with pearl millet flour.

Jowar Roti or Bhakri: Jowar rotis or bhakris are unleavened flatbreads made with sorghum flour. They are consumed in summer with a gram flour curry called pitla and a green chutney in Maharashtra, Rajasthan and some parts of Karnataka as jolada rotis, and as jonna rotis in Andhra Pradesh. Hard breads made with sorghum flour, called baatis, are served in the tribal communities of Andhra Pradesh.

Ragi Roti or Bhakri: Ragi rotis or nachni bhakris are unleavened flatbreads made with finger millet or red millet flour in Maharashtra. The Gujarati khakra is also made with finger millet flour.

Jowar Bajra Roti: Jowar bajra rotis are unleavened flatbreads made with a mixture of sorghum and pearl millet flours in Gujarat and Maharashtra.

Breads Made with Multigrain Flour

Multigrain flours can contain from three to seven types of flours including cereal, millet, pulse and legume flours. These are served plain or stuffed, toasted or fried, in Gujarat and Maharashtra. Satpadi rotlis, dhebras, thalipeeths, vadas and khakras are made with multigrain flours. Moreover, vegetables and dairy products are added to the dough to make the flatbreads.

Breads Made with Wheat Flour and Ground Legumes/Pulses

Flatbreads are often made with wheat and gram or soya flour in equal proportions mixed with herbs, or stuffed with vegetables or dairy products.

Missi Roti: Missi rotis are unleavened flatbreads made with wholewheat flour and gram flour. They are popular in Rajasthan.

Rotis Stuffed with Legumes: These are unleavened flatbreads made with wholewheat flour and stuffed with boiled legumes. Rajma roti is one such flatbread in Mughlai cuisine.

Cooked Dal Paratha: Cooked dal parathas are unleavened flatbreads made with wholewheat flour and stuffed with boiled dals. Chana dal paratha and mung dal paratha are consumed in the western states of India, especially in Rajasthan, as is choorie ka paratha, which is stuffed with husked split mung paste. Urad dal paratha is popular in Uttar Pradesh.

Parathas Stuffed with Pulses: These are unleavened wholewheat flour flatbreads stuffed with ground roasted pulses. Sattu paratha, stuffed with roasted gram flour, is consumed in Bihar.

Dal Dhokli: This is a popular dish in Gujarat, where wheat flour flatbreads are broken into pieces and cooked with a dal.

Soft Bread Rolls (Pav) Made with Whole and Refined Wheat Flour

Pav is a soft, leavened bread made with refined wheat flour. It is toasted with butter till crisp and consumed with tea. Jam, cheese or paneer spread on toasted pavs are popular among teenagers and several snacks are made with pav.

Pav Bhaji: Pav bhaji is a well-known street food in Maharashtra. A hot spicy mixed vegetable curry is served with buttered toasted pavs.

Masala Pav: The pav is sliced horizontally, toasted on both sides with butter and the spicy bhaji is spread evenly on the inside.

Vada Pav: The pav is sliced horizontally, toasted with butter and a garlic-chilli paste, and stuffed with a spicy, batter-fried potato fritter.

Dabeli: The pav is sliced horizontally, toasted with butter and stuffed with a spicy curry, peanuts and pomegranate seeds.

Usal Pav: Usal is a spicy legume curry made with moth beans (matki) and served with hot pav toasted with butter.

Misal Pav: Misal means mixture in Marathi. Usal is topped with crisp sev, chivda, chopped onions, tomatoes and coriander leaves and lime wedges and served with hot pav toasted with butter. Sometimes thick curd is spooned over the dish.

Vegetarian, Non-Vegetarian and Fasting Flatbreads

Vegetarian Flatbreads: Vegetarian flatbreads are made with single or multigrain flour. They may be leavened or unleavened and are stuffed with vegetables, herbs, nuts, seeds, pulses, legumes and dairy products, or these may be mixed into the dough.

Non-Vegetarian Flatbreads: These are similar to vegetarian flatbreads, but are stuffed with eggs, fish, prawns, chicken and mutton.

Egg Flatbreads: Omelettes and scrambled eggs are folded into flatbread wraps; raw eggs are added to the flour — anda naan, tava paratha and Mughlai lachha paratha; curried eggs are mixed into the dough — parottas of Kerala. Baida rotis, parathas stuffed or layered with eggs, are typical of Mughlai cuisine.

Seafood Flatbreads: Flatbreads stuffed with seafood, such as chemmeen paratha and meen pathiri are popular in Kerala. Fish curry is also added to rice flour dough to make meen orotti in Kerala.

Chicken Flatbreads: Baida rotis stuffed with chicken are typical fare in Mughlai cuisine. Chicken curry mixed with flaky parottas or added to rice flour dough (chicken orotti) are served in Kerala.

Mutton Flatbreads: Flatbreads stuffed with mince — kheema parathas — are typical of Mughlai and Punjabi cuisines and kheema naans are enjoyed in Punjab. Baida rotis are also stuffed with kheema in Mughlai cuisine. Curried kheema added to flaky parottas are regularly served in Kerala. Rice flatbreads stuffed with minced meat — erachi pathiri — and curried mince added to the rice flour dough to make erachi orotti are served in Kerala.

Flatbreads as Fasting Foods: Fasting foods in the form of parathas and puris are made with pseudo grains such as buckwheat flour (kuttu), amaranth seed flour (rajgira) and with sago (sabudana) and water chestnut flour (singhada).

Unleavened and Leavened Breads

Unleavened flatbreads are made with a dough to which no leavening agents are added. They can be made quickly as the dough does not need to rise.

Leavening is the process of producing carbon dioxide which causes the dough to rise. A leavening agent that is activated in the presence of moisture, heat or acidity is added to the dough to produce carbon dioxide.

The biological leavening agent used is usually yeast, a fungus which is a unicellular micro-organism. Yeast requires sugar as a substrate (food) and heat to produce carbon dioxide. Active dried yeast is added to warm milk or water along with sugar. It uses the carbohydrates in the dough to multiply rapidly and causes the dough to rise.

Chemical leavening agents are baking powder and baking soda. Baking powder is a mixture of an acid, cream of tartar (potassium hydrogen tartrate) and an alkaline, baking soda (sodium bicarbonate). Cream of tartar is a by-product of the wine industry. When combined with baking soda, it increases leavening abilities. Baking soda alone has less leavening abilities. So it is added to the flour with sour curd or buttermilk, which provides moisture and acid to increase its leavening abilities.

Self-raising flour contains baking powder, which causes the dough to rise before the flatbread is cooked as well as during cooking.

The texture of leavened flatbreads remains the same whatever cooking methods are employed: they are soft, light and fluffy.

There are many disadvantages to leavened flatbreads. They cannot be cooked as soon as the dough is made as it has to be left to rise. Further, if the dough is left too long, it can become sour and taste stale. In addition, many people show sensitivity or allergy to food containing yeast in the form of fungal infections.

GUIDELINES FOR INDIAN BREADS

Follow these guidelines while making Indian breads.

1 Avoid sifting the flour as it results in a loss of fibre and other important nutrients, most of which are in the bran.

2 When a mixture of vegetables, salt and flour are left for some time, the salt drains the water from the vegetables and so the dough is kneaded without water. If the dough is very hard and dry, add a little water.

3 Flatbreads made with dough in a food processor are softer and fluffier than those prepared manually. However, only dough made with wheat flour and multigrain flour can be made in a processor. Rice and millet flour doughs have to be kneaded manually.

4 If the dough is soft and smooth, the flatbread is also soft and smooth.

5 If the dough is firm and hard, the flatbread is crisp.

6 Add hot water to rice flour and millet flours while preparing the dough to increase binding capacity as they lack gluten.

7 The dough can be rolled out immediately if it is unleavened, but leaving it aside for 20-30 mins produces soft, fluffy flatbreads.

8 For leavened flatbreads use only one leavening agent — biological or chemical. Don't mix them.

9 Eggs tend to act as a leavening agent. They make moist, delicate flatbreads.

10 If the recipe demands baking powder, it can be added to the flour even if egg is an ingredient.

11 While making naans with egg, use baking powder rather than yeast, because a dough containing egg should not be left to rise. Eggs spoil easily.

12 Rolling out each dough portion and cooking it immediately produces softer fluffier flatbreads, than rolling out all the portions and then cooking them. This is because the dough dries out and the breads become slightly hard.

13 Add a little more flour, if the dough sticks to the rolling pin.

14 If the dough contains fat, do not toast them in fat — ghee, oil or butter.

15 Do not grease the baking tray if the dough contains fat.

16 If the flatbreads have to be fried, do not add fat to the dough.

17 Always drain fried flatbreads on layers of tissue paper.

18 Flatbreads cooked on high heat burn and become crisp. Cooking on low heat leaves a raw taste in the mouth. Always cook them on medium heat.

19 Flatbreads made with flours other than wheat flour are thick and take a longer time to cook. They should be cooked on low heat.

20 To store flatbreads, roll them individually in aluminium foil to keep them warm.

21 If you find it difficult to stuff and roll flatbreads, cook them partially, place the stuffing between 2 flatbreads and gently seal their edges.

NUTRITIONAL VALUES OF BREADS MADE WITH WHOLE GRAIN CEREALS AND MILLETS

Flatbreads made with whole grain cereals and millets are more nutritious and have a better flavour than those made with rice flour and refined wheat flour.

They are milled with all three parts of the kernel: the bran, endosperm and germ. The bran or outer protective covering of the kernel is a good source of B-complex vitamins (thiamine, riboflavin, niacin, pantothenic acid, pyridoxine), fibre, proteins, minerals and essential fatty and amino acids. The endosperm makes up the largest part of the kernel and contains starch and proteins. The germ provides proteins, fats, B1 and B2 vitamins, folic acid, phosphorus and iron. These are thus good sources of energy, high in complex carbohydrates and dietary fibre, and low in fat.

Millets are small grains with a thick seed coat and contain good-quality protein. Finger millets are the richest source of calcium. Most cereals and millets lack vitamin A, C, D and B12. However, corn contains a carotene, beta-carotene called pro-vitamin A, which is converted to vitamin A in the body.

The bran and germ of cereals and millets contain abundant phytochemicals, which reduce the risk of heart diseases, diabetes, hypertension, cancer and arthritis. They contain antioxidants in the form of alpha-lipoic acid (ALA) and co-enzyme Q10. They are rich in soluble fibres. Insoluble fibres add bulk to the diet and prevent constipation, while soluble fibres reduce blood sugar, total blood cholesterol and LDL or bad cholesterol levels. They also improve the low density/high density lipoprotein (LDL/HDL) ratio and help to reduce weight.

Whole grain flatbreads contribute 50 to 60 per cent of the total energy intake and 50 per cent of the daily protein and essential fatty acid requirements. They supply calories, carbohydrates, proteins, invisible fat, phosphorus, potassium, chloride, sodium, iron, thiamine, riboflavin and niacin and are a good source of fibre, magnesium, zinc and other essential minerals, vitamin B complex and vitamin E.

Who Should Avoid Flatbreads Rich in Fibre and Gluten

Oats, barley, rye and wheat contain a complex protein called gluten. People who are allergic to gluten suffer from celiac disease, which results in the inflammation of the small intestine and prevents the absorption of nutrients. So these people should avoid food containing wheat, oats, barley and rye. Similarly, those who have digestive problems such as irritable bowel syndrome, need to avoid the high fibre in these flatbreads.

VEGETARIAN FLATBREADS

Flatbreads Made with Wholewheat Flour

Botanically known as Triticum aestivum (the most common species) of the family Poaceae or Graminaceae, wheat is a staple food the world over. It is available in the market as a grain, wholewheat flour, bulgur wheat, wheat bran, wheat germ, refined flour, vermicelli and semolina.

Wheat is consumed as leavened breads, pasta, noodles and as breakfast cereal. In south India, pancakes are prepared with wholewheat flour batter. In north India, Gujarat and Maharashtra, it is used to make unleavened flatbreads.

If not properly stored, wholewheat flour is subject to rapid deterioration, which is why refined flour is used to make snacks.

PARATHA
Pan-fried flatbread

Preparation time: 20 mins; Cooking time: 5 mins

Parathas are pan-fried flatbreads with a few layers of pastry and are made from wholewheat flour. They are plain, stuffed or shallow-fried; circular, square or triangular. Parathas can be made with more or less any vegetable by mixing them into the flour or by stuffing them. Parathas are also made with dairy products, seeds and nuts by mixing them into the flour or stuffing them.

Dough for Parathas

The dough can be prepared manually or in the food processor.

Ingredients for 2 parathas

1 cup wholewheat flour
A pinch of salt or to taste
1 tsp oil

Method

Place the flour in a flat plate or bowl.

Dissolve the salt in about 5 tbsp of water.

Rub the oil into the flour.

Add the salt water gradually to the flour. Knead for 5-10 mins to make a smooth dough. Add more water if the dough is dry.

Cover the dough and leave it aside for about 20 mins.

Knead it again for a few mins.

Notes: 1 cup of flour indicates 100g wholewheat flour. When salt water is added to the flour, the dough weighs approximately 170g-180g

Preparation time does not include soaking, sprouting, marinating and the resting and rising times for the dough)

Nutritive values of the dough for 2 parathas: Calories: 388.0kcal; Carbohydrate: 69.4g; Protein: 12.2g; Fat: 6.8g; Minerals: 2.8g; Fibre: 1.9g.

SADA PARATHA
Plain pan-fried flatbread

Preparation time: 15 mins; Cooking time: 4 mins

Sada paratha is a plain, unleavened, traditional, north Indian, pan-fried flatbread. Sada means plain. Sada paratha served with sooji halwa (semolina halwa), called halwa paratha, is popular in Uttar Pradesh.

Ingredients for 2 parathas

Dough to make 2 sada parathas (p. 22)
2 tsp oil

Method

Divide the dough into 2 portions and shape them into balls.

Roll out a portion of the dough on a lightly floured board into a 5" circle.

Fold it into a semicircle and then into a quarter circle.

Roll it out again into a 6" circle.

To pan-fry the parathas: Put a non-stick pan on medium heat and place the rolled dough on it.

When spots appear on the surface, flip it over and spoon ½ tsp oil along the edges.

When the base is golden brown, flip it over again and spoon another ½ tsp oil along the edges. Cook till the other side is golden brown.

Repeat with the second portion of dough.

Serve hot with any curry or dal.

Nutritive values for 1 paratha: Calories: 239.0kcal; Carbohydrate: 34.7g; Protein: 6.1g; Fat: 8.4g; Minerals: 1.3g; Fibre: 0.95g.

Healthy modifications: Avoid adding fat to the flour while preparing the dough. This will reduce 2.5g fat and 23kcal from each paratha.

Toast the parathas in a non-stick pan without oil. This will further reduce 5g fat and 45 kcal from each paratha.

TAVA PARATHA

Rich pan-fried flatbread

Preparation time: 20 mins; Cooking time: 5 mins

Tava paratha is an unleavened traditional, north Indian flatbread. A tava is an iron griddle on which the paratha is toasted. This flatbread is as large as your griddle.

Ingredients for 2 parathas

Dough to make 4 parathas (p. 22)
2 tsp ghee
4 tsp vegetable oil

Method

Divide the dough into 2 portions.

Roll out a portion of the dough as given for sada paratha (p. 22), spreading ½ tsp of ghee over the surface every time you fold the dough; the final size should be 10"- 12" wide.

Put a large iron griddle on medium heat and place the rolled out dough on it.

Pan-fry it with 2 tsp oil till golden brown on both sides (p. 22).

Repeat with the second portion of dough.

Serve hot with onion slices, lime wedges and any curry or dal.

Nutritive values for 1 paratha: Calories: 523.0kcal; Carbohydrate: 69.4g; Protein: 12.2g; Fat: 21.8g; Minerals: 2.8g; Fibre: 1.9g.

Healthy modifications: Avoid adding oil to the flour while preparing the dough. This will reduce 2.5g fat and 23kcal from each paratha.

Replace ghee with vegetable oils such as soya bean oil (omega-3 fatty acids), sunflower or safflower oil (omega-6 fatty acids), olive oil, groundnut oil or mustard oil (MUFA fat).

Toast the parathas in a non-stick pan without oil. This will further reduce 10g fat and 90 kcal from each paratha.

SHALLOW-FRIED PARATHA

Preparation time: 15 mins; Cooking time: 3 mins

Shallow-fried parathas are unleavened, traditional flatbreads, typical of north Indian and Mughlai cuisines.

Ingredients for 2 parathas

Dough to make 2 sada parathas (p. 22)
Oil for shallow-frying

Method

Divide the dough into 2 portions and shape them into balls.

Roll out the dough as given for sada paratha (p. 22).

Heat the oil in a pan and shallow-fry the paratha on both sides, till golden brown. Drain.

Repeat with the second portion of dough.

Serve hot with any curry or dal.

Nutritive values for 1 paratha: Calories: 284.0kcal; Carbohydrate: 34.7g; Protein: 6.1g; Fat: 13.4g; Minerals: 1.4g; Fibre: 0.95g.

Healthy modifications: Avoid adding fat to the flour while preparing the dough. This will reduce 2.5g fat and 23kcal from each flatbread.

PAN-FRIED AND TOASTED PARATHAS WITH LEAFY GREENS

Leaves used to make parathas include green and Chinese cabbage, amaranth leaves, colocasia leaves, fenugreek leaves, lettuce, mustard leaves, radish leaves, red, green and sour spinach, turnip greens, kale, collard greens, Brussels sprouts and watercress. Leafy greens are rich sources of beta-carotene, B vitamins including folate, vitamin C, calcium, potassium and fibre.

PALAK PARATHA
Pan-fried spinach flatbread

Preparation time: 15 mins; Cooking time: 4 mins

Palak paratha is an unleavened, traditional, north Indian flatbread.

Ingredients for 2 parathas

To make the dough
200g spinach
1 cup wholewheat flour
1 tsp ginger paste
½ tsp coriander powder
¼ tsp red chilli powder
2 tsp oil
A pinch of salt or to taste
To pan-fry the parathas
2 tsp oil

Method

Wash the spinach leaves, drain and chop them.

To make the dough and roll it out:

Mix all the dough ingredients in a bowl.

Knead for 5-10 mins to make a smooth dough.

Cover the dough and leave aside for about 20 mins.

Knead it again for a few mins. Add a little water if the dough is dry.

Divide dough into 2 portions and shape into balls.

Roll out a portion of the dough on a lightly floured board into a 6" circle.

To pan-fry the parathas: Pan-fry each paratha with 1 tsp oil, as given for sada paratha (p. 22).

Repeat with the second portion of dough.

Serve hot with curd, onion slices, lemon wedges and any curry or dal.

Nutritive values for 1 paratha: Calories: 245.0kcal; Carbohydrate: 38.3g; Protein: 8.2g; Fat: 6.6g; Minerals: 3.1g; Fibre: 1.6g.

Healthy modifications: See band gobi paratha (p. 25).

BAND GOBI PARATHA

Pan-fried flatbread with green cabbage filling

Preparation time: 20 mins; Cooking time: 10 mins

Band gobi paratha is an unleavened, traditional, north Indian flatbread stuffed with fresh cabbage leaves.

Ingredients for 2 parathas

The filling
1 tsp ghee
1 tsp ginger-garlic-green chilli paste
2 cups shredded cabbage
A pinch of salt or to taste
To make the parathas
Dough to make 2 sada parathas (p. 22)
2 tsp oil

Method

The filling: Heat the ghee in a pan and sauté the ginger-garlic-green chilli paste for a few seconds.

Mix in the cabbage and salt.

Cover the pan with a lid and simmer, till the cabbage is tender.

Divide the filling into 2 portions. Allow it to cool.

To prepare the stuffed parathas:

Divide the dough into 2 portions and shape them into balls.

Roll out a portion of the dough on a lightly floured board into a 3" circle.

Place a portion of the filling in the centre and pull up the dough from around it to cover the filling. Gently seal the edges with moist fingertips.

Roll it out again into a 6" circle.

To pan-fry the parathas: Pan-fry the stuffed paratha with 1 tsp oil, as given for sada paratha (p. 22).

(Method Cont.)

Repeat with the second portion of dough and filling.

Serve hot with curd, onion slices, lemon wedges and any curry or dal.

Nutritive values for 1 paratha: Calories: 250.0kcal; Carbohydrate: 40.5g; Protein: 8.3g; Fat: 6.0g; Minerals: 2.1g; Fibre: 2.2g.

Healthy modifications: Avoid adding fat to the flour while preparing the dough. This will reduce 2.5g fat and 23kcal from each paratha.

Toast the parathas in a non-stick pan without oil. This will further reduce 5g fat and 45 kcal from each paratha.

METHI PARATHA

Pan-fried fenugreek leaf flatbread

Preparation time: 15 mins; Cooking time: 4 mins

Methi paratha is an unleavened, traditional, north Indian flatbread made with fresh fenugreek leaves. Use fresh fenugreek leaves instead of mustard leaves and make 2 parathas as given for sarson ka saag paratha (p. 27); pan-fry each paratha in 1 tsp oil as given sada paratha (p. 22). Serve them hot with curd, onion slices, lemon wedges and any curry or dal.

Nutritive values for 1 paratha: Calories: 265.0kcal; Carbohydrate: 40.7g; Protein: 10.5g; Fat: 6.8g; Minerals: 2.9g; Fibre: 2.1g.

Healthy modifications: See band gobi paratha (p. 25).

CHINI BAND GOBI PARATHA

Toasted Chinese cabbage flatbread

Preparation time: 15 mins; Cooking time: 4 mins

This is an innovative flatbread made with Chinese cabbage.

Ingredients for 2 parathas

1 cup wholewheat flour
2 cups shredded Chinese cabbage
¼ tsp black pepper powder
½ tsp cumin powder
A pinch of salt or to taste

Method

Make the dough and roll it out as given for palak paratha (p. 24).

Toast each paratha in a non-stick pan on medium heat, till golden brown on both sides.

Serve hot with chopped onions, a tomato salad and any curry or dal.

Nutritive values for 1 paratha: Calories: 182.0kcal; Carbohydrate: 36.3g; Protein: 6.7g; Fat: 1.1g; Minerals: 1.6g; Fibre: 1.4g.

Healthy modifications: See band gobi paratha (p. 25).

BATHUA PARATHA

Pan-fried chenopodium flatbread

Preparation time: 15 mins; Cooking time: 4 mins

Bathua paratha is an unleavened, traditional, north Indian flatbread.

Ingredients for 2 parathas

The dough
200g bathua leaves
1 cup wholewheat flour
1 tsp garlic paste
½ tsp cumin powder
¼ tsp red chilli powder
A pinch of salt or to taste
To pan-fry the parathas
2 tsp oil

Method

Wash the bathua leaves, drain and chop them.

Make the dough and roll it out as given for palak paratha (p. 24).

Pan-fry each paratha with 1 tsp oil, as given for sada paratha (p. 22).

Serve hot with curd, onion slices, lemon wedges and any curry or dal.

Nutritive values for 1 paratha: Calories: 254.0kcal; Carbohydrate: 37.8g; Protein: 10.1g; Fat: 6.5g; Minerals: 4.1g; Fibre: 1.9g.

Healthy modifications: See band gobi paratha (p. 25).

SARSON KA SAAG PARATHA

Toasted mustard leaf flatbread

Preparation time: 15 mins; Cooking time: 4 mins

Sarson ka saag paratha is an unleavened and innovative flatbread made with wholewheat flour and fresh mustard greens.

Ingredients for 2 parathas

200g mustard leaves
1 cup wholewheat flour
¼ tsp red chilli powder
A pinch of salt or to taste

Method

Wash the mustard leaves, drain and chop them.

Make the dough and roll it out as given for palak paratha (p. 24).

Toast each paratha in a non-stick pan on medium heat, till golden brown on both sides.

Serve hot with curd, onion slices, lemon wedges and any curry or dal.

Nutritive values for 1 paratha: Calories: 205.0kcal; Carbohydrate: 37.9g; Protein: 10.1g; Fat: 1.5g; Minerals: 3.0g; Fibre: 1.8g.

Healthy modifications: See band gobi paratha (p.25).

GONGURA PARATHA

Toasted sorrel leaf flatbread

Preparation time: 15 mins; Cooking time: 4 mins

Gongura paratha is an unleavened, innovative flatbread made with fresh, sour sorrel leaves.

Ingredients for 2 parathas

1 cup wholewheat flour
2 cups sorrel leaves, chopped
¼ tsp cumin powder
¼ tsp coriander powder
¼ tsp red chilli powder
A pinch of salt or to taste

Method

Make the dough and roll it out as given for palak paratha (p. 24).

Toast each paratha in a non-stick pan on medium heat, till golden brown on both sides.

Serve hot with curd, onion slices, lemon wedges and any curry or dal.

Nutritive values for 1 paratha: Calories: 194.0kcal; Carbohydrates: 38.1g; Protein: 6.9g; Fat: 1.5g; Minerals: 1.7g; Fibre: 1.5g.

Healthy modifications: See band gobi paratha (p. 25).

PAN-FRIED AND TOASTED PARATHAS WITH ROOT VEGETABLES

Root vegetables contain phytochemicals in the form of carotenoids. They are a rich source of some antioxidant nutrients, beta-carotene, vitamin C, folate, potassium and fibre. Turnips are a useful source of vitamin C. Parsnips contain vitamin E while carrots are rich in beta-carotene. Since root vegetables grow underground, scrub them thoroughly before peeling. Select fresh, firm, unbruised vegetables.

MULI PARATHA

Pan-fried radish flatbread

Preparation time: 15 mins; Cooking time: 4 mins

Muli paratha is an unleavened, traditional, north Indian flatbread made with grated fresh white radish.

Ingredients for 2 parathas

The dough
2 medium-sized white radishes
1 cup wholewheat flour
1 tsp ginger paste
¼ tsp red chilli powder
A pinch of salt or to taste
To pan-fry the parathas
2 tsp oil

Method

Scrub the radishes, wash, peel and grate them.

Make the dough and roll it out as given for palak paratha (p. 24).

Pan-fry each paratha with 1 tsp oil as given for sada paratha (p. 22).

Serve hot with curd, onion slices, lemon wedges and any curry or dal.

Nutritive values for 1 paratha: Calories: 236.0kcal; Carbohydrate: 38.8g; Protein: 6.9g; Fat: 6.0g; Minerals: 2.0g; Fibre: 1.8g.

Healthy modifications: See band gobi paratha (p. 25).

GAJAR PARATHA

Toasted carrot flatbread

Preparation time: 15 mins; Cooking time: 4 mins

Gajar paratha is an unleavened, innovative flatbread made with fresh carrots.

Ingredients for 2 parathas

2 medium-sized sweet or regular carrots
1 cup wholewheat flour
½ tsp green chilli paste
½ tsp garam masala powder
A pinch of salt or to taste

Method

Scrub the carrots, wash, peel and grate them.

Make the dough and roll it out as given for palak paratha (p. 24).

Toast each paratha in a non-stick pan on medium heat, till golden brown on both sides.

Serve hot with curd, onion slices, lemon wedges and any curry or dal.

Nutritive values for 1 paratha: Calories: 224.0kcal; Carbohydrate: 45.3g; Protein: 7.0g; Fat: 1.1g; Minerals: 2.5g; Fibre: 2.2g.

CHUKANDAR PARATHA

Toasted beetroot flatbread

Preparation time: 15 mins; Cooking time: 4 mins

Chukandar paratha is an unleavened, innovative flatbread made with fresh beetroot.

Ingredients for 2 parathas

2 medium-sized beetroots
1 cup wholewheat flour
1 tsp garlic paste
½ tsp garam masala powder
A pinch of salt or to taste

Method

Scrub the beetroots, wash, peel and grate them.

Make the dough and roll it out as given for palak paratha (p. 24).

Toast each paratha in a non-stick pan on medium heat, till golden brown on both sides.

Serve hot with curd, onion slices, cucumber and carrots and any curry or dal.

Nutritive values for 1 paratha: Calories: 217.0kcal; Carbohydrate: 45.0g; Protein: 7.9g; Fat: 1.0g; Minerals: 2.2g; Fibre: 1.9g.

SHALGAM PARATHA

Toasted turnip flatbread

Preparation time: 15 mins; Cooking time: 4 mins

Shalgam paratha is an unleavened, innovative flatbread made with fresh turnips.

Ingredients for 2 parathas

2 medium-sized pink or regular turnips
1 cup wholewheat flour
1 cup parsley, chopped
½ tsp garam masala powder
A pinch of salt or to taste

Method

Scrub the turnips, wash, peel and grate them.

Make the dough and roll it out as given for palak paratha (p. 24).

Toast each paratha in a non-stick pan on medium heat, till golden brown on both sides.

Serve hot with curd, onion slices, lemon wedges and any curry or dal.

Nutritive values for 1 paratha: Calories: 206.0kcal; Carbohydrate: 42.0g; Protein: 6.9g; Fat: 1.1g; Minerals: 2.2g; Fibre: 2.6g.

SHAKHARKAND PARATHA

Pan-fried flatbread with sweet potato filling

Preparation time: 20 mins; Cooking time: 5 mins

Shakharkand paratha is an unleavened, innovative flatbread made with sweet potatoes.

Ingredients for 2 parathas

The filling
2 medium-sized sweet potatoes
A pinch of salt or to taste
1 tsp oil
1 tsp ginger-garlic-green chilli paste
½ tsp garam masala powder
2 tsp chopped mint leaves
The dough
Dough to make 2 sada parathas (p. 22)

Method

Scrub the sweet potatoes, wash, peel and chop them roughly.

Boil the sweet potatoes with a pinch of salt, till tender. Drain well and mash thoroughly.

Heat the oil in a pan and sauté the ginger-garlic-green chilli paste for a few seconds.

Mix in the mashed sweet potatoes, garam masala powder and mint leaves.

Divide the filling into 2 portions and leave aside, till cool.

Divide the dough into 2 portions and shape them into balls.

Make the parathas as given for band gobi paratha (p. 25).

Toast each paratha in a non-stick pan on medium heat, till golden brown on both sides.

Serve hot with curd, onion slices, lemon wedges and any curry.

Nutritive values for 1 paratha: Calories: 336.0kcal; Carbohydrate: 62.9g; Protein: 7.3g; Fat: 6.2g; Minerals: 2.4g; Fibre: 1.8g.

PAN-FRIED AND TOASTED PARATHAS WITH STEM VEGETABLES

Many stems and stem tubers are consumed as vegetables. Stem tubers are modified stems that grow underground. Asparagus and kohlrabi (knoll kohl) are stem vegetables. Tapioca, colocasia, yam, potato and Jerusalem artichoke are tubers.

They contain phytochemicals in the form of carotenoids and are a rich source of some antioxidant nutrients, beta-carotene, vitamin C, folate, potassium and fibre. Potatoes are a useful sources of vitamin C. Yellow varieties of yam are a good source of beta-carotene and potassium.

Since stem vegetables grow underground, treat them in the same way as root vegetables.

ALOO PARATHA

Pan-fried flatbread with potato filling

Preparation time: 20 mins; Cooking time: 20 mins

Aloo paratha is an unleavened, traditional, north Indian flatbread stuffed with potatoes. Prepare them in the same way as given for shakharkand paratha (p. 30). Use 4 medium-sized potatoes instead of the sweet potatoes and substitute ghee for oil and coriander leaves for mint to make the filling. Pan-fry in 2 tsp of oil as given for sada paratha (p. 22). Serve them hot with curd, onion slices, lemon wedges and any curry or dal.

Nutritive values for 1 paratha: Calories: 358.0kcal; Carbohydrate: 57.3g; Protein: 7.7g; Fat: 11.0g; Minerals: 2.0g; Fibre: 1.4g.

Healthy modifications: Replace the ghee for the filling with oil.

Avoid fat while preparing the filling. This will reduce 2.5g fat and 23kcal from each paratha.

Toast the parathas in a non-stick pan without oil. This will further reduce 5g fat and 45kcal from each paratha.

SURAN PARATHA

Toasted flatbread with yam filling

Preparation time: 20 mins; Cooking time: 20 mins

Suran paratha is an unleavened, innovative flatbread stuffed with yam. Prepare them in the same way as given for shakharkand paratha (p. 30). Use 200g yam instead of the sweet potatoes and add a pinch of turmeric powder while boiling them. Substitute ghee for oil and mixed herbs (mint, coriander, celery, parsley) for mint to make the filling. Toast them in a non-stick pan on medium heat, till golden brown on both sides. Serve them hot with curd, onion slices, lemon wedges and any curry or dal.

Nutritive values for 1 paratha: Calories: 330.0kcal; Carbohydrate: 61.0g; Protein: 7.7g; Fat: 6.0g; Minerals: 3.1g; Fibre: 2.1g.

GANTH GOBI PARATHA

Toasted knoll kohl/kohlrabi flatbread

Preparation time: 15 mins; Cooking time: 4 mins

Ganth gobi paratha is an unleavened, innovative flatbread made with knoll kohl/kohlrabi.

Ingredients for 2 parathas

2 medium-sized knoll kohls
1 cup wholewheat flour
1 tsp garlic-ginger-green chilli paste
2 tbsp coriander leaves, chopped
½ tsp garam masala powder
A pinch of salt or to taste

Method

Scrub the knoll kohls, wash, peel and grate them.

Make the dough and roll it out as given for palak paratha (p. 24).

Toast each paratha in a non-stick pan on medium heat, till golden brown on both sides.

Serve hot with curd, onion slices, lemon wedges and any curry or dal.

Nutritive values for 1 paratha: Calories: 195.0kcal; Carbohydrate: 38.8g; Protein: 7.3g; Fat: 1.1g; Minerals: 2.2g; Fibre: 2.5g.

PAN-FRIED AND TOASTED PARATHAS WITH BULBS AND RHIZOMES

Bulbs grow underground and comprise many fleshy leaves which surround a very short stem. The swollen base of these leaves is the part usually consumed. These vegetables include onion, shallot, garlic, spring onion, leek. Ginger is a rhizome similar to turmeric and galangal.

The aromatic underground vegetables, ginger, garlic and onion are used as vegetables and as flavouring agents in Indian cuisines. These have hypotensive (blood pressure lowering), hypoglycaemic (blood sugar lowering) and cholesterol reducing properties and should be included in the daily diet. Chopped or puréed garlic, ginger and onion can be added to flatbread doughs. Cooking does not alter their beneficial effects.

Garlic contains sulphur compounds and essential oils, which have antioxidant properties. It is advisable to eat at least 10g (3-4 cloves or 2 tsp of paste) of raw garlic a day and 100g of onions (1 large or 2 medium-sized) a day. Ginger contains several phenolic compounds and is also anti-inflammatory.

HARA PYAZ PARATHA

Toasted spring onion flatbread

Preparation time: 15 mins; Cooking time: 4 mins

Hara pyaz paratha is an unleavened, innovative flatbread made with fresh spring onions or leeks.

Ingredients for 2 parathas

200g spring onion or leek bulbs with some of the tender green
1 cup wholewheat flour
1 tsp coriander-cumin powder
¼ tsp red chilli powder
A pinch of salt or to taste

Method

Wash the spring onions, drain and chop them.

Make the dough and roll it out as given for palak paratha (p.24).

Toast each paratha in a non-stick pan on medium heat, till golden brown on both sides.

Serve hot with curd, onion slices, lemon wedges and any curry or dal.

Nutritive values for 1 paratha: Calories: 248.0kcal; Carbohydrate: 51.9g; Protein: 7.9g; Fat: 5.0g; Minerals: 2.1g; Fibre: 2.3g.

ADRAK PARATHA

Toasted ginger flatbread

Preparation time: 15 mins; Cooking time: 4 mins

Adrak paratha is an unleavened, innovative flatbread made with fresh ginger. Use fresh ginger instead of garlic and make 2 parathas as given for lassoon paratha (p. 34). Serve them hot with curd, and any curry.

Nutritive values for 1 paratha: Calories: 174.0kcal; Carbohydrate: 35.3g; Protein: 6.2g; Fat: 0.9g; Minerals: 1.4g; Fibre: 1.1g.

KOKI ROTI

Pan-fried onion flatbread

Preparation time: 15 mins; Cooking time: 4 mins

Koki roti is an unleavened, traditional, Sindhi flatbread made with onions, also popular in north India and often served for breakfast.

Ingredients for 2 parathas

1 cup wholewheat flour
2 onions, chopped
1 tsp ginger-garlic-green chilli paste
2 tbsp coriander leaves, chopped
¼ tsp red chilli powder
1 tsp cumin seeds
2 tsp ghee
A pinch of salt or to taste
To pan-fry the parathas
2 tsp oil

Method

Make the dough and roll it out as given for palak paratha (p. 24).

Pan-fry each paratha with 1 tsp oil, as given for sada paratha (p. 22).

Serve hot with curd, pickles, papads and any curry or dal.

Nutritive values for 1 paratha: Calories: 295.0kcal; Carbohydrate: 41.2g; Protein: 7.2g; Fat: 11.3g; Minerals: 1.8g; Fibre: 1.6g.

Healthy modifications: See aloo paratha (p. 31).

LASSOON PARATHA

Toasted garlic flatbread

Preparation time: 15 mins; Cooking time: 4 mins

Lassoon paratha is an unleavened, innovative flatbread made with wholewheat flour and garlic.

Ingredients for 2 parathas

1 cup wholewheat flour
2 tsp garlic paste
A pinch of salt or to taste

Method

Mix the flour and garlic paste in a bowl.

Make the dough and roll it out as given for sada paratha (p. 22).

Toast each paratha in a non-stick pan on medium heat, till golden brown on both sides.

Serve hot with a salad, curd and any curry or dal.

Nutritive values for 1 paratha: Calories: 178.0kcal; Carbohydrate: 36.2g; Protein: 6.4g; Fat: 0.9g; Minerals: 1.4g; Fibre: 0.99g.

HARA LASSOON PARATHA

Toasted green garlic flatbread

Preparation time: 15 mins; Cooking time: 4 mins

Hara lassoon paratha is an unleavened, innovative flatbread made with fresh green garlic. Prepare them in the same way as given for hara pyaz paratha (p. 33), substituting fresh green garlic leaves and their bulbs. Serve them hot with curd, onion slices, lemon wedges and any curry or dal.

Nutritive values for 1 paratha: Calories: 218.0kcal; Carbohydrate: 44.2g; Protein: 7.4g; Fat: 1.3g; Minerals: 1.9g; Fibre: 1.9g.

PAN-FRIED AND TOASTED PARATHAS WITH OTHER VEGETABLES

Some vegetables comprise a cluster of flowers — broccoli, cauliflower and globe artichoke; some, like pumpkin, tomato and aubergine are actually fruits, while others, such as green peas and broad beans are called seed vegetables.

These vegetables are rich sources of phytochemicals and contain antioxidant-rich nutrients. Puréed tomatoes mixed into the dough makes the breads attractive and appetizing.

PHOOL GOBI PARATHA

Pan-fried flatbread with cauliflower filling

Preparation time: 15 mins; Cooking time: 20 mins

Phool gobi paratha is an unleavened, traditional, north Indian flatbread stuffed with cauliflower.

Ingredients for 2 parathas

The filling
250g cauliflower florets
1 tsp ghee
1 onion, puréed
½ tsp garam masala powder
A pinch of salt or to taste
To prepare the parathas
Dough to make 2 sada parathas (p. 22)
2 tsp oil

Method

Wash the cauliflower and shred or grate it.

Heat the ghee in a pan and sauté the onion purée for a few seconds.

Mix in cauliflower, garam masala powder and salt.

Cover the pan with a lid and simmer, till the cauliflower is tender and dry.

Remove the pan from the heat and mash the mixture thoroughly.

Divide the filling into 2 portions and leave aside, till cool.

Divide the dough into 2 portions and shape them into balls.

Make the parathas and pan-fry them as given for band gobi paratha (p. 25).

Serve hot with onion slices, lemon wedges, curd and any curry or dal.

Nutritive values for 1 paratha: Calories: 311.0kcal; Carbohydrate: 42.5g; Protein: 9.6g; Fat: 11.4g; Minerals: 2.7g; Fibre: 2.5g.

Healthy modifications: See aloo paratha (p. 31).

MATTAR PARATHA

Pan-fried flatbread stuffed with green peas

Preparation time: 15 mins; Cooking time: 15 mins

Mattar paratha is an unleavened, traditional, north Indian and Rajasthani flatbread stuffed with fresh green peas.

Ingredients for 2 parathas

The filling
250g green peas, shelled
1 tsp ghee
1 tsp ginger-garlic-green chilli paste
½ garam masala powder
1 tbsp lime juice
A pinch of salt or to taste
To prepare the parathas
Dough to make 2 sada parathas (p. 22)
2 tsp oil

Method

Parboil the green peas, drain well and mash thoroughly.

Heat the ghee in a pan and sauté the ginger-garlic-green chilli paste for a few seconds.

Mix in the green peas, garam masala powder, lime juice and salt.

Divide the filling into 2 portions and leave aside, till cool.

Divide the dough into 2 portions and shape them into balls.

Make the parathas and pan-fry them as given for band gobi paratha (p. 25).

Serve hot with curd and any curry or dal.

Nutritive values for 1 paratha: Calories: 378.0kcal; Carbohydrate: 54.6g; Protein: 15.1g; Fat: 11.0g; Minerals: 2.4g; Fibre: 6.0g.

Healthy modifications: See aloo paratha (p. 31).

KELA PARATHA

Toasted flatbread with banana filling

Preparation time: 20 mins; Cooking time: 20 mins

Kela paratha is an unleavened, innovative flatbread stuffed with cooking bananas.

Ingredients for 2 parathas

The filling
2 medium-sized cooking bananas
A pinch of salt or to taste
A pinch of turmeric powder
1 tsp oil
1 tsp ginger-garlic-green chilli paste
½ tsp powdered mustard seeds
2 tbsp mixed herbs (sweet basil, rosemary, thyme, sage), chopped
1 tbsp lime juice
The dough
Dough to make 2 sada parathas (p. 22)

Method

Wash the bananas, peel and chop them.

Boil the bananas in salted water with a pinch of turmeric powder, till tender. Drain thoroughly and mash well.

Heat the oil in a pan and sauté the ginger-garlic-green chilli paste, till fragrant.

Mix in the bananas, mustard seeds, herbs and lime juice.

Divide the filling into 2 portions and leave aside, till cool.

Divide the dough into 4 portions and shape them into balls.

To prepare the parathas: Roll out 2 portions of the dough on a lightly floured board into 5" circles.

Toast one side of each paratha, till light brown.

Place a paratha on a plate or a plastic sheet, toasted side up.

(Method Cont.)

Spread a portion of the filling evenly over the paratha.

Cover the filling with the second paratha, toasted side down. Press the edges firmly to seal.

To toast the parathas: Toast each paratha in a non-stick pan on medium heat, till golden brown on both sides.

Repeat with the remaining dough and filling.

Serve hot with onion slices, lemon wedges and any curry or dal.

Nutritive values for 1 paratha: Calories: 325.0kcal; Carbohydrate: 60.0g; Protein: 7.6g; Fat: 6.8g; Minerals: 2.0g; Fibre: 2.9g.

SHIMLA MIRCH PARATHA

Toasted capsicum flatbread

Preparation time: 15 mins; Cooking time: 4 mins

Shimla mirch paratha is an unleavened, innovative flatbread made with fresh multicoloured capsicums.

Ingredients for 2 parathas

1 each of red, green and yellow capsicums, minced
1 cup wholewheat flour
¼ tsp black pepper powder
A pinch of salt or to taste

Method

Make the dough and roll it out as given for palak paratha (p. 24).

Toast each paratha in a non-stick pan on medium heat, till golden brown on both sides.

Serve hot with curd and any curry or dal.

Nutritive values for 1 paratha: Calories: 195.0kcal; Carbohydrate: 39.0g; Protein: 7.4g; Fat: 1.2g; Minerals: 2.1g; Fibre: 2.0g.

LAUKI PARATHA

Pan-fried bottle gourd flatbread

Preparation time: 15 mins; Cooking time: 4 mins

Lauki paratha is an unleavened, traditional, Gujarati and Rajasthani flatbread made with bottle gourd.

Ingredients for 2 parathas

1 small bottle gourd
1 cup wholewheat flour
1 cup coriander and mint leaves, chopped
½ tsp garam masala powder
A pinch of salt or to taste
To pan-fry the parathas
2 tsp oil

Method

Wash the gourd, peel and grate it.

Make the parathas and pan-fry them as given for palak paratha (p. 24).

Serve hot with onion slices, curd and any curry or dal.

Nutritive values for 1 paratha: Calories: 230.0kcal; Carbohydrate: 37.3g; Protein: 6.6g; Fat: 6.0g; Minerals: 2.0g; Fibre: 1.6g.

Healthy modifications: Toast the parathas in a non-stick pan without oil. This will reduce 5g fat and 45kcal from each paratha.

PETHA PARATHA

Toasted ash gourd flatbread

Preparation time: 15 mins; Cooking time: 4 mins

Petha paratha is an unleavened, innovative flatbread with fresh ash gourd. Prepare them in the same way as given for lauki paratha (alongside). Substitute 1 cup of grated ash gourd for the bottle gourd and use parsley instead of the herbs. Toast them in a non-stick pan on medium heat, till golden brown on both sides. Serve hot with a salad, curd and any curry or dal.

Nutritive values for 1 paratha: Calories: 180.0kcal; Carbohydrate: 36.4g; Protein: 6.6g; Fat: 1.0g; Minerals: 1.7g; Fibre: 1.4g.

SHAHI SABJI PARATHA

Pan-fried flatbread with mixed vegetable filling
Preparation time: 20 mins; Cooking time: 25 mins

Shahi vegetable paratha is an unleavened, traditional, Mughlai flatbread stuffed with mixed vegetables.

Ingredients for 2 parathas

The filling
2 tbsp cashew nuts
2 cups chopped vegetables (carrot, green pea, cabbage, capsicum, cauliflower)
A pinch of salt or to taste
2 tsp ghee
2 tsp ginger-garlic-green chilli paste
½ tsp garam masala powder
To prepare the parathas
Dough to make 2 sada parathas (p. 22)
2 tsp ghee

Method

Soak the cashew nuts in water for 1 hour and grind them with little water.

Pressure-cook the vegetables with a little salted water (just enough to cover), on low heat for 2 mins after the cooker reaches full pressure.

Drain thoroughly and mash well.

Heat the ghee and sauté the ginger-garlic-green chilli paste for 1 minute.

Add the cashew nut paste and sauté for a few mins.

Stir in the garam masala powder and sauté for a second.

Mix in the mashed vegetables and cook, till the mixture is dry.

Divide the filling into 2 portions and leave aside, till cool.

Divide the dough into 2 portions and shape them into balls.

(Method Cont.)

Make the parathas and pan-fry them as given for band gobi paratha (p. 25).

Serve hot with any curry or dal.

Nutritive values for 1 paratha: Calories: 388.0kcal; Carbohydrates: 48.5g; Protein: 12.5g; Fat: 20.9g; Minerals: 2.7g; Fibre: 3.5g.

Healthy modifications: See aloo paratha (p. 31).

KACHA AAM PARATHA

Toasted raw mango flatbread
Preparation time: 15 mins; Cooking time: 4 mins

Kacha aam paratha is an unleavened, tangy, innovative flatbread prepared with seasonal raw mangoes.

Ingredients for 2 parathas

1 cup grated raw mango
1 cup wholewheat flour
2 tsp ginger-garlic-green chilli paste
¼ tsp red chilli powder
A pinch of salt or to taste

Method

Make the dough and roll it out as given for palak paratha (p. 24).

Toast each paratha in a non-stick pan on medium heat, till golden brown on both sides.

Serve hot with any curry or dal.

Nutritive values for 1 paratha: Calories: 200.0kcal; Carbohydrates: 40.9g; Protein: 6.6g; Fat: 0.99g; Minerals: 1.7g; Fibre: 1.8g.

PAN-FRIED AND TOASTED PARATHAS WITH HERBS

Herbs aid in digestion, add flavour and make food more appetizing. All herbs are low in calories and are fat-free. They are good sources of phytochemicals, such as carotenoids, antioxidant-rich nutrients, vitamin C and iron. They are available fresh or dried. Herbs used in Indian cuisines are coriander, mint, dill, bay leaves and curry leaves, while those in Western cuisines include basil, parsley, celery, thyme, rosemary, sage, oregano, fennel, chives and chervil and are also used in Indian cuisines.

All herbs, except celery, are low in sodium. Most have anti-carcinogenic, anti-inflammatory and antioxidant properties. Celery leaves are a natural diuretic which help lower blood pressure by eliminating water and salt from the body.

HARA DHANIA PARATHA

Toasted coriander leaf flatbread

Preparation time: 15 mins; Cooking time: 4 mins

Hara dhania paratha is an unleavened, innovative flatbread made with fresh coriander leaves.

Ingredients for 2 parathas

200g coriander leaves
1 cup wholewheat flour
½ tsp coriander powder
¼ tsp red chilli powder
A pinch of salt or to taste

Method

Chop off the roots of the coriander leaves and discard. Wash the leaves, drain and chop them.

Make the dough and roll it out as given for palak paratha (p. 24).

Toast each paratha in a non-stick pan on medium heat, till golden brown on both sides.

Serve hot with curd, onion slices, lemon wedges and any curry or dal.

Nutritive values for 1 paratha: Calories: 215.0kcal; Carbohydrate: 41.0g; Protein: 9.4g; Fat: 1.5g; Minerals: 3.7g; Fibre: 2.2g.

PUDINA PARATHA

Toasted mint leaf flatbread

Preparation time: 15 mins; Cooking time: 4 mins

Pudina paratha is an unleavened, innovative flatbread made with fresh mint leaves. Use mint and cumin powder instead of coriander leaves and coriander powder and make the parathas as given for hara dhania paratha (p. 39). Serve them hot with curd, onion slices, lemon wedges and any curry or dal.

Nutritive values for 1 paratha: Calories: 217.0kcal; Carbohydrate: 40.0g; Protein: 10.9g; Fat: 1.5g; Minerals: 8.3g; Fibre: 3.0g.

CELERY PARATHA

Toasted celery leaf flatbread

Preparation time: 15 mins; Cooking time: 4 mins

Celery paratha is an unleavened, innovative flatbread made with fresh celery leaves. Use a medium-sized head of celery instead of coriander leaves, omit the coriander powder and make the parathas as given for hara dhania paratha (p. 39). Serve them hot with onion, cucumber and carrot slices and a raita.

Nutritive values for 1 paratha: Calories: 208.0kcal; Carbohydrate: 36.3g; Protein: 12.4g; Fat: 1.5g; Minerals: 3.5g; Fibre: 2.4g.

PARSLEY PARATHA

Toasted parsley flatbread

Preparation time: 15 mins; Cooking time: 4 mins

Parsley paratha is an unleavened, innovative flatbread made with fresh parsley leaves. Use parsley instead of coriander leaves, omit the coriander powder and make 2 parathas as given for hara dhania paratha (p. 39). Serve them hot with curd, onion slices, lemon wedges and a vegetable curry.

Nutritive values for 1 paratha: Calories: 258.0kcal; Carbohydrate: 48.2g; Protein: 12.0g; Fat: 1.9g; Minerals: 4.6g; Fibre: 2.8g.

PAN-FRIED AND TOASTED PARATHAS WITH DAIRY PRODUCTS

Dairy products are the highest source of calcium and provide calories, fat, protein, carbohydrates, phosphorus, potassium, chloride, sodium, magnesium, zinc and various other essential trace minerals, the B-complex vitamins (thiamine, riboflavin, niacin, vitamin B6, vitamin B12) and vitamins A, D and E.

Non-vegetarians should opt for low-fat dairy products, as they get vitamin A, B12 and D from several non-vegetarian foods. Vegetarians should also generally choose low-fat dairy products, but can occasionally consume high-fat ones, such as milk and curd, since vitamins A, B12 and D are present only in these and are absent in plant foods. Vegans should consume high-fat dairy products a few times a week and should not avoid milk or curd, because it is an animal product.

Flatbreads made with wholewheat flour and dairy products are one-dish meals as they contribute good-quality macro and micro nutrients.

MAKHAN PARATHA
Buttered flatbread

Preparation time: 15 mins; Cooking time: 4 mins

Makhan paratha is a rich, unleavened, traditional, Punjabi flatbread made with fresh, home-made, white butter. (Restaurants make them with processed butter.)

Ingredients for 2 parathas
Dough to make 2 sada parathas (p. 22)
2 tsp + 1 tsp fresh home-made white butter

Method
Roll out the dough as given for tava paratha (p. 23), using butter instead of ghee.

Toast each paratha in a non-stick pan on medium heat, till golden brown on both sides.

Smear each paratha with ¼ tsp butter on both sides.

Serve hot with curd.

Nutritive values for 1 paratha: Calories: 230.0kcal; Carbohydrate: 34.7g; Protein: 6.1g; Fat: 7.4g; Minerals: 1.5g; Fibre: 0.95g.

Health Tip : Butter is a saturated fat and rich in cholesterol. Limit its intake.

CHEESE PARATHA

Pan-fried flatbread with cheese filling

Preparation time: 15 mins; Cooking time: 8 mins

Cheese paratha is an unleavened, traditional flatbread, stuffed with cheese slices.

Ingredients for 2 parathas

Dough to make 2 sada parathas (p. 22)
2 tsp oil
The filling
4 cheese slices
¼ tsp black pepper powder
¼ tsp cumin powder

Method

Roll out the dough and make the parathas as given for kela paratha (p. 36).

Pan-fry each paratha with 1 tsp oil, as given for sada paratha (p. 22).

Serve hot with any curry or dal.

Nutritive values for 1 paratha: Calories: 382.0kcal; Carbohydrate: 37.7g; Protein: 15.9g; Fat: 13.6g; Minerals: 3.1g; Fibre: 1.1g.

Healthy modifications: Use low-fat cheese.

See sada paratha (p. 22) for further modifications.

CHEESE-PANEER-LAL MIRCH PARATHA

Cheese-paneer-chilli roll

Preparation time: 15 mins; Cooking time: 4 mins

Cheese-paneer-lal mirch paratha is an unleavened roll, filled with cheese, paneer and chilli flakes and is on several restaurant menus.

Ingredients for 2 rolls

2 hot sada parathas (p. 22)
The filling
4 tsp cheese spread
4 tsp grated paneer
2 tsp red chilli flakes
2 tsp mixed herbs (rosemary, thyme, sweet basil, sage), chopped

Method

Lay the parathas on a flat work surface.

Spread 2 tsp cheese spread and 2 tsp paneer evenly over each paratha.

Sprinkle the chilli flakes and herbs on top.

Gently roll the parathas and serve immediately with any curry or dal.

Nutritive values for 1 roll: Calories: 309.0kcal; Carbohydrate: 35.7g; Protein: 10.9g; Fat: 13.0g; Minerals: 2.3g; Fibre: 1.1g.

Healthy modifications: Use low-fat cheese.

Use low-fat paneer made with skimmed milk.

See sada paratha (p. 22) for further modifications.

PANEER PARATHA

Pan-fried flatbread with paneer filling

Preparation time: 15 mins; Cooking time: 5 mins

Paneer paratha is an unleavened, traditional, Punjabi flatbread, stuffed with paneer.

Ingredients for 2 parathas

The filling
100g low-fat paneer
2 onions, minced
3 cloves garlic, minced
1 green chilli, minced
1 tsp grated ginger
½ tsp garam masala powder
A pinch of salt or to taste
To prepare the parathas
Dough to make 2 sada parathas (p. 22)
2 tsp oil

Method

Grate the paneer and mix it with the remaining filling ingredients.

Divide the filling into 2 portions.

Divide the dough into 2 portions and shape them into balls.

Make the parathas and pan-fry them as given for band gobi paratha (p. 25).

Serve hot with curd and any curry or dal.

Nutritive values for 1 paratha: Calories: 406.0kcal; Carbohydrate: 42.7g; Protein: 16.2g; Fat: 18.8g; Minerals: 2.9g; Fibre: 1.4g.

Healthy modifications: Use low-fat paneer made with skimmed milk.

See sada paratha (p. 22) for further modifications.

KASHMIRI PARATHA

Kashmiri flatbread

Preparation time: 20 mins; Cooking time: 6 mins

Kashmiri paratha is an unleavened, traditional flatbread stuffed with paneer, fresh pineapple and cherries.

Ingredients for 2 parathas

The filling
100g cottage cheese, grated
1 cup grated pineapple
1 cup chopped and seeded cherries
To prepare the parathas
Dough to make 2 sada parathas (p. 22)
2 tsp oil

Method

Mix all the filling ingredients in a bowl.

Prepare the parathas as given for kela paratha (p. 36).

Pan-fry each paratha with 1 tsp oil, as given for sada paratha (p. 22).

Serve hot with onion slices, lemon wedges and any curry or dal.

Nutritive values for 1 paratha: Calories: 427.0kcal; Carbohydrate: 47.6g; Protein: 16.0g; Fat: 19.1g; Minerals: 2.0g; Fibre: 1.4g.

Healthy modifications: Use low-fat paneer made with skimmed milk.

HARA SABJI-PANEER PARATHA

Toasted flatbread with vegetable and paneer filling

Preparation time: 15 mins; Cooking time: 5 mins

Hara sabji paneer-paratha is an unleavened, traditional, Punjabi flatbread stuffed with mixed leafy vegetables and paneer. Use spinach, red spinach, sour spinach, fenugreek leaves and radish leaves.

Ingredients for 2 parathas

The filling
100g paneer
1 onion, minced
2 cups mixed leafy green vegetables, chopped
3 cloves garlic, minced
1 green chilli, minced
1 tsp grated ginger
½ tsp garam masala powder
A pinch of salt or to taste
To prepare the paratha
Dough to make 2 sada parathas (p. 22)

Method

Grate the paneer and mix it with the remaining filling ingredients.

Make the parathas as given for band gobi paratha (p. 25).

Toast each paratha in a non-stick pan on medium heat, till golden brown on both sides.

Serve hot with curd and any curry or dal.

Nutritive values for 1 paratha: Calories: 361.0kcal; Carbohydrate: 42.7g; Protein: 16.2g; Fat: 13.8g; Minerals: 2.9g; Fibre: 1.4g.

Healthy modifications: Use a low-fat paneer made with skimmed milk.

Use tofu instead of paneer.

PAN-FRIED AND TOASTED PARATHAS WITH SEEDS AND SPICES

Though whole grain cereals, legumes and nuts are also seeds, for culinary purposes, only the seeds of fruits, vegetables, spices and oilseeds are considered as seeds. Water melon, musk melon and jackfruit seeds are examples of fruit seeds. Pumpkin and lotus seeds are examples of vegetable seeds. Sesame, mustard and flax seeds are examples of oil seeds. Some pseudo grains such as amaranth (rajgira) and garden cress (sabja) are also considered as seeds. Flatbreads made with amaranth seeds are consumed during fasts in western India.

Seeds are good sources of phytochemicals, especially flavonoids and are rich in some antioxidant nutrients. A few are good sources of carbohydrates (amaranth), protein (pumpkin, sesame and melon) and fat (oilseeds such as sesame, mustard and flax). In addition, seeds contain minerals such as calcium, phosphorus, potassium, magnesium, iron, zinc (sesame, amaranth, garden cress, pumpkin, jackfruit) and vitamins E and B and dietary fibre. Pumpkin and flax seeds are good sources of omega-3 fatty acids. Sesame seeds contain monounsaturated fatty acids (MUFA) and polyunsaturated fatty acids (PUFA).

Flatbreads made with wholewheat flour and seeds are one-dish meals as they contribute good-quality macro and micro nutrients.

Some mild spices are also seeds, and those that contribute to health benefits should be included in the daily diet. Cumin, coriander, caraway, nigella, carom, fenugreek, celery, pepper, and aniseed are examples of spice seeds. Add them to flatbreads for flavour.

Most spices have therapeutic values, stimulate the appetite and aid in digestion by relieving flatulence, colic problems and constipation. Some, like fenugreek seeds reduce blood sugar, blood cholesterol and blood triglyceride levels.

TIL PARATHA

Toasted sesame seed flatbread

Preparation time: 15 mins; Cooking time: 4 mins

Til paratha is an unleavened, innovative flatbread made with sesame seeds.

Ingredients for 2 parathas

1 cup wholewheat flour
4 tsp sesame seeds
A pinch of salt or to taste

Method

Mix the flour and sesame seeds in a bowl.

Prepare the dough as given for sada paratha (p. 22), without adding the oil and roll out the parathas.

Toast each paratha in a non-stick pan on medium heat, till golden brown on both sides.

Serve hot with curd and any curry or dal.

Nutritive values for 1 paratha: Calories: 227.0kcal; Carbohydrate: 37.2g; Protein: 7.9g; Fat: 5.2g; Minerals: 1.9g; Fibre: 1.2g.

KALONJI PARATHA

Toasted flatbread with nigella seeds

Preparation time: 15 mins; Cooking time: 4 mins

Kalonji paratha is an unleavened, innovative flatbread made with nigella seeds. Use 2 tsp of nigella seeds instead of 4 tsp of sesame and make 2 parathas as given for til paratha (alongside). Serve them hot with curd and any curry or dal.

Nutritive values for 1 paratha: Calories: 189.0kcal; Carbohydrate: 36.0g; Protein: 6.9g; Fat: 2.0g; Minerals: 1.8g; Fibre: 2.0g.

AJWAIN PARATHA

Pan-fried flatbread with carom seeds

Preparation time: 4 mins; Cooking time: 4 mins

Ajwain paratha is an unleavened, traditional north Indian and Rajasthani flatbread, made with carom seeds. Use 2 tsp of carom seeds instead of 4 tsp of sesame and make 2 parathas as given for til paratha (alongside). Serve them hot with curd and a dry vegetable curry.

Nutritive values for 1 paratha: Calories: 234.0kcal; Carbohydrate: 36.0g; Protein: 6.9g; Fat: 7.0g; Minerals: 1.8g; Fibre: 2.0g.

BHOPLA PARATHA

Toasted flatbread with pumpkin

Preparation time: 15 mins; Cooking time: 4 mins

Bhopla paratha is an unleavened, innovative flatbread, made with fresh pumpkin and dried seeds. The latter offer omega-3 fatty acids. Avoid salted or fried seeds.

Ingredients for 2 parathas

1 cup wholewheat flour
1 cup red pumpkin purée
4 tsp pumpkin seeds
A pinch of salt or to taste

Method

Make the dough and roll it out as given for palak paratha (p. 24).

Toast each paratha in a non-stick pan on medium heat, till golden brown on both sides.

Serve hot with curd and any curry or dal.

Nutritive values for 1 paratha: Calories: 241.0kcal; Carbohydrate: 38.6g; Protein: 9.2g; Fat: 5.6g; Minerals: 2.1g; Fibre: 1.3g.

ALSI PARATHA

Toasted flatbread with flax seeds

Preparation time: 15 mins; Cooking time: 4 mins

Alsi paratha is an unleavened, innovative flatbread made with flax seeds. Flax seeds offer omega-3 fatty acids, the essential fatty acids for vegetarians. Use 4 tsp of coarsely powdered flax seeds instead of 4 tsp of sesame and make 2 parathas as given for til paratha (facing page). Serve them hot with curd and any curry or dal.

Nutritive values for 1 paratha: Calories: 224.0kcal; Carbohydrate: 37.6g; Protein: 8.1g; Fat: 4.6g; Minerals: 1.6g; Fibre: 1.4g.

KHAS-KHAS PARATHA

Toasted flatbread with poppy seeds

Preparation time: 15 mins; Cooking time: 4 mins

Khas-khas paratha is an unleavened, traditional flatbread, made with poppy seeds. Use 4 tsp of poppy seeds instead of 4 tsp of sesame and add ½ tsp of garam masala powder. Make 2 parathas as given for til paratha (facing page). Serve them hot with curd and any curry or dal.

Nutritive values for 1 paratha: Calories: 212.0kcal; Carbohydrate: 38.4g; Protein: 8.2g; Fat: 2.8g; Minerals: 2.4g; Fibre: 1.8g.

Health tip: Poppy seeds are high in calories. Limit their intake.

SAUNF PARATHA

Toasted flatbread with fennel

Preparation time: 15 mins; Cooking time: 4 mins

Saunf paratha is an unleavened, innovative flatbread, made with fresh fennel and dried seeds. Use 4 tsp of fennel seeds and 1 cup of shredded fennel bulb and leaves instead of the pumpkin seeds and pumpkin purée, and make 2 parathas as given for bhopla paratha (alongside). Serve them hot with curd and any curry or dal.

Nutritive values for 1 paratha: Calories: 220.0kcal; Carbohydrate: 41.3g; Protein: 8.4g; Fat: 2.4g; Minerals: 2.0g; Fibre: 2.2g.

MASALA PARATHA

PAN-FRIED SPICY FLATBREAD

Preparation time: 15 mins; Cooking time: 4 mins

Masala paratha is a spicy unleavened, traditional, north Indian flatbread.

Ingredients for 2 parathas

1 cup wholewheat flour
1 onion, puréed
2 tsp ginger-garlic-green chilli paste
2 tsp garam masala powder
A pinch of salt or to taste
To pan-fry the parathas
2 tsp oil

Method

Mix all the ingredients, except the salt, in a bowl.

Prepare the dough as given for sada paratha (p. 22), without adding the oil and roll out the parathas.

Pan-fry each paratha with 1 tsp oil, as given for sada paratha.

Serve hot with curd and any curry or dal.

Nutritive values for 1 paratha: Calories: 264.0kcal; Carbohydrate: 42.2g; Protein: 7.6g; Fat: 7.1g; Minerals: 2.1g; Fibre: 2.3g.

Healthy modifications: Toast the parathas in a non-stick pan without oil. This will reduce 5g fat and 45kcal from each paratha.

PAN-FRIED AND TOASTED PARATHAS WITH NUTS

Flatbreads made with nuts are higher in calories than others. Nuts are a good source of high-quality protein, B-complex vitamins, vitamin E, minerals such as calcium, magnesium, potassium, phosphorus, manganese, copper, iron, zinc, selenium and fibre. They are high in antioxidants and many phytochemicals.

The fat found in most nuts contain monounsaturated fatty acids (MUFA). Walnuts contain polyunsaturated fats such as omega-3 fatty acids. So nuts are low in saturated fats and cholesterol. Since they are rich in fats, they are high in calories and are energy-rich foods. Nuts are also a good source of fibre, but contain very little carbohydrates. So they are foods of low glycemic index. Peanuts are used in Marathi and Mughlai cuisines; cashewnuts and almonds in Punjabi and Mughlai cuisines; and walnuts are used in Kashmir and Himachal Pradesh. Parathas with nuts are good for growing children, especially vegetarians, who require good-quality proteins in their diet.

They are one-dish meals, as they offer good-quality macro and micro nutrients.

BADAM PARATHA

Toasted almond flatbread

Preparation time: 15 mins; Cooking time: 4 mins

Badam paratha is an unleavened, innovative flatbread, using powdered almonds, and is commonly consumed in Punjab.

Ingredients for 2 parathas

A pinch of salt or to taste
1 cup wholewheat flour
2 tbsp powdered almonds
1 tsp red chilli flakes

Method

Make the dough and roll it out as given for masala paratha (alongside).

Toast each paratha in a non-stick pan on medium heat, till golden brown on both sides.

Serve hot with curd and any curry or dal.

Nutritive values for 1 paratha: Calories: 269.0kcal; Carbohydrate: 36.3g; Protein: 9.2; Fat: 9.7g; Minerals: 1.8g; Fibre: 1.2g;

MUNGPHALI PARATHA

Toasted peanut flatbread

Preparation time: 15 mins; Cooking time: 4 mins

Mungphali paratha is an unleavened, innovative flatbread, made in the same way as badam paratha (p. 50), using powdered peanuts instead of almonds. Serve them hot with curd and any curry or dal.

Nutritive values for 1 paratha: Calories: 258.0kcal; Carbohydrate: 38.9g; Protein: 9.9g; Fat: 6.9g; Minerals: 1.7g; Fibre: 1.5g.

KAJU PARATHA

Toasted cashewnut flatbread

Preparation time: 15 mins; Cooking time: 4 mins

Kaju paratha is an unleavened, innovative flatbread, made in the same way as badam paratha (alongside), using powdered cashewnuts instead of almonds. Serve them hot with a salad, curd and any curry or dal.

Nutritive values for 1 paratha: Calories: 266.0kcal; Carbohydrate: 38.9g; Protein: 9.6g; Fat: 8.1g; Minerals: 1.9g; Fibre: 1.9g

AKHROT PARATHA

Toasted walnut flatbread

Preparation time: 15 mins; Cooking time: 4 mins

Akhrot paratha is an unleavened, innovative flatbread, made in the same way as badam paratha (p. 49), using powdered walnuts instead of almonds, and is served in Kashmir. Serve them hot with a salad, curd and any curry or dal.

Nutritive values for 1 paratha: Calories: 277.0kcal; Carbohydrate: 37.1g; Protein: 8.6g; Fat: 10.6g; Minerals: 1.7g; Fibre: 1.4g.

PISTA PARATHA

TOASTED PISTACHIO FLATBREAD

Preparation time: 15 mins; Cooking time: 4 mins

Pista paratha is an unleavened, innovative flatbread found in Mughlai cuisine. It is made in the same way as badam paratha (p. 49), using powdered pistachios instead of almonds. Serve them hot with a salad, curd and any curry or dal.

Nutritive values for 1 paratha: Calories: 265.0kcal; Carbohydrate: 37.2g; Protein: 9.0; Fat: 8.9g; Minerals: 1.8g; Fibre: 1.3g.

OTHER PAN-FRIED AND TOASTED PARATHAS

Flatbreads are often made with a mixture of vegetables, herbs, seeds, spices and nuts. These are one-dish meals and offer good-quality macro and micro nutrients.

TOFU-HARA PYAZ PARATHA

Flatbread with tofu, spring onion filling

Preparation time: 15 mins; Cooking time: 4 mins

Tofu-hara pyaz paratha is an unleavened, innovative flatbread made with wholewheat flour and stuffed with tofu and spring onion.

Ingredients for 2 parathas

The filling
100g tofu
6-8 spring onion stems
2 tsp oil
1 tsp garam masala powder
A pinch of salt or to taste
The dough
Dough to make 2 sada parathas (p. 22)

Method

Squeeze the water out of the tofu and crumble it.

Wash the spring onion leaves and chop them fine. (Reserve the bulbs for another use.)

Heat the oil in a pan and sauté the spring onion leaves for a few mins.

Mix in the tofu, garam masala powder and salt. Simmer for a few mins.

Divide the filling into 2 portions and leave aside, till cool.

Divide the dough into 4 portions and shape them into balls.

Prepare and cook the parathas as given for kela paratha (p. 36).

Serve hot with any curry or dal.

Nutritive values for 1 paratha: Calories: 256.0kcal; Carbohydrate: 45.4g; Protein: 11.2g; Fat: 3.5g; Minerals: 1.9g; Fibre: 1.9g.

SOYA-HARA MATTAR PARATHA

Flatbread with soya, green pea filling

Preparation time: 15 mins; Cooking time: 20 mins

Soya-hara mattar paratha is an unleavened, innovative flatbread stuffed with soya granules and green peas.

Ingredients for 2 parathas

The filling
2 cups soya granules
1 cup shelled green peas
2 tsp oil
2 onions, puréed
2 tsp ginger-garlic-green chilli paste
A pinch of salt or to taste
The dough
Dough to make 2 sada parathas (p. 22)

Method

Soak the soya granules in boiling hot water for 10 mins.

Squeeze well and rinse twice in fresh water. Squeeze again.

Grind the green peas to make a purée.

Heat the oil in a pan and sauté the onions and ginger-garlic-green chilli paste for a few mins.

Mix in the soya granules, green peas and salt and sauté for 2 mins longer.

Divide the filling into 2 portions and leave aside, till cool.

Divide the dough into 4 portions and shape them into balls.

Prepare and cook the parathas as given for kela paratha (p. 36).

Serve hot with sliced spring onions, shredded cabbage and any curry or dal.

Nutritive values for 1 paratha: Calories: 300.0kcal; Carbohydrate: 49.3g; Protein: 12.4g; Fat: 5.9g; Minerals: 2.2g; Fibre: 3.4g.

KHUMB PARATHA

Button mushroom flatbread

Preparation time: 15 mins; Cooking time: 4 mins

Khumb paratha is an unleavened, innovative flatbread made with chopped button mushrooms.

Ingredients for 4 parathas

8 button mushrooms
1 cup wholewheat flour
2 tsp fresh rosemary leaves
2 tsp fresh thyme leaves
A pinch of salt or to taste

Method

Wash the mushrooms thoroughly. Wipe well. Remove and discard the stalks. Chop the heads fine.

Mix all the ingredients in a bowl.

Make the dough as given for palak paratha (p. 24).

Divide the dough into 4 portions and shape them into balls.

Press each dough ball on a greased plastic sheet with your fingertips into a 3"- 4" circle.

Toast each paratha in a non-stick pan on medium heat, till golden brown on both sides.

Serve hot with shredded cabbage and any curry or dal.

Nutritive values for 1 paratha: Calories: 192.0kcal; Carbohydrates: 36.9g; Protein: 7.6g; Fat: 1.3g; Minerals: 2.1g; Fibre: 1.2g.

TEEKHA, MEETHA AND KHATTA PARATHA

Toasted hot, sweet and sour flatbread

Preparation time: 10 mins; Cooking time: 4 mins

Tikka, meetha and khatta paratha is an unleavened, innovative flatbread — pungent, sweet, sour and mouth watering!

Ingredients for 2 parathas

1 cup wholewheat flour
1 cup grated red pumpkin flesh
1 green chilli, minced
½ tsp red chilli powder
2 tsp grated jaggery, dissolved in little water
2 tbsp tamarind pulp
¼ tsp coriander-cumin powder
A pinch of salt or to taste

Method

Make the dough and roll it out as given for palak paratha (p. 24).

Toast each paratha in a non-stick pan on medium heat, till golden brown on both sides.

Serve hot with curd and any curry or dal.

Nutritive values for 1 paratha: Calories: 201.0kcal; Carbohydrate: 41.3g; Protein: 6.8g; Fat: 0.9g; Minerals: 1.8g; Fibre: 1.3g.

SABJI PARATHA

Toasted mixed vegetable flatbread

Preparation time: 15 mins; Cooking time: 4 mins

Sabji paratha is an unleavened, innovative flatbread made with mixed vegetables.

Ingredients for 2 parathas

1 cup wholewheat flour
1 cup grated or shredded mixed vegetables (carrot, bell peppers, cabbage, cauliflower)
2 tbsp puréed mixed herbs (coriander, mint, celery, parsley)
½ tsp garam masala powder
A pinch of salt or to taste

Method

Make the dough and roll it out as given for palak paratha (p. 24).

Toast each paratha in a non-stick pan on medium heat, till golden brown on both sides.

Serve hot with onion slices, lemon wedges and a fruit raita.

Nutritive values for 1 paratha: Calories: 202.0kcal; Carbohydrate: 39.8g; Protein: 7.9g; Fat: 1.2g; Minerals: 1.9g; Fibre: 2.2g.

PALAK-PANEER PARATHA

Toasted spinach flatbread with paneer filling

Preparation time: 15 mins; Cooking time: 4 mins

Palak-paneer paratha is an unleavened, traditional flatbread made with spinach and stuffed with paneer.

Ingredients for 2 parathas

The dough
1 cup wholewheat flour
100g spinach leaves, chopped
½ tsp coriander powder
½ tsp red chilli powder
½ tsp dried mango powder
A pinch of salt or to taste
The filling
100g paneer, grated
½ tsp garam masala powder
A pinch of salt or to taste

Method

Make the dough as given for palak paratha (p. 24).

Mix all the filling ingredients in another bowl.

Make the parathas as given for band gobi paratha (p. 25).

Toast each paratha in a non-stick pan on medium heat, till golden brown on both sides.

Serve hot with onion slices, lemon wedges and a raita.

Nutritive values for 1 paratha: Calories: 334.0kcal; Carbohydrate: 38.6g; Protein: 17.2g; Fat: 12.4g; Minerals: 3.8g; Fibre: 2.5g.

Healthy modifications: Use low-fat paneer.
Use tofu instead of paneer.

METHI-ALOO PARATHA

Toasted fenugreek flatbread with potato filling

Preparation time: 15 mins; Cooking time: 20 mins

Methi-aloo paratha is an unleavened, innovative flatbread made with fresh fenugreek leaves and stuffed with spicy potatoes.

Ingredients for 2 parathas

The dough
1 cup wholewheat flour
100g fenugreek leaves, chopped
½ tsp cumin seeds powder
½ tsp black pepper powder
A pinch of salt or to taste
The filling
Potato filling for 2 parathas (see aloo paratha; p. 31)

Method

Mix all the dough ingredients in a bowl.

Make the dough as given for palak paratha (p. 24).

Make the parathas as given for band gobi paratha (p. 25).

Toast each paratha in a non-stick pan on medium heat, till golden brown on both sides.

Serve hot with tomato slices, lemon wedges and any curry or dal.

Nutritive values for 1 paratha: Calories: 324.0kcal; Carbohydrate: 61.8g; Protein: 10.4g; Fat: 4.4g; Minerals: 2.9g; Fibre: 2.3g.

MAKKAI-PUDINA PARATHA

Toasted flatbread with corn and mint filling

Preparation time: 15 mins; Cooking time: 4 mins

Makkai-pudina paratha is an unleavened, innovative flatbread stuffed with tender corn kernels and mint.

Ingredients for 2 parathas

The filling
1 cup tender sweet corn kernels
A pinch of salt or to taste
4 cups mint leaves
1 tsp oil
1 red chilli, chopped
1 green chilli, chopped
The dough
Dough to make 2 sada parathas (p. 22)

Method

Boil the corn in salted water, till tender. Drain thoroughly.

Lightly roast the mint leaves in a pan on low heat for a few mins.

Heat the oil in a pan and sauté the chillies, till fragrant.

Grind the mint leaves, sautéed chillies and salt to make a smooth paste.

Mix in the corn kernels.

Divide the filling into 2 portions.

Divide the dough into 4 portions and shape them into balls.

Prepare and cook the parathas as given for kela paratha (p. 36).

Serve hot with any raita.

Nutritive values for 1 paratha: Calories: 280.0kcal; Carbohydrate: 49.9g; Protein: 10.8g; Fat: 4.1g; Minerals: 2.7g; Fibre: 2.9g.

KOPRA PARATHA

Toasted dried coconut flatbread

Preparation time: 15 mins; Cooking time: 4 mins

Kopra paratha is an unleavened, traditional flatbread made with desiccated coconut powder or grated dried coconut. These flatbreads have a nutty flavour and are popular in the cuisines of some hilly areas.

Ingredients for 2 parathas

2 tsp coriander seeds
1 tsp cumin seeds
A pinch of salt or to taste
1 cup wholewheat flour
2 tbsp desiccated coconut powder
2 tsp red chilli flakes
1 tsp garam masala powder (clove, cinnamon, black cardamom, caraway seeds)

Method

Roast the coriander and the cumin seeds and powder them.

Prepare the parathas and toast them as given for til paratha (p. 46).

Serve hot with any raita.

Nutritive values for 1 paratha: Calories: 276.0kcal; Carbohydrate: 38.2g; Protein: 7.5g; Fat: 10.4g; Minerals: 1.7g; Fibre: 2.7g.

Healthy modifications: Coconut is rich in saturated fat. Limit its intake.

Replace dried coconut with flax seeds which have a nutty taste but good-quality fat (omega-3 fatty acids).

NARIYAL PARATHA

Toasted fresh coconut flatbread

Preparation time: 15 mins; Cooking time: 4 mins

Nariyal paratha is an unleavened, traditional flatbread made with fresh coconut in the coastal regions of the country.

Ingredients for 2 parathas

1 cup wholewheat flour
2 tbsp grated fresh coconut
2 tsp ginger-garlic-green chilli paste
A pinch of salt or to taste
¾ cup thick coconut milk

Method

Mix all the dry ingredients in a bowl.

Prepare the parathas and toast them as given for til paratha (p. 46), using the coconut milk to make the dough.

Serve hot with any raita.

Nutritive values for 1 paratha: Calories: 237.0kcal; Carbohydrate: 36.7g; Protein: 6.8g; Fat: 7.1g; Minerals: 1.5g; Fibre: 1.5g.

Healthy modifications: Coconut is high in calories and provides saturated fat. Limit its intake.

Replace fresh coconut with a nutty-flavoured tofu.

Replace coconut milk with skimmed milk. While 100 ml of coconut milk provides 430kcal, 100 ml skimmed milk provides only 29kcal.

FRUIT PARATHA

Toasted mixed fruit flatbread

Preparation time: 15 mins; Cooking time: 4 mins

Mixed fruit paratha is an unleavened, innovative flatbread made with puréed mixed fruits.

Ingredients for 2 parathas

2 cups chopped mixed fruits (apple, pear, banana, papaya, peach, fig)
1 cup wholewheat flour

Method

Blend the fruits in the mixer to make a paste.

Make the dough and roll it out as given for palak paratha (p. 24).

Toast each paratha in a non-stick pan on medium heat, till golden brown on both sides.

Serve hot with a mixed vegetable raita.

Nutritive values for 1 paratha: Calories: 237.0kcal; Carbohydrate: 49.7g; Protein: 6.9g; Fat: 1.2g; Minerals: 1.9g; Fibre: 1.9g.

LACHHA PARATHAS (MULTILAYERED FLATBREADS)

Lachha parathas are multilayered, flaky, fluffy, unleavened flatbreads made with wholewheat flour. Each paratha requires 120-130g of dough. Cooking techniques for lachha parathas vary from place to place and can be quite laborious. They are made plain or with leafy greens, herbs or dairy products. They are best toasted on a hot pan. In some parts of north India, especially in Punjab, lachha parathas are fried (Amritsari lachha paratha; p. 59) or cooked in a tandoor.

They have a higher calorific value than parathas, chapattis or phulkas, since they require more dough and fat. So they are heavier and more filling than the other flatbreads.

SADA LACHHA PARATHA

Plain multilayered flatbread

Preparation time: 30-40 mins; Cooking time: 5 mins

Sada lachha paratha is an unleavened, traditional, Punjabi flatbread.

Ingredients for 2 parathas

The dough
A pinch of salt or to taste
1 tbsp ghee
1½ cups wholewheat flour
To roll the parathas
1 tbsp ghee
To pan-fry the parathas
2 tsp oil

Method

Dissolve the salt in about 110 ml of water.

Rub the ghee into the flour in a bowl.

Gradually add the salt water and knead for about 15 mins to make a smooth dough.

Cover the dough and leave it aside for about 30 mins.

Knead it again for about 10 mins, grease it with few drops of ghee and leave it aside for another 15 mins.

Divide the dough into 2 portions and shape them into balls.

Roll out a portion of the dough on a lightly floured board, as thin as possible.

Apply 1 tsp ghee evenly over it.

Fold the dough in the form of a fan or roll it tightly into a rope.

Stretch it at both ends and twist it.

Apply ½ tsp ghee on the inner surface of the twisted rope and on the 2 ends.

(Method Cont.)

Coil the twisted rope at both ends to meet at the centre.

Place the 2 circular coils one over the other and gently press the top.

Roll the dough into a 6" circle.

Pan-fry the paratha as given for sada paratha (p. 22).

Pat the flatbread at the edges with your palms to make it flakier.

Repeat with the second portion of dough.

Serve hot with a mixed vegetable pickle, baby onions and any curry or dal.

Nutritive values for 1 paratha: Calories: 436.0kcal; Carbohydrate: 52.1g; Protein: 9.1g; Fat: 21.3g; Minerals: 2.0g; Fibre: 1.4g.

Healthy modifications: Ghee is high in calories and is a saturated fat. Replace it with oil.

Avoid applying ghee on the rolled out dough. This will reduce 15g fat and 135kcal from each paratha. However, it will not be flaky and fluffy.

Toast the paratha in a non-stick pan without oil. This will further reduce 5g fat and 45kcal from each paratha.

MAKHAN LACHHA PARATHA

Multilayered flatbread with butter

Preparation time: 30-40 mins; Cooking time: 4 mins

Makhan lachha paratha is an unleavened, traditional, Punjabi flatbread. It is made in the same way as sada lachha paratha (facing page), replacing the ghee with melted home-made white butter. Serve them hot with a salad, curd and any curry or dal.

Nutritive values for 1 paratha: Calories: 411.0kcal; Carbohydrate: 52.1g; Protein: 9.1g;

Fat: 18.5g; Minerals: 2.4g; Fibre: 1.4g.

Healthy modifications: White butter is a saturated fat, rich in cholesterol.

Toast the paratha in a non-stick pan without oil. This will reduce 5g fat and 45kcal from each paratha.

HARA BHAJI LACHHA PARATHA

Multilayered flatbread with leafy greens

Preparation time: 30-40 mins; Cooking time: 5 mins

Hara bhaji lachha paratha is an unleavened, traditional, multilayered, Punjabi flatbread made with fresh leafy greens.

Ingredients for 2 parathas

The dough
A pinch of salt or to taste
1½ cups wholewheat flour
1 cup mixed fresh leafy greens (spinach, leek, fenugreek leaves), chopped
½ tsp garam masala powder
2 green chillies, minced
1 tbsp ghee
To roll the parathas
1 tbsp ghee
To pan-fry the parathas
2 tsp oil

Method

Dissolve the salt in about 50 ml of water.

Combine the flour with the remaining dough ingredients.

Prepare the dough, roll out the parathas and cook them as given for sada lachha paratha (facing page).

Serve hot with any curry or dal.

Nutritive values for 1 paratha: Calories: 450.0kcal; Carbohydrate: 53.7g; Protein: 10.2g; Fat: 21.7g; Minerals: 3.0g; Fibre: 2.1g.

Healthy modifications: See sada lachha paratha (p. 58).

AMRITSARI LACHHA PARATHA

Shallow-fried multilayered flatbread

Preparation time: 30-40 mins; Cooking time: 4 mins

Amritsari lachha paratha is an unleavened, traditional, multilayered, Punjabi flatbread. Make regular lachha parathas, shallow-fry them in ghee and drain them on tissue paper. Serve them hot with curd and any curry or dal.

Nutritive values for 1 paratha: Calories: 526.0kcal; Carbohydrate: 52.1kcal; Protein: 9.1g; Fat: 31.3g; Minerals: 2.0g; Fibre: 1.4g.

Healthy modifications: See sada lachha parathas (p. 56).

PANEER LACHHA PARATHA

Multilayered flatbread with paneer

Preparation time: 30-40 mins; Cooking time: 5 mins

Paneer lachha paratha is an unleavened, traditional north Indian and Mughlai flatbread made with paneer.

Ingredients for 2 parathas

The dough
A pinch of salt or to taste
1½ cups wholewheat flour
½ cup grated paneer
½ tsp garam masala powder
2 green chillies, minced
2 tbsp coriander leaves, chopped
1 tbsp ghee
To roll the parathas
1 tbsp ghee
To pan-fry the parathas
2 tsp oil

Method

Dissolve the salt in about 75 ml of water.

Combine the flour with the remaining dough ingredients.

Prepare the dough, roll out the parathas and cook them as given for sada lachha paratha (p. 56).

Serve hot with a light vegetable curry.

Nutritive values for 1 paratha: Calories: 479.0kcal; Carbohydrate: 52.9g; Protein: 12.1g; Fat: 24.4g; Minerals: 2.6g; Fibre: 2.0g.

Healthy modifications: Use low-fat paneer.

Replace paneer with tofu.

See sada lachha parathas (p. 56) for further modifications.

KASOORI METHI LACHHA PARATHA

Multilayered flatbread with dried fenugreek leaves

Preparation time: 30-40 mins; Cooking time: 5 mins

Kasoori methi lachha paratha is an unleavened, traditional, north Indian and Mughlai flatbread made with dried fenugreek leaves.

Ingredients for 2 parathas

The dough
1 cup dried fenugreek leaves
A pinch of salt or to taste
1½ cups wholewheat flour
½ tsp garam masala powder
2 green chillies, minced
To roll the parathas
1 tbsp ghee
To pan-fry the parathas
2 tsp oil

Method

Soak the fenugreek leaves in 50 ml of hot water for about 10 mins.

Dissolve the salt in the same hot water.

Combine the flour with the soaked fenugreek leaves and remaining dough ingredients.

Prepare the dough, roll out the parathas and cook them as given for sada lachha paratha (p. 56).

Serve hot with curd and any curry or dal.

Nutritive values for 1 paratha: Calories: 461.0kcal; Carbohydrate: 55.3g; Protein: 11.4g; Fat: 21.7g; Minerals: 2.9g; Fibre: 2.3g.

Healthy modifications: See sada lachha parathas (p. 56).

MASALA TIKADIA

Spicy multilayered flatbread

Preparation time: 30-40 mins; Cooking time: 5 mins

Masala tikadia is an unleavened, traditional, spicy, crisp, Rajasthani flatbread, which somewhat resembles the Mughlai lachha paratha.

Ingredients for 2 parathas

The dough
A pinch of salt or to taste
2 tsp ghee
1 cup wholewheat flour
To roll the parathas
2 tsp ghee
1 tsp roasted cumin powder
½ tsp red chilli powder
To pan-fry the parathas
4 tsp oil

Method

Dissolve the salt in 50 ml of water.

Prepare the dough, roll out the parathas and cook them as given for sada lachha paratha (p. 56). Sprinkle ½ tsp cumin powder and ¼ tsp red chilli powder over each paratha before rolling it into a rope.

Serve hot with any curry or dal.

Nutritive values for 1 paratha: Calories: 364.0kcal; Carbohydrates: 36.1g; Protein: 6.7g; Fat: 21.5g; Minerals: 1.6g; Fibre: 1.4g.

Healthy modifications: See sada lachha paratha (p. 56).

SATPURO PHULKO
Multilayered Sindhi flatbread
Preparation time: 30-40 mins; Cooking time: 5 mins

Satpuro phulko is an unleavened, traditional, Sindhi, flaky flatbread. It resembles the Punjabi lachha paratha, but the technique of rolling the dough differs.

Ingredients for 2 phulkos

The dough
A pinch of salt or to taste
1½ cups wholewheat flour
¼ tsp black pepper powder
1 tbsp oil
To roll the dough
2 tbsp oil

Method

Dissolve the salt in 110 ml water.

Mix the flour with the pepper in a bowl.

Prepare the dough as given for sada lachha paratha (p. 56).

Divide the dough into 2 portions and shape them into balls.

Roll out a portion of the dough on a lightly floured board into a 6"- 7" circle.

Sprinkle a little flour and 2 tsp oil over the surface.

Cut the rolled out dough vertically into 5 strips.

Roll out 1 strip.

Place it over a second strip and roll it again.

Repeat, till all the strips are used.

(Method Cont.)

Press it gently on top and roll out again into a 6" circle.

Pan-fry the phulko as given for sada paratha (p. 22), using 1 tsp oil.

Repeat with the second portion of dough.

Serve hot with any curry or dal.

Nutritive values for 1 phulko: Calories: 458.0kcal; Carbohydrates: 52.1g; Protein: 9.1g; Fat: 23.8g; Minerals: 2.0g; Fibre: 1.4g.

Healthy modifications: Avoid adding oil to the flour while making the dough. This will reduce 7.5g fat and 67 kcal from each paratha.

Avoid sprinkling oil while rolling the dough. This will reduce an additional 10g fat and 90kcal from each paratha.

Toast the paratha in a non-stick pan without oil. This will further reduce 5g fat and 45kcal from each paratha.

TANDOORI & TAVA ROTIS (BAKED & TOASTED FLATBREADS)

Tandoori rotis are slapped on to the inner walls of a tandoor (clay oven). They cook rapidly and are peeled off with the help of a long iron rod.

MAKHAN TANDOORI ROTI

Tandoori flatbread with butter

Preparation time: 15 mins; Cooking time: 4 mins

Makhan tandoori roti is a rich, creamy, soft, unleavened, traditional, Punjabi and Mughlai flatbread.

Ingredients for 2 rotis

1 cup wholewheat flour
A pinch of salt or to taste
½ cup warm milk
2 tbsp home-made white butter, melted

Method

Mix the flour and salt in a bowl.

Add warm milk and melted butter to the flour.

To make the rotis and cook them: Knead it for 5-10 mins to make a smooth dough.

Cover the dough and leave it aside for about 20 mins.

Knead it again for a few mins.

Divide the dough into 2 portions and shape them into balls.

Roll them on a lightly floured board into 5" circles.

Stretch the rotis on one side to give it an oval shape.

Bake them in a clay, gas or electric tandoor, till golden brown on both sides.

Alternatively, toast each paratha in a non-stick pan on medium heat, till golden brown on both sides.

Serve hot with a salad, curd and any Mughlai curry or dal.

Nutritive values for 1 roti: Calories: 304.0kcal; Carbohydrate: 34.7g; Protein: 7.1g; Fat: 14.6g; Minerals: 1.9g; Fibre: 0.95g.

Healthy modifications: Butter is high in calories and provides saturated fat. Replace it with oil.

Replace the butter with curd, and if required apply ½ tsp butter over the roti before serving them. This will reduce 9.1g fat and 91kcal from each roti.

MALAI TANDOORI ROTI

Tandoori flatbread with cream

Preparation time: 15 mins; Cooking time: 4 mins

Malai tandoori roti is an unleavened, traditional, Punjabi and Mughlai flatbread.

Ingredients for 2 rotis

1 cup wholewheat flour
A pinch of salt or to taste
2 tbsp curd
2 tbsp fresh cream

Method

Mix the flour and salt in a bowl.

Add the curd and cream.

Make the rotis and cook them as given for makhan tandoori roti (alongside).

Serve hot with a salad, curd and any Mughlai curry or dal.

Nutritive values for 1 roti: Calories: 233.0kcal; Carbohydrate: 35.7g; Protein: 7.6g; Fat: 6.8g; Minerals: 1.5g; Fibre: 0.95g.

Healthy modifications: Use light cream instead of double or whipping cream.

Replace cream with curd in the flour.

KHAMIRI ROTI

Leavened baked flatbread

Preparation time: 20 mins; Cooking time: 10-12 mins

Khamiri roti is a traditional, Mughlai flatbread, using yeast as a leavening agent. Khamir means yeast.

Ingredients for 4 rotis

1 tsp sugar
½ tsp active dried yeast
2 tbsp warm milk
1 cup wholewheat flour
A pinch of salt or to taste
2 tsp ghee or home-made white butter, melted
To serve
2 tsp ghee or home-made white butter

Method

Mix the sugar, yeast and warm milk in a bowl and leave it aside for 10 mins, till frothy.

Mix the flour, salt and 2 tsp ghee or butter in a bowl.

Add the yeast mixture.

Knead the mixture for 10-15 mins to make a smooth dough.

Cover the dough and leave it aside for about 1 hour to rise.

Knead the dough again, divide it into 4 portions and shape them into balls.

Leave aside again for 10-20 mins.

Knead each ball for about 10 mins.

Roll out each portion of the dough on a lightly floured board into a thick, 4" round.

Bake the rotis in a clay, gas or electric tandoor, till golden brown and fluffy.

(Method Cont.)

Alternatively, place the rotis on a baking sheet and bake them in an electric or gas oven preheated to 180°-200° for 5-6 mins.

Smear each flatbread with ½ tsp ghee or butter before serving.

Serve hot with any Mughlai curry or dal.

Nutritive values for 1 roti: Calories: 143.0kcal; Carbohydrate: 19.0g; Protein: 3.4g; Fat: 5.9g; Minerals: 0.74g; Fibre: 0.95g.

Healthy modifications: Avoid adding ghee or butter to the dough. This will reduce 10g fat and 90kcal from the rotis.

Avoid applying the ghee or butter on the rotis before serving them. This will further reduce 2.5g fat and 27kcal from each roti.

KHOOBA ROTI

Puffed flatbread

Preparation time: 25 mins; Cooking time: 5 mins

Khooba roti is an unleavened, traditional, Rajasthani flatbread. The roti is pinched all over the surface before a final cooking, giving it a puffed look.

Ingredients for 2 rotis

A pinch of salt or to taste
1 cup wholewheat flour
3 tsp ghee
To serve
1 tsp ghee

Method

Dissolve the salt in 50 ml water.

Prepare the dough as given for sada lachha paratha (p. 56).

Divide the dough into 2 portions.

Roll out a portion of the dough on a lightly floured board into a 7"- 8" circle.

Put a non-stick pan on medium heat and toast the roti for 1 minute on each side.

Transfer the roti to a plate. Pinch it all over the surface in a circular pattern.

Toast it again on the hot pan for a few seconds on both sides.

Cook the roti directly over the fire on both sides, till it puffs and turns golden brown.

Roll and cook the second dough portion in the same way.

Smear each roti with ½ tsp ghee.

Serve hot with any curry or dal.

Nutritive values for 1 roti: Calories: 261.0kcal; Carbohydrates: 34.7g; Protein: 6.1g; Fat: 10.1g; Minerals: 1.4g; Fibre: 0.9g.

Healthy modifications: See khamiri roti (p. 63).

KASHMIRI ROTI

Preparation time: 15 mins; Cooking time: 4 mins

Kashmiri roti is an unleavened, traditional, shallow-fried, spicy flatbread.

Ingredients for 4 rotis

¼ tsp saffron strands

¾ cup milk

1½ cups wholewheat flour

1 tbsp powdered walnuts

½ tsp Kashmiri red chilli powder

2 tsp aniseed, coarsely crushed

A pinch of salt or to taste

1 tbsp ghee or home-made white butter, melted

Ghee for shallow-frying

Method

Dissolve the saffron in a little hot milk.

Mix the dry ingredients in a bowl with 1 tbsp ghee or butter.

Add the milk and saffron milk gradually and prepare the dough as given for sada paratha (p. 22).

Divide the dough into 4 portions and shape them into balls.

Roll out a portion of the dough on a lightly floured board into a thick 4" round.

Shallow-fry it in ghee, till golden brown on both sides.

Repeat with the remaining portions of dough.

Serve hot with any curry or dal.

Nutritive values for 1 roti: Calories: 267.0kcal; Carbohydrates: 28.8g; Protein: 6.7g; Fat: 13.9g; Minerals: 1.5g; Fibre: 1.3g.

Healthy modifications: Replace ghee with oil.

See khamiri roti (p. 63) for further modifications.

CHAPATTIS (PAN-FRIED FLATBREADS)

Chapattis are only made with wholewheat flour. Each chapatti requires 70-75g of dough. Chapattis are similar in shape and size to phulkas, but are slightly thicker. They are pan-fried with oil, ghee or home-made white butter and puffed. Chapattis are a staple diet in Maharashtra, Gujarat, Rajasthan and Uttar Pradesh.

DOUGH FOR CHAPATTIS

Ingredients for 4 chapattis

A pinch of salt or to taste

1¼ cups wholewheat flour

Method

Dissolve the salt in about 5 tbsp of water.

Place the flour in a bowl.

Add salt water gradually to the flour and knead it to make a smooth dough.

Knead it for 5-10 mins longer.

Cover the dough with a damp cloth and leave it aside for 20 mins.

Nutritive values of the dough for 4 chapattis: Calories: 426.0 kcal; Carbohydrate: 6.8g; Protein: 15.1g; Fat: 2.1g; Minerals: 3.2g; Fibre: 2.4g.

GHEE CHAPATTI

Plain flatbread pan-fried in ghee

Preparation time: 15 mins; Cooking time: 8 mins

Ghee chapatti is an unleavened, traditional flatbread made in the same way as sada chapatti (p. 66), using ghee instead of oil to pan-fry. Serve them hot with any curry or dal.

Nutritive values for 1 chapatti: Calories: 152.0kcall Carbohydrate: 21.7g; Protein: 3.8g; Fat: 5.5g; Minerals: 0.8g; Fibre: 0.53g;

SADA CHAPATTI

Plain flatbread pan-fried in oil

Preparation time: 15 mins; Cooking time: 8 mins

Sada chapatti is an unleavened, traditional flatbread pan-fried in oil and is served for lunch and dinner in most homes across the country.

Ingredients for 4 chapattis

Dough to make 4 chapattis (p. 65)
4 tsp oil

Method

Divide the dough into 4 portions and shape them into balls.

Roll out a portion of the dough on a lightly floured board into a 6" circle.

To pan-fry the chapatti: Heat a pan and place the rolled dough on it.

When brown spots appear on the surface, flip it over and spoon ½ tsp oil over its edges. Gently press the edges and centre of the chapatti with a spatula and rotate it, so that it puffs up.

When the base is golden brown, flip it over again and spoon another ½ tsp oil over its edges. Press the edges and centre again and cook till the base is golden brown.

Repeat with the remaining portions of dough.

Serve hot with cucumber slices, grated carrot and beetroot salad and any curry or dal.

Nutritive values for 1 chapatti: Calories: 152.0kcal; Carbohydrate: 21.7g; Protein: 3.8g; Fat: 5.5g; Minerals: 0.8g; Fibre: 0.53g.

Healthy modifications: Toast the chapattis in a non-stick pan without oil. This will reduce 5g fat and 45kcal from each chapatti.

LASSOON CHUTNEY CHAPATTI

Garlic chutney flatbread wrap

Preparation time: 20 mins; Cooking time: 10 mins

Lassoon chutney chapatti is an unleavened, innovative flatbread wrap smeared with garlic chutney and filled with vegetables.

Ingredients for 4 wraps

The garlic chutney
1 head garlic flakes
1 onion
1 tomato
1 tbsp tamarind pulp
A pinch of red chilli powder
A pinch of salt or to taste
The seasoning
1 tsp sesame oil
½ tsp mustard seeds
¼ tsp fenugreek seeds
¼ tsp asafoetida
The filling
2 cups grated, shredded or chopped mixed vegetables (cabbage, carrot, capsicum)
The wraps
4 hot sada chapattis prepared without oil (alongside)

Method

Grind the garlic, onion and tomato for the chutney to make a paste.

Heat the oil for the seasoning in a pan and sauté the seasoning ingredients for a minute.

Add the garlic paste, tamarind pulp, chilli powder and salt. Mix the contents well and cook for 10 mins.

Cool and store in an airtight jar in the refrigerator if not using immediately.

(Method Cont.)

Divide the garlic chutney and the filling into 4 portions.

Smear the garlic chutney evenly on the chapattis. Spread the filling along one side of the chapattis and roll them gently.

Serve immediately with plenty of curd.

Nutritive values for 1 wrap: Calories: 168.0kcal; Carbohydrates: 34.1g; Protein: 6.3g; Fat: 0.7g; Minerals: 1.6g; Fibre: 1.6g.

BUTTER CHAPATTI

Plain flatbread pan-fried in white butter

Preparation time: 15 mins; Cooking time: 8 mins

Butter chapatti is an unleavened, traditional flatbread made in the same way as sada chapatti (p. 66), using home-made white butter instead of oil to pan-fry. Serve them hot with any curry or dal.

Nutritive values for 1 chapatti: Calories: 144.0kcal; Carbohydrate: 21.7g; Protein: 3.8g; Fat: 4.5g; Minerals: 0.8g; Fibre: 0.53g.

ADRAK CHUTNEY CHAPATTI

Ginger chutney flatbread wrap

Preparation time: 20 mins; Cooking time: 10 mins

Adrak chutney chapatti is an unleavened, innovative flatbread wrap smeared with ginger chutney and filled with mixed sprouts. Cook the chutney as given below and make the wraps as given for lassoon chutney chapatti (p. 66), using mixed sprouts as the filling.

Ingredients for ginger chutney for 4 wraps

The seasoning
1 tbsp sesame oil
½ tsp mustard seeds
¼ tsp fenugreek seeds
¼ tsp asafoetida powder
1 dried red chilli
The ginger chutney
100g ginger, chopped
2 tbsp tamarind pulp
1 tbsp grated jaggery
A pinch of salt or to taste

Method

Heat the oil for the seasoning in a pan and sauté the seasoning ingredients for a minute. Allow it to cool.

Grind the chutney ingredients with the seasoning to make a smooth paste.

Store in an airtight jar in the refrigerator if not using immediately.

Nutritive values for 1 wrap: Calories: 197.0 kcal; Carbohydrates: 38.2g; Protein: 7.7g; Fat: 1.5g; Minerals: 1.7g; Fibre: 1.6g.

MADAKKU CHAPATTI

Malabar flatbread

Preparation time: 20 mins; Cooking time: 5 mins

Madakku chapatti is an unleavened, traditional, Malabari flatbread.

Ingredients for 2 chapattis

A pinch of salt or to taste
1 cup wholewheat flour
4 tsp ghee

Method

Make the dough and knead it as given for sada chapatti (p. 66).

Divide the dough into 2 portions and shape them into balls.

Roll out a portion of the dough on a lightly floured board into a 6" circle.

Spread 1 tsp of ghee evenly on the surface and sprinkle some flour over it.

Fold the circle into 3 to form a rectangle and fold it again into half to form a square.

Spread ½ tsp ghee on the surface and sprinkle with flour.

Roll it out again into a square.

Pan-fry the chapatti as given for sada chapatti (p. 66), using ghee instead of oil.

Repeat with the second portion of dough.

Serve hot with any curry or dal.

Nutritive values for 1 chapatti: Calories: 261.0 kcal; Carbohydrates: 34.7g; Protein: 6.1g; Fat: 10.9g; Minerals: 1.4g; Fibre: 0.95g.

Healthy modifications: Avoid layering the rolled out dough with ghee. This will reduce 7.5g fat and 67kcal from each chapatti.

Toast the chapatti in a non-stick pan without fat. This will further reduce 2.5g fat and 23 kcal from each chapatti.

PHULKAS (FIRE-ROASTED PUFFED FLATBREADS)

Skill is required to make soft, thin, fluffy phulkas, which are always made with wholewheat flour. Around 35-45g of dough is needed for each phulka. They are served in Maharashtra and Gujarat and are called rotlis in Gujarati.

DOUGH FOR PHULKAS

Ingredients for 4 phulkas

A pinch of salt or to taste

1 cup (100g) wholewheat flour

Method

Make the dough and knead it as given for sada chapatti (p. 66).

Nutritive values for the dough for 4 phulkas: Calories: 341.0kcal; Carbohydrate: 69.4g; Protein: 12.1g; Fat: 1.7g; Minerals: 2.7g; Fibre: 1.9g.

PHULKA

Fire-roasted puffed flatbread

Preparation time: 15 mins; Cooking time: 8 mins

Phulka is an unleavened, traditional flatbread served in Maharashtra and Gujarat.

Ingredients for 4 phulkas

Dough to make 4 phulkas (alongside)

2 tsp ghee

Method

Divide the dough into four portions and shape them into balls.

Roll out a portion of the dough on a lightly floured board into a 5" circle.

Toast the rolled out dough on a hot pan.

When the base is slightly cooked and bubbles appear on the upper surface, flip it over directly on to the fire to puff.

Flip it over again on the fire, till the other side puffs up.

Repeat with the remaining portions of dough.

Smear each phulka with ½ tsp ghee.

Serve hot with any curry or dal.

Nutritive values for 1 phulka: Calories: 108.0kcal; Carbohydrate: 17.4g; Protein: 3.0g; Fat: 2.9g; Minerals: 0.68g; Fibre: 0.48g.

Healthy modifications: Avoid smearing the phulkas with ghee. This will reduce 2.5g fat and 27kcal from each phulka.

PAD ROTI

Double-layered flatbread

Preparation time: 15 mins; Cooking time: 4 mins

Pad roti is an unleavened, traditional, Gujarati flatbread. Two portions of dough are rolled out together, cooked on a pan and then roasted directly on the fire, like phulkas. They are then tapped with both palms to separate the layers.

Ingredients for 4 rotis

Dough to make 4 phulkas (p. 69)
1 tsp oil
A pinch of salt or to taste

Method

Divide the dough into four portions and shape them into balls.

Roll out 2 portions of the dough on a lightly floured board into 4" circles.

Sprinkle ½ tsp oil over one roti and spread it evenly.

Place the second roti on top.

Roll out into a 5" circle.

Cook the roti as given for phulkas (p. 69).

Repeat with the remaining portions of dough.

Pat the edges of the rotis with both palms to separate the layers.

Serve hot with any curry or dal.

Nutritive values for 1 phulka: Calories: 97.0kcal; Carbohydrate: 17.4g; Protein: 3.0g; Fat: 1.7g; Minerals: 0.68g; Fibre: 0.48g.

THEPLAS (THIN FLATBREADS)

Theplas are made only from wholewheat flour. Each thepla requires 30-35g of dough. They are thinner and softer than phulkas.

SADA THEPLA

Plain flatbread

Preparation time: 15 mins; Cooking time: 12 mins

Sada thepla is an unleavened, traditional, Gujarati flatbread.

Ingredients for 6 theplas

The dough
1 cup wheat flour
¾ cup curd
¼ tsp turmeric powder
¼ tsp red chilli powder
1 tsp sugar
A pinch of salt or to taste
1 tsp oil
To pan-fry the theplas
6 tsp oil

Method

Combine all the dough ingredients in a bowl and prepare the dough as given for palak paratha (p. 24).

Divide the dough into 6 portions and shape them into balls.

Roll out a portion of the dough on a lightly floured board into a circle as thin as possible.

Put a non-stick pan on medium heat and toast the thepla with 1 tsp oil, till just golden on both sides.

Repeat with the remaining portions of dough.

Serve hot with any curry or dal.

Nutritive values for 1 thepla: Calories: 135.0kcal; Carbohydrate: 12.6g; Protein: 2.7g; Fat: 8.2g; Minerals: 0.54g; Fibre: 0.32g.

Healthy modifications: Toast the thepla in a non-stick pan without oil. This will reduce 5g fat and 45kcal from each flatbread.

METHI THEPLA

Fenugreek leaf flatbread

Preparation time: 15 mins; Cooking time: 12 mins

Methi thepla is an unleavened, traditional, Gujarati flatbread made with fresh fenugreek leaves and spices. Add 100g finely chopped fenugreek leaves to the ingredients for sada thepla (alongside) and make 6 theplas.

Nutritive values for 1 thepla: Calories: 137.0kcal; Carbohydrate: 13.0g; Protein: 2.6g; Fat: 8.2g; Minerals: 0.61g; Fibre: 0.36g.

DOODHI THEPLA

Bottle gourd flatbread

Preparation time: 15 mins; Cooking time: 12 mins

Doodhi thepla is an unleavened, traditional, Gujarati flatbread made with grated bottle gourd and spices. Add ½ cup of grated bottle gourd to the ingredients for sada thepla (alongside) and make 6 theplas.

Nutritive values for 1 thepla: Calories: 136.0kcal; Carbohydrate: 13.0g; Protein: 2.4g; Fat: 8.2g; Minerals: 0.58g; Fibre: 0.37g.

MULI THEPLA

Radish flatbread

Preparation time: 15 mins; Cooking time: 12 mins

Muli thepla is an unleavened, traditional, Gujarati flatbread made with grated white radish and spices. Add ½ cup of grated white radish to the ingredients for sada thepla (alongside) and make 6 theplas.

Nutritive values for 1 thepla: Calories: 136.0kcal; Carbohydrate: 13.1g; Protein: 2.5g; Fat: 8.2g; Minerals: 0.59g; Fibre: 0.38g.

BHAKRIS (SMALL FLATBREADS)

Two types of bhakris, which are 2"- 2½" in diameter, are prepared in Gujarati cuisine: one is puffed while cooking and the other is the 'biscuit bhakri' which has a crisp coating and soft inside. The latter is usually consumed as a teatime snack.

METHI BHAKRI

Fenugreek leaf flatbread

Preparation time: 15 mins; Cooking time: 12 mins

Methi bhakri is an unleavened, traditional, Gujarati and Rajasthani flatbread made with fresh fenugreek leaves. Add 50g of chopped fenugreek leaves to the ingredients for sada bhakri (alongside) and make 6 bhakris but do not add any water while making the dough. Serve them hot with any curry or dal.

Nutritive values for 1 bhakri: Calories: 84.0kcal; Carbohydrate: 12.1g; Protein: 2.4g; Fat: 2.9g; Minerals: 0.59g; Fibre: 0.41g.

Healthy modifications: See sada bhakri (alongside).

SADA BHAKRI

Plain flatbread

Preparation time: 15 mins; Cooking time: 12 mins

Sada bhakri is an unleavened, traditional, Gujarati and Rajasthani flatbread.

Ingredients for 6 bhakris

A pinch of salt or to taste
1 cup wholewheat flour
To serve
3 tsp ghee

Method

Make the dough and knead it as given sada chapatti (p. 66).

Divide the dough into 6 portions and shape them into balls.

Roll out a portion of the dough into a 3" circle.

Put a non-stick pan on medium heat and toast the bhakri, pressing the edges with a spatula to make it puff up.

When the base is firm and golden brown, flip it over and cook the other side, till golden brown.

Repeat with the remaining portions of dough.

Smear each bhakris with ½ tsp ghee.

Serve hot with any curry or dal.

Nutritive values for 1 bhakri: Calories: 79.0kcal; Carbohydrate: 11.6g; Protein: 2.0g; Fat: 2.8g; Minerals: 0.45g; Fibre: 0.32g.

Healthy modifications: Replace ghee with oil.

Avoid smearing the bhakris with ghee. This will reduce 2.5g fat and 23kcal from each bhakri.

PURI (FRIED PUFFED FLATBREAD)

Puris are fried flatbreads made with wholewheat or refined flour or multigrain flour. They are served plain or stuffed. Each puri requires 15-20g dough. Puri bhaji (a spicy potato curry) is a popular breakfast dish in north India. Puri korma curry is another familiar breakfast dish in north Indian and Mughlai cuisines. In Uttar Pradesh and Rajasthan, puri is served with sooji (semolina) halwa. In Maharashtra and Gujarat, it is served with aamras (flavoured mango pulp) during the summer. The dough for puris is also flavoured with vegetables such as tomatoes, mint, spinach; spices, dals, etc.

DOUGH FOR PURIS

Ingredients for 10 puris
A pinch of salt or to taste
1 cup wholewheat flour

Method

Dissolve the salt in 5 tbsp water.

Place the flour in a flat plate or bowl.

Add the salt water gradually to the flour and knead it for 5-10 mins to make a smooth dough.

Cover the dough with a damp cloth and leave it aside for about 20 mins.

Knead it again for a few mins.

Nutritive values for the dough to make 10 puris: Calories: 341.0kcal; Carbohydrate: 69.4g; Protein: 12.1g; Fat: 1.7g; Minerals: 2.7g; Fibre: 1.9g.

SADA PURI

Plain fried puffed flatbread

Preparation time: 15 mins; Cooking time: 5 mins

Sada puri is an unleavened, traditional, deep-fried flatbread served throughout India.

Ingredients for 10 puris
Dough to make 10 puris (alongside)
Oil for deep-frying

Method

Divide the dough into 10 portions and shape them into balls.

Roll out all the dough portions on a lightly floured board into 2"- 3" circles.

Heat the oil in a kadhai or wok and deep-fry 2-3 puris at a time, till light brown on both sides. Keep pressing the puris with a spatula to make them puff up.

Drain them on layers of tissue paper.

Serve hot with a potato curry.

Nutritive values for 1 puri: Calories: 79.0kcal; Carbohydrate: 6.9g; Protein: 1.2g; Fat: 5.2g; Minerals: 0.27g; Fibre: 0.19g.

PUDINA PURI

Mint-flavoured fried puffed flatbread

Preparation time: 20 mins; Cooking time: 5 mins

Pudina puri is an unleavened, traditional, deep-fried flatbread flavoured with fresh mint leaves. Grind 100g of mint leaves with salt and prepare the dough without any water as given for sada puri (p. 73). Roll out and cook 10 puris as given for sada puri. Serve them hot with any curry or dal.

Nutritive values for 1 puri: Calories: 82.0kcal; Carbohydrate: 7.2g; Protein: 1.5g; Fat: 5.2g; Minerals: 0.36g; Fibre: 0.29g.

METHI PURI

Fresh fenugreek flavoured fried puffed flatbread

Preparation time: 20 mins; Cooking time: 5 mins

Methi puri is an unleavened, traditional, deep-fried flatbread flavoured with fresh fenugreek leaves. Grind 100g of fenugreek leaves with salt and prepare the dough without any water as given for sada puri (p. 73). Roll out and cook 10 puris as given for sada puri. Serve them hot with aamras (puréed mango).

Nutritive values for 1 puri: Calories: 82.0kcal; Carbohydrate: 7.2g; Protein: 1.4g; Fat: 5.2g; Minerals: 0.35g; Fibre: 0.25g.

TOMATO PURI

Tomato-flavoured fried puffed flatbread

Preparation time: 20 mins; Cooking time: 5 mins

Tomato puri is an unleavened, traditional, deep-fried flatbread flavoured with puréed tomatoes and spices. Make the dough as given for sada puri (p. 73), using 2 puréed tomatoes, instead of water and add ½ tsp garam masala powder to the flour. Roll out and cook 10 puris as given for sada puri. Serve them hot with any curry or dal.

Nutritive values for 1 puri: Calories: 83.0kcal; Carbohydrate: 7.7g; Protein: 1.4g; Fat: 5.2g; Minerals: 0.37g; Fibre: 0.35g.

MASALA PURI

Spicy fried puffed flatbread

Preparation time: 20 mins; Cooking time: 5 mins

Masala puri is an unleavened, traditional, deep-fried, Marathi and Gujarati flatbread flavoured with spices. Add 1 tsp carom seeds (ajwain) and nigella seeds (kalonji), a pinch of asafoetida powder and turmeric powder and ¼ tsp red chilli powder to the flour. Make 10 puri as given for sada puri (p. 73). Serve them hot with srikhand.

Nutritive values for 1 puri: Calories: 83.0kcal; Carbohydrate: 7.2g; Protein: 1.4g; Fat: 5.4g; Minerals: 0.35g; Fibre: 0.39g.

PALAK PURI

Spinach-flavoured fried puffed flatbread

Preparation time: 20 mins; Cooking time: 5 mins

Palak puri is an unleavened, traditional, deep-fried flatbread flavoured with fresh spinach leaves and is popular in Uttar Pradesh. Chop 100g of spinach leaves and prepare the dough without any water as given for sada puri (p. 73). Roll out and cook 10 puris as given for sada puri. Serve them hot with any curry or dal.

Nutritive values for 1 puri: Calories: 80.0kcal; Carbohydrate: 7.1g; Protein: 1.3g; Fat: 5.2g; Minerals: 0.36g; Fibre: 0.22g.

PAKWAN

Fried flatbread

Preparation time: 25 mins; Cooking time: 3 mins

Pakwan is an unleavened, traditional, crisp flatbread. It is dipped in a gravied Bengal gram (chana dal) dish and served as dal pakwan in Sindhi cuisine.

Ingredients for 6 pakwans

½ cup wholewheat flour
½ cup refined wheat flour
1 tsp cumin seeds
A pinch of salt or to taste
To fry the pakwan
Oil for deep-frying

Method

To make the pakwan

Mix the flours and the cumin seeds in a bowl.

Prepare the dough and knead it as given for sada puris (p. 73).

Divide the dough into 6 portions and shape them into balls.

Roll out each portion of dough on a lightly floured board into a 4"- 5" circle.

Heat the oil in a kadhai or wok and deep-fry 2-3 pakwans at a time, till crisp and golden.

Drain it on layers of tissue paper.

Serve hot with chana dal.

Nutritive values for 1 pakwan: Calories: 105.0kcal; Carbohydrates: 12.2g; Protein: 2.1g; Fat: 5.4g; Minerals: 0.32g; Fibre: 0.28g.

Healthy modifications: Avoid the refined wheat flour; use only wholewheat flour.

Toast the pakwan in a non-stick pan without fat instead of deep-frying in oil.

BEDMI PURI

Fried flatbread with black gram filling

Preparation time: 25 mins; Cooking time: 8 mins

Bedmi puri is a famous, leavened, traditional fried flatbread stuffed with spicy black gram. It is popular in Uttar Pradesh and Delhi as street food and is served with sooji halwa and aloo masala. It is similar to radhaballabhi of Bengal, but the latter is made with refined wheat flour.

Ingredients for 8 puris

The filling
1 cup husked, split black gram (urad dal)
A pinch of salt or to taste
2 tsp ginger-garlic-green chilli paste
¼ tsp red chilli powder
½ tsp garam masala powder
A pinch of asafoetida powder
1 tbsp oil
The dough
1 cup wholewheat flour
2 tbsp semolina
¼ tsp sodium bicarbonate (baking soda)
A pinch of salt or to taste
To fry the puris
Oil for deep-frying

Method

The filling: Wash the dal and soak it in water for a few hours.

Drain the dal and grind it with salt to make a smooth paste.

Mix it with the ginger-garlic-green chilli paste and spice powders in a bowl.

Heat the oil in a frying pan and sauté the filling, till dry.

Divide the filling into 8 portions and leave aside, till cool.

(Method Cont.)

The dough: Mix the dry ingredients in a bowl.

Make the dough and knead it as given for sada puri (p. 73).

Divide the dough into 8 portions and shape them into balls.

To prepare the stuffed puris: Roll out a portion of dough on a lightly floured board into a 2" circle.

Place a portion of filling in the centre and gently pull up the dough from the sides to cover the filling completely. Press gently to seal the edges and roll out into a 3" circle.

Repeat with the remaining portions of dough and filling.

Heat the oil for deep-frying in a kadhai or wok and fry 2-3 puris at a time, till golden brown on both sides.

Drain them on layers of tissue paper.

Serve hot with sooji halwa (p. 218).

Nutritive values for 1 puri: Calories: 165.0kcal; Carbohydrate: 19.5g; Protein: 5.1g; Fat: 7.5g; Minerals: 0.82g; Fibre: 0.49g.

MUNG DAL PURI

Fried flatbread with mung filling

Preparation time: 25 mins; Cooking time: 8 mins

Mung dal puri is an unleavened, traditional, fried flatbread stuffed with spicy husked, split mung.

Ingredients for 10 puris

The filling
1 cup husked, split mung
2 tsp ginger-garlic-green chilli paste
½ tsp cumin powder
½ tsp powdered aniseed
¼ tsp black pepper powder
½ tsp coriander powder
¼ tsp red chilli powder
½ tsp turmeric powder
¼ tsp asafoetida powder
A pinch of salt or to taste
The seasoning
1 tsp ghee
1 tsp mustard-cumin seeds
To make the puris
Dough to make 10 puris (p. 73)
Oil for deep-frying

(Recipe Cont.)

Method

Wash the dal and pressure cook it with 1 cup of water on low heat for 10 mins after the cooker reaches full pressure.

Heat the ghee for the seasoning in a pan and sauté the seasoning ingredients, till fragrant.

Add the ginger-garlic-green chilli paste and sauté for a minute.

Stir in the cooked dal and all the spice powders and cook, till dry.

Divide the filling into 10 portions and leave aside, till cool.

Divide the dough into 10 portions and shape them into balls.

Prepare the stuffed puris and fry them as given for bedmi puri (p. 76).

Serve hot with any curry.

Nutritive values for 1 puri: Calories: 125.0kcal; Carbohydrate: 13.6g; Protein: 4.0g; Fat: 6.0g; Minerals: 3.6g; Fibre: 2.4g.

BESAN PURI

Fried flatbread with gram flour filling

Preparation time: 25 mins; Cooking time: 8 mins

Besan puri is a Rajasthani, unleavened, traditional, fried flatbread stuffed with gram flour.

Ingredients for 8 puris

The filling
1 tbsp ghee
½ cup gram flour (besan)
½ tsp red chilli powder
2 tbsp coriander powder
1 tbsp cumin powder
½ tsp dried mango powder
1 tsp aniseed, coarsely ground
½ tsp garam masala powder
A pinch of salt or to taste
The dough
A pinch of salt or to taste
1 cup wholewheat flour
To fry the puris
Oil for deep-frying

(Recipe Cont.)

Method

Heat the ghee in a pan and roast the gram flour, till light brown.

Add all the remaining filling ingredients and mix well.

Divide the filling into 8 portions and leave aside, till cool

Prepare the dough and knead it as given for sada puri (p. 73).

Divide the dough into 8 portions and shape them into balls.

Prepare the stuffed puris and fry them as given for bedmi puri (p. 76).

Serve hot with any curry.

Nutritive values for 1 puri: Calories: 151.0kcal; Carbohydrates: 14.5g; Protein: 4.0g; Fat: 8.5g; Minerals: 0.86g; Fibre: 2.0g.

Healthy modifications: Replace ghee with oil while preparing the filling.

FLATBREADS MADE WITH REFINED WHEAT FLOUR

Flatbreads made with refined wheat flour are delicious, but not nutritious. The by-products of the milling process are the wheat bran and germ, which are lost when the grains are polished and refined. Food made with refined flour lack minerals and are low in fibre. They do not contain protein, minerals and vitamins which are concentrated in the bran and the germ.

NAAN (BAKED FLATBREAD)

Naans are leavened flatbreads baked in a tandoor. Each naan requires 150g-160g of dough. They are served in Punjabi and Mughlai cuisines and are often smeared with butter. They can be prepared with dairy products and fresh herbs, stuffed and sprinkled with sesame seeds and even dried fruits.

CHEESE NAAN

Cheese-flavoured baked flatbread

Preparation time: 30 mins; Cooking time: 2 mins

To make cheese naan sprinkle 1 tbsp of grated cheese over a sada naan (p. 81) and press it in gently with the back of a spoon after it is cooked. Serve hot with any Mughlai curry.

Nutritive values for 1 naan: Calories: 420.0kcal; Carbohydrate: 60.8g; Protein: 13.4g; Fat: 13.6g; Minerals: 1.5g; Fibre: 1.0g.

Healthy modifications: Use low-fat cheese.

See sada naan (p. 81) for further modifications.

DOUGH FOR NAANS

Ingredients for 2 naans

1 tsp dried yeast

1 tsp sugar

2 tbsp warm milk

1½ cups refined wheat flour

½ cup curd

1 tbsp ghee or oil

A pinch of salt or to taste

Method

Add the yeast and sugar to the warm milk and leave it aside for about 10 mins, till it froths up.

Mix the flour, curd, ghee or oil and salt in a bowl.

Add the yeast mixture and mix well.

To prepare a leavened dough

Knead the contents for 15-20 mins to make a smooth dough.

Cover the dough with a damp cloth and leave it aside for about 1 hour to rise.

Knead it again for 5-10 mins and leave it aside for another 20-30 mins, till the dough is double in volume.

Nutritive values for the dough for 2 naans: Calories: 736.0 kcal; Carbohydrate: 18.8g; Protein: 19.3g; Fat: 20.4g; Minerals: 1.5g; Fibre: 0.48g.

BUTTER NAAN

Buttered baked flatbread

Preparation time: 30 mins; Cooking time: 2 mins

To make butter naan smear a sada naan (p. 81) with 1 tsp of home-made white butter after it is cooked. Serve hot with any Mughlai curry or dal.

Nutritive values for 1 naan: Calories: 405.0kcal; Carbohydrate: 59.3g; Protein: 9.7g; Fat: 14.1g; Minerals: 0.88g; Fibre: 0.25g.

Healthy modifications: Smear the naans with peanut or hazelnut butter instead of ghee. See sada naan (p. 81) for further modifications.

SADA NAAN

Plain baked flatbread

Preparation time: 30 mins; Cooking time: 2 mins

Sada naan is a leavened flatbread, traditionally baked in a tandoor.

Ingredients for 2 naans

Dough to make 2 naans (p. 80)

Method

Divide the dough into 2 portions and shape them into balls.

Roll each portion of dough on a lightly floured board into an oval shape, 7"- 8" long.

Bake the naans in a clay, gas or electric tandoor for about 2 mins, till light golden on both sides.

Alternatively, place them on a baking tray and bake them in an oven preheated to 200°C for 2-3 mins, till light golden on top. Turn them over and cook till the other side is light golden.

Serve hot with any Mughlai curry or dal.

Nutritive values for 1 naan: Calories: 368.0kcal; Carbohydrate: 59.4g; Protein: 9.7g; Fat: 10.2g; Minerals: 0.75g; Fibre: 0.24g.

Healthy modifications: Avoid adding fat to the dough. This will reduce 7.5g of fat and 68kcal for each naan.

Replace half the refined flour with wholewheat flour.

CHEESE-LAL-MIRCH NAAN

Cheese-red chilli-flavoured baked flatbread

Preparation time: 30 mins; Cooking time: 2 mins

Mix 2 tsp of red chilli flakes with the cheese and make 2 naans in the same way as given for cheese naan (p. 80).

Nutritive values for 1 naan: Calories: 433.0kcal; Carbohydrate: 62.4g; Protein: 14.2g; Fat: 13.9g; Minerals: 1.8g; Fibre: 2.5g.

Healthy modifications: See cheese naan (p. 80).

LASSOON NAAN

Garlic-flavoured baked flatbread

Preparation time: 35 mins; Cooking time: 2 mins

Add 2 tsp of garlic paste to the dough and make 2 naans in the same way as given for sada naan (alongside). Sprinkle ½ cup of minced garlic on the hot naans and gently press it in. Serve hot with onion slices, a pickle and any Mughlai curry or dal.

Nutritive values for 1 naan: Calories: 412.0kcal; Carbohydrate: 68.3g; Protein: 11.6g; Fat: 10.1g; Minerals 0: 1.0g; Fibre: 0.49g.

Healthy modifications: See sada naan (alongside).

TIL NAAN

Baked flatbread with sesame seeds

Preparation time: 30 mins; Cooking time: 2 mins

Make sada naans as given on (alongside) and sprinkle 1 tsp of sesame seeds on each naan before baking them. Serve them with curd and any Mughlai curry or dal.

Nutritive values for 1 naan: Calories: 396.0kcal; Carbohydrate: 60.6g; Protein: 10.6g; Fat: 12.4g; Minerals: 0.96g; Fibre: 0.40g.

Healthy modifications: Sesame seeds are oilseeds. Limit their use.

See sada naan (alongside) for further modifications.

AMRITSARI NAAN

Baked flatbread with a potato filling

Preparation time: 40 mins; Cooking time: 2 mins

Amritsari naan is a leavened, flatbread stuffed with potatoes and traditionally baked in a tandoor.

Ingredients for 2 naans

The filling
250g potatoes
A pinch of salt or to taste
1 tsp ginger-garlic-green chilli paste
½ tsp garam masala powder
2 tsp coriander leaves, chopped
The seasoning
2 tsp oil
1 tsp mustard-cumin seeds
2 tsp curry leaves
The dough
Dough to make 2 naans (p. 80)

Method

The filling: Wash the potatoes, peel and cut them into small cubes.

Boil the potatoes in salt water, till just tender. Drain and leave aside.

Heat the oil for the seasoning in a pan and sauté the seasoning ingredients, till fragrant.

Add the ginger-garlic-green chilli paste and sauté for a minute.

Add the boiled potatoes, garam masala powder and the coriander leaves.

Mix the contents and simmer for a few mins.

Divide the filling into 2 portions and leave aside, till cool.

To prepare the naans: Divide the dough into 2 portions and shape them into balls.

Make the naans as given for band gobi paratha (p. 25).

Bake the naans as given for sada naan (p. 81).

(Method Cont.)

Serve hot with a pickle, curd and any Mughlai curry or dal.

Nutritive values for 1 naan: Calories: 542.0kcal; Carbohydrate: 89.0g; Protein: 12.0g; Fat: 15.5g; Minerals: 1.6g; Fibre: 1.0g.
Healthy modifications: See sada naan (p. 81).

KASHMIRI NAAN

Baked flatbread with dried fruit filling

Preparation time: 40 mins; Cooking time: 2 mins

Kashmiri naan is a leavened, flatbread stuffed with dried fruits and baked in a tandoor. It is similar to Peshawari naan, which is also stuffed with dried fruits.

Ingredients for 2 naans

The filling
1 tbsp almonds
1 tbsp cashew nuts
1 tbsp walnuts
1 tbsp dried fruits (raisins, dates, apricots etc), ground to a paste
The dough
Dough to make 2 naans (p. 80)

Method

Powder half the nuts coarsely and powder the rest fine. Reserve the coarsely powdered nuts for the topping.

Mix the finely powdered nuts with the dried fruits.

Make the stuffed naans and bake them as given for Amritsari naan (alongside).

Sprinkle the reserved powdered nuts on each naan and press it in gently with the back of a spatula.

Serve hot with any curry or dal.

Nutritive values for 1 naan: Calories: 519.0kcal; Carbohydrate: 65.4g; Protein: 13.9g; Fat: 21.0g; Minerals: 1.5g; Fibre: 0.75g.
Healthy modifications: Limit the use of nuts.
See sada naan (p. 81) for further modifications.

SHEERMAL

Baked sweet flatbread

Preparation time: 40 mins; Cooking time: 5 mins

Sheermal is a leavened, traditional flatbread, brushed with sweetened saffron milk and baked. It is called meetha naan in Mughlai cuisine.

Ingredients for 4 sheermals

The saffron milk
½ cup full-cream milk, boiled and cooled
1 tsp saffron strands
A few drops of rose essence
2 tbsp sugar
The dough
½ tsp active dried yeast
1 tsp sugar
2 tbsp warm milk
1½ cups refined flour
1 tbsp ghee, melted
A pinch of salt or to taste
2 tbsp raisins, chopped
The topping
1 tbsp ghee, melted
2 tsp poppy seeds

Method

Warm the milk and soak the saffron in it for about 10 mins.

Add the rose essence and sugar and stir, till the sugar dissolves.

Divide the saffron milk into 2 portions.

Make the dough as given for sada naans (p. 81), adding 1 portion of the saffron milk and the raisins to the flour along with the yeast mixture.

Divide the dough into 4 portions and shape them into balls.

(Method Cont.)

Roll out each portion of dough into a 4"- 5" circle.

Place a baking sheet on a tray and place the rotis on the baking sheet.

Prick them all over with a fork. Brush with a little ghee and the reserved saffron milk. Sprinkle poppy seeds on top and press them in gently with the back of a spatula.

Bake them in an oven preheated to 180°C for 4-5 mins.

Remove them from the oven and brush them again with ghee and saffron milk and continue to bake for 4-5 mins longer, till cooked.

Brush them again with saffron milk before serving.

Serve hot with any curry.

Nutritive values for 1 sheermal: Calories: 264.0kcal; Carbohydrates: 39.3g; Protein: 5.0g; Fat: 9.5g; Minerals: 0.71g; Fibre: 0.36g.

Healthy modifications: Replace refined wheat flour with wholewheat flour.

Replace ghee with oil.

Avoid adding fat to the flour while preparing the dough. This will reduce 15g fat and 135kcal from each naan.

Avoid brushing the naans with fat. This will further reduce 15g fat and 135kcal from them.

KULCHAS (BAKED ROUND FLATBREADS)

Kulchas are leavened flatbreads made with refined wheat flour. They are often seen on restaurant menus and are an important part of Punjabi and Mughlai cuisines. The dough to prepare kulchas is similar to that used to make naans

DOUGH FOR KULCHAS

Ingredients for 2 kulchas

1½ cups refined wheat flour
1 tsp sugar
½ tsp baking powder
½ cup curd
1 tbsp ghee or oil
A pinch of salt or to taste

Method

Mix all the ingredients in a bowl.

Knead the dough as given for sada paratha (p. 22).

Nutritive values for the dough for 2 kulchas: Calories: 707.0kcal; Carbohydrate: 117.2g; Protein: 18.1g; Fat: 18.3g; Minerals: 1.2g; Fibre: 0.5g.

SADA KULCHA

Plain baked flatbread

Preparation time: 30 mins; Cooking time: 2 mins

Sada kulcha is a leavened flatbread traditionally baked in a tandoor.

Ingredients for 2 kulchas

Dough to make 2 kulchas (alongside)
2 tsp ghee

Method

Divide the dough into 2 portions and shape them into balls.

Roll out each portion of dough into a 6"- 7" circle.

Cook them as given for sada naan (p. 81).

Kulchas can also be toasted on a hot pan on both sides, till light golden.

Smear each kulcha with 1 tsp ghee.

Serve hot with curd and any curry.

Nutritive values for 1 kulcha: Calories: 399.0kcal; Carbohydrate: 58.6g; Protein: 9.1g; Fat: 14.2g; Minerals: 0.6g; Fibre: 0.25g.

Healthy modifications: Avoid adding ghee or oil to the dough. This will reduce 7.5g of fat and 68kcal from each kulcha.

Avoid smearing the kulchas with ghee. This will further reduce 5g fat and 45kcal from each kulcha.

Smear the kulchas with peanut or hazelnut butter instead of ghee.

Replace half the refined flour with wholewheat flour.

BUTTER KULCHA
Buttered baked flatbread
Preparation time: 30 mins; Cooking time: 2 mins

To make butter kulchas replace the ghee in the kulcha dough (p. 84) with home-made white butter. Cook 2 kulchas as given for sada kulcha (p. 84) and smear them with 1 tsp of butter. Serve them hot with curd and a dry vegetable curry.

Nutritive values for 1 kulcha: Calories: 391.0kcal; Carbohydrate: 41.0g; Protein: 6.9g; Fat: 17.1g; Minerals: 1.0g; Fibre: 0.15g.

Healthy modifications: Smear the kulchas with peanut or hazelnut butter instead of butter.

Replace half the refined flour with wholewheat flour.

HARA DHANIA KULCHA
Coriander-flavoured baked flatbread
Preparation time: 35 mins; Cooking time: 2 mins

Hara dhania kulcha is a leavened flatbread sprinkled with fresh coriander leaves and traditionally baked in a tandoor. Make 2 kulchas as given for pyaz kulcha (alongside) replacing the onion with 2 tbsp of chopped fresh coriander leaves. Serve them with curd and any curry.

Nutritive values for 1 kulcha: Calories: 401.0kcal; Carbohydrate: 58.9g; Protein: 9.2g; Fat: 14.2g; Minerals: 0.8g; Fibre: 0.22g.

Healthy modifications: See sada kulcha (p. 84).

PYAZ KULCHA
Onion-flavoured baked flatbread
Preparation time: 35 mins; Cooking time: 2 mins

To make pyaz kulcha, sprinkle 1 minced onion over sada kulchas (p. 84) before baking them, and press it in gently with the back of a spoon. Smear the cooked kulchas with 1 tsp of home-made white butter and serve them hot with any curry.

Nutritive values for 1 kulcha: Calories: 412.0kcal; Carbohydrate: 61.4g; Protein: 9.4g; Fat: 14.2g; Minerals: 0.7g; Fibre: 0.3g.

Healthy modifications See sada kulcha (p. 84).

KASOORI METHI KULCHA
Fenugreek-flavoured baked flatbread
Preparation time: 35 mins; Cooking time: 2 mins

Kasoori methi kulcha is a leavened flatbread flavoured with dried fenugreek leaves and traditionally baked in a tandoor. Make 2 kulchas as given for pyaz kulcha (alongside) replacing the onion with 2 tbsp of chopped dried fenugreek leaves. Serve them with any curry.

Nutritive values for 1 kulcha: Calories: 403.0kcal; Carbohydrate: 59.3g; Protein: 9.3g; Fat: 14.3g; Minerals: 0.8g; Fibre: 0.4g.

Healthy modifications: See sada kulcha (p. 84).

MASALA KULCHA

Baked flatbread with potato and capsicum filling

Preparation time: 40 mins; Cooking time: 2 mins

Masala kulcha is a leavened flatbread stuffed with vegetables and traditionally baked in a tandoor. Make the potato filling given in Amritsari naan (p. 82) and add 2 chopped and sautéed capsicums to it. Make the dough for sada kulcha (p. 84) and stuff 2 kulchas as given for Amritsari naan. Sprinkle with 2 tbsp chopped coriander leaves and cook them as given for sada kulcha. Smear with 1 tsp ghee and serve hot with a pickle, curd and any dal.

Nutritive values for 1 kulcha: Calories: 553.0kcal; Carbohydrate: 87.5g; Protein: 10.8g; Fat: 18.6g; Minerals: 1.3g; Fibre: 0.95g.

Healthy modifications: See pyaz kulcha (p. 85).

PANEER KULCHA

Baked flatbread with paneer filling

Preparation time: 30 mins; Cooking time: 2 mins

Paneer kulcha is a leavened flatbread stuffed with paneer and traditionally baked in a tandoor. Make the filling by mixing 4 tbsp of grated paneer with ½ tsp of garam masala powder and 1 minced onion. Make 2 kulchas as given for masala kulcha (p. 86). Serve them hot with any curry.

Nutritive values for 1 kulcha: Calories: 495.0kcal; Carbohydrate: 65.3g; Protein: 15.2g; Fat: 19.9g; Minerals: 1.4g; Fibre: 0.45g.

Healthy modifications: Use low-fat paneer.

See pyaz kulcha (p. 85) for further modifications.

CHEESE-LAL MIRCH KULCHA

Cheese-red chilli-flavoured baked flatbread

Preparation time: 30 mins; Cooking time: 2 mins

Cheese-lal mirch kulcha is a leavened flatbread flavoured with cheese and red chilli flakes traditionally baked in a tandoor. Make 2 kulchas as given for sada kulcha (p. 84) and sprinkle them with 4 tbsp cheese and 2 tsp red chilli flakes before baking them. Smear each kulcha with 1 tsp ghee when it is removed from the oven. Serve them with any curry.

Nutritive values for 1 kulcha: Calories: 510.0kcal; Carbohydrate: 61.4g; Protein: 16.8g; Fat: 21.9g; Minerals: 2.0g; Fibre: 0.9g.

Healthy modifications: Use low-fat cheese.

See pyaz kulcha (p. 85) for further modifications.

PAROTTAS (FLAKY, FLUFFY FLATBREADS)

Parottas are unleavened flaky, fluffy flatbreads similar to lachha parathas made with refined wheat flour and plenty of ghee. In Kerala, plain parottas are served with any curry and are even shredded and added to it. Kothu parottas of Tamil Nadu are consumed as street food and are similar to those of Kerala. Kothu means mince, and the parottas are minced and added to a curry as in Kerala.

DOUGH FOR PAROTTAS

Ingredients for 2 parottas

A pinch of salt or to taste

1½ cups refined flour

3 tsp + 1 tsp ghee

Method

Dissolve the salt in 100 ml water.

Mix the flour and 3 tsp ghee in a bowl.

Add the salt water gradually and knead it for 10-15 mins to make a smooth dough.

Cover the dough and leave it aside for 30 mins.

Knead the dough again for about 5 mins and add 1 tsp ghee gradually.

Beat the dough on the flat surface or with a rolling pin for 15-20 mins.

The nutritive values for the dough to make 2 parottas: Calories: 351.0kcal; Carbohydrate: 55.4g; Protein: 8.3g; Fat: 10.7g; Minerals: 0.45g; Fibre: 0.23g.

MALABAR PAROTTA

Plain flaky flatbread

Preparation time: 30 mins; Cooking time: 5 mins

Malabar parotta is an unleavened, traditional, flaky, fluffy flatbread.

Ingredients for 2 parottas

Dough to make 2 parottas (p. 87)
3 tsp + 1 tsp ghee
A pinch of salt or to taste

Method

Roll out the parottas as given for sada lachha paratha (p. 56).

Pan-fry them on a hot pan with 1 tsp ghee, till golden brown on both sides.

Beat the parottas on the sides with both hands to make them flaky.

Serve hot with curd and any curry.

Nutritive values for 1 parotta: Calories: 441.0kcal; Carbohydrate: 55.4g; Protein: 8.3g; Fat: 20.7g; Minerals: 0.45g; Fibre: 0.23g.

Healthy modifications: Replace the ghee with oil while preparing the dough.

Avoid adding fat to the dough. This will reduce 10g fat and 90kcal from each parotta.

Avoid adding fat while rolling the parotta. This will further reduce 10g fat and 90kcal from each one.

Use wholewheat flour or replace half the refined flour with it.

VEECHU PAROTTA

Flaky flatbread

Preparation time: 30 mins; Cooking time: 5 mins

Veechu parotta is an unleavened, traditional flaky and fluffy flatbread from Kerala, similar to Malabar parottas, but they are folded differently. Veechu parotta is also part of Tamil Nadu cuisine, but it resembles a roomali roti; it is stretched as thin as possible and is cooked on a large flat pan with plenty of oil.

Ingredients for 2 parottas

Dough to make 2 sada parottas (p. 87)
2 tsp ghee
2 tsp oil

Method

Divide the dough into 2 portions and shape them into balls.

Roll out a portion of the dough on a lightly floured board, as thin as possible.

Spread 1 tsp ghee evenly over it.

Fold the opposite ends towards the centre to make a square. Roll it out again.

Pan-fry the parotta on a hot pan with 1 tsp oil, till golden on both sides.

Repeat with the remaining portion of dough.

Pat the parottas on the sides with the palms to separates the layers.

Serve hot with any curry.

Nutritive values for 1 parotta: Calories: 441.0kcal; Carbohydrate: 55.4g; Protein: 8.3g; Fat: 20.7g; Minerals: 0.45g; Fibre: 0.23g.

Healthy modifications: See Malabar parotta (alongside).

OTHER FLATBREADS MADE WITH REFINED FLOUR

TANDOORI ROTI

Tandoori flatbread

Preparation time: 30 mins; Cooking time: 5 mins

Tandoori roti made with refined wheat flour is a leavened, traditional, Punjabi and Mughlai flatbread.

Ingredients for 2 rotis

A pinch of salt or to taste
½ cup curd
¼ tsp baking soda
1 cup refined wheat flour
1 tsp sugar
1 tbsp oil
1 tsp ghee or home-made white butter for topping

Method

Dissolve the salt in 1 tbsp water.

Mix the curd and the baking soda in a small bowl and leave it aside for about 10 mins.

Mix the flour, sugar and oil in another bowl.

Stir in the curd.

Add a little salt water at a time and mix well.

Prepare the dough as given for sada naan (p. 81).

Divide the dough into 2 portions and shape them into balls. Knead it again for 5-10 mins.

Roll out each portion of dough on a lightly floured board into a thick, 5" circle.

Bake them in a clay, gas or electric tandoor for about 5 mins, till golden on both sides.

Brush the rotis with ghee or butter before serving.

Serve hot with any curry.

Nutritive values for 1 roti: Calories: 298.0kcal; Carbohydrate: 40.8g; Protein: 6.8g; Fat: 12.1g; Minerals: 0.62g; Fibre: 0.15g.

Healthy modifications: Avoid adding fat to the dough. This will reduce 7.5g fat and 68kcal for each roti.

Avoid brushing the cooked roti with ghee or butter. This will further reduce 2.5g fat and 27 kcal from each roti.

Use wholewheat flour or replace half the refined flour with it.

ROOMALI ROTI

Handkerchief flatbread

Preparation time: 40 mins; Cooking time: 5 mins

Roomali roti is a leavened, traditional, Punjabi and Mughlai flatbread. It is very thin, 12"- 14" in diameter and is folded like a handkerchief before serving.

Ingredients for 2 rotis

¾ cup curd
½ tsp baking soda
1½ cups refined flour
A pinch of salt or to taste

Method

Mix the curd and the baking soda in a small bowl and leave it aside for about 10 mins.

Mix the flour and the salt in another bowl.

Add the curd to the flour and knead it to make a soft dough for about 5 mins. Add a little more curd if the dough is dry.

Cover the dough and leave it aside for about 1 hour to rise.

Knead it again for 5-10 mins and leave it aside for 15-20 mins.

Divide the dough into 2 portions and shape them into balls.

Roll out a portion of the dough on a lightly floured board as thin as possible and stretch it from all sides to make it even thinner.

Cook it on a large inverted wok or tava, till light brown on both sides.

Repeat with the remaining portion of dough.

Fold each roti like a handkerchief.

Serve immediately with curd and any curry.

Nutritive values for 1 roti: Calories: 277.0kcal; Carbohydrate: 56.3g; Protein: 9.0g; Fat: 1.7g; Minerals: 0.75g; Fibre: 0.42g.

Healthy modifications: Use wholewheat flour or replace half the refined flour with it.

SADA MUGHLAI LACHHA PARATHA

Plain multilayered flatbread

Preparation time: 40 mins; Cooking time: 5 mins

Sada Mughlai lachha paratha is a leavened, traditional flatbread made with refined wheat flour. Punjabi lachha parathas made with wholewheat flour are unleavened.

Ingredients for 2 parathas

The dough
1½ cups refined flour
A pinch of salt or to taste
2 tsp + 1 tsp ghee
½ tsp baking powder
1 tsp sugar
½ cup milk
To make the parathas
1 tbsp ghee
2 tsp oil

Method

Mix the flour, salt, 2 tsp ghee and the baking powder in a bowl.

Dissolve the sugar in the milk and add it to the flour mixture.

Knead it for 10-15 mins to make a smooth dough.

Smear the dough with 1 tsp ghee, cover it with a damp cloth and leave it aside for about 1 hour.

Knead it again for about 10 mins and leave it aside again for about 15 mins.

Roll out the dough and cook the parathas as given for sada lachha paratha (p. 56).

Serve hot with any curry.

Nutritive values for 1 paratha: Calories: 475.0kcal; Carbohydrate: 59.2g; Protein: 9.3g; Fat: 22.3g; Minerals: 0.65g; Fibre: 0.23g.

Healthy modifications: See tandoori roti (p. 94).

RESHMI PARATHA

Sweet multilayered flatbread

Preparation time: 40 mins; Cooking time: 5 mins

Reshmi paratha is a leavened, traditional sweet flatbread.

Ingredients for 2 parathas

1½ cups refined flour
½ tsp baking powder
2 tbsp + 1 tsp ghee
1 tbsp sugar, powdered
½ tsp saffron strands
A few drops of yellow food colouring (optional)
½ cup milk
The topping
½ cup chopped sweet cherries
½ cup chopped pineapple
To cook the parathas
2 tsp oil

Method

Mix the flour, baking powder and 2 tbsp ghee in a bowl.

Dissolve the sugar, saffron and the food colouring in the milk and add it to the flour mixture.

Prepare the dough as given for sada naan (p. 81) but smearing it with 1 tsp ghee.

Divide the dough into 2 portions and roll them out as given for sada lachha paratha (p. 56).

Sprinkle the cherries and pineapples on the parathas and press it gently into the dough.

Pan-fry the paratha on a hot pan with 1 tsp oil, till golden on both sides.

Pat the paratha from the sides with the palms to make it flakier.

Repeat with the remaining portion of dough.

Serve hot with any curry.

Nutritive values for 1 paratha: Calories: 523.0kcal; Carbohydrate: 70.4g; Protein: 9.7g; Fat: 22.5g; Minerals: 0.95g; Fibre: 0.43g.

Healthy modifications: See Sada Mughlai lachha paratha (alongside).

FRIED FLATBREADS MADE WITH REFINED WHEAT FLOUR

BHATURA

Fried large flatbread

Preparation time: 30 mins; Cooking time: 5 mins

Bhatura is a leavened, thick, fried flatbread popularly served with chola (spicy chickpea curry) in Punjabi cuisine.

Ingredients for 2 bhaturas

A pinch of salt or to taste
1 tsp sugar
1 tsp active dried yeast
2 tbsp warm water
1½ cups refined wheat flour
¾ cup curd
Oil for deep-frying

Method

Dissolve the salt in 1 tbsp of water.

Add the sugar and yeast to the warm water and leave it aside for about 10 mins to froth up.

Mix the flour, curd and yeast mixture.

Add the salt water slowly to the flour and mix well.

Prepare the dough as given for sada naan (p. 81).

Divide the dough into 2 portions and shape them into balls.

Roll out a portion of the dough on a lightly floured board into a thick, 8"- 9" circle.

Heat the oil in a kadhai or wok and deep-fry the bhatura, till light brown.

Drain on layers of tissue paper.

Repeat with the remaining portion of dough.

Serve hot with onion rings, lime wedges, raita, chola and a pickle.

Nutritive values for 1 bhatura: Calories: 376.0kcal; Carbohydrate: 58.7g; Protein: 9.0g; Fat: 11.7g; Minerals: 0.65g; Fibre: 0.23g.

Healthy modifications: Toast the bhaturas in a non-stick pan without fat. This will reduce 10g fat and 90kcal from each bhatura.

Use wholewheat flour or replace half the refined flour with it.

LUCHI
Fried puffed flatbread

Preparation time: 20 mins; Cooking time: 5 mins

Luchi is an unleavened, traditional fried flatbread served in Bengal at breakfast. Luchais from Uttar Pradesh are similar and are fried in any oil other than mustard oil. They are served with sooji halwa (p. 218).

Ingredients for 10 luchis
A pinch of salt or to taste
1 tbsp home-made white butter
1 cup refined wheat flour
Mustard oil for deep-frying

Method
Dissolve the salt in 4 tbsp of water.

Prepare the dough as given for sada paratha (p. 22), using 1 tbsp of butter instead of the oil.

Divide the dough into 10 portions and shape them into balls.

Prepare the luchi as given for sada puri (p. 73).

Serve hot with any curry.

Nutritive values for 1 luchi: Calories: 80.0kcal; Carbohydrate: 7.4g; Protein: 1.1g; Fat: 5.1g; Minerals: 0.10g; Fibre: 0.03g.

Healthy modifications: Avoid adding fat to the flour while making the dough.

Use wholewheat flour or replace half the refined flour with it.

MATARSHUTIR KACHORI
Fried flatbread with green pea filling

Preparation time: 25 mins; Cooking time: 3 mins

Matarshutir kachori is an unleavened, traditional, fried flatbread stuffed with green peas. A similar flatbread is made in Rajasthan, but with wholewheat flour.

Ingredients for 6 kachoris
The filling
1 cup shelled green peas
A pinch of salt or to taste
1 tsp ginger-green chilli paste
A pinch of asafoetida powder
The dough
A pinch of salt or to taste
1 cup refined wheat flour
To fry the kachoris
Ghee for deep-frying

Method
Boil the green peas in a little salted water, till just tender and dry.

Mix all the filling ingredients and grind them to make a smooth paste.

Divide the filling into 6 portions.

Prepare the dough as given for sada puri (p. 73).

Prepare the stuffed kachoris and fry them as given for bedmi puri (p. 76).

Serve hot with a spicy dal.

Nutritive values for 1 kachori: Calories: 119.0kcal; Carbohydrate: 15.0g; Protein: 3.0g; Fat: 5.2g; Minerals: 0.23g; Fibre: 0.72g.

Healthy modifications: Fry the kachoris in oil instead of ghee.

Toast the kachoris in a non-stick pan without fat. This will reduce 5g fat and 45kcal from each kachori.

Use wholewheat flour or replace half the refined flour it.

ALOO KACHORI

Fried flatbread with potato filling

Preparation time: 25 mins; Cooking time: 10 mins

Aloo kachori is an unleavened, traditional fried flatbread stuffed with potatoes.

Ingredients for 6 kachoris

The filling
4 medium-sized potatoes
1 tsp ginger-green chilli paste
A pinch of asafoetida
A pinch of salt or to taste
The dough
1 cup refined wheat flour
A pinch of salt or to taste
To fry the kachoris
Ghee for deep-frying

Method

Wash the potatoes, peel and cube them.

Boil the potatoes in a little salted water, till just tender and dry.

Mash the potatoes and mix them with the remaining filling ingredients.

Divide the filling into six portions.

Prepare the dough as given for sada puri (p. 73).

Prepare the stuffed kachoris and fry them as given for bedmi puri (p. 76).

Serve hot with a tomato chutney (p. 219).

Nutritive values for 1 kachori: Calories: 135.0kcal; Carbohydrate: 19.9g; Protein: 2.4g; Fat: 5.2g; Minerals: 0.3g; Fibre: 0.18g.

Healthy modifications: See matarshutir kachori (p. 93).

RADHABALLABHI

Fried flatbread with black gram filling

Preparation time: 25 mins; Cooking time: 3 mins

Kachori stuffed with husked, split black gram is an unleavened, traditional fried flatbread, similar to bedmi puri of Rajasthan, which is spicier.

Ingredients for 6 kachoris

The filling
1 cup husked, split black gram (urad dal)
A pinch of salt or to taste
1" piece ginger
1 tsp aniseed
A pinch of asafoetida powder
¼ tsp red chilli powder
1 tbsp oil
The dough
1 cup refined flour
A pinch of salt or to taste
To fry the kachoris
Ghee for deep-frying

Method

Wash the gram and soak it in water for a few hours.

Drain and grind it with salt, ginger and aniseed to make a smooth paste.

Mix in the asafoetida powder and chilli powder.

Heat the oil in a pan and sauté the gram paste, till dry.

Divide the filling into 6 portions and leave aside, till cool.

Prepare the dough as given for sada puri (p. 73).

Prepare the stuffed kachoris and fry them as given for bedmi puri (p. 76).

Serve hot with any potato curry.

Nutritive values for 1 kachori: Calories: 188.0kcal; Carbohydrate: 22.8g; Protein: 6.0g; Fat: 8.0g; Minerals: 0.7g; Fibre: 0.34g.

Healthy modifications: See matarshutir kachori (p. 93).

FLATBREADS MADE WITH REFINED WHEAT FLOUR AND SEMOLINA

KHASTA ROTI

Flaky flatbread

Preparation time: 30 mins; Cooking time: 2 mins

Khasta roti is an unleavened, traditional, flaky flatbread, popular in Rajasthan and north India.

Ingredients for 2 rotis

A pinch of salt or to taste
1 cup refined wheat flour
½ cup semolina
2 tsp sugar, powdered
1 tsp carom seeds (ajwain)
2 tbsp ghee

Method

Dissolve the salt in 6 tbsp of water.

Mix the flour, semolina, sugar, carom seeds and ghee in a bowl.

Prepare the dough as given for sada paratha (p. 22).

Divide the dough into 2 portions and shape them into balls.

Roll out each portion of dough into a 6"- 7" circle and prick it all over with a fork.

Bake them in a clay, gas or electric tandoor, till golden brown on both sides.

Serve hot with any curry or dal.

Nutritive values for 1 roti: Calories: 405.0kcal; Carbohydrate: 56.3g; Protein: 8.5g; Fat: 16.2g; Minerals: 0.55g; Fibre: 0.65g.

Healthy modifications: Avoid adding ghee to the dough. This will reduce 7.5g fat and 68kcal for each flatbread. Use khasta rotis made with wholewheat flour and semolina.

KHASTA PURI

Fried flatbread

Preparation time: 20 mins; Cooking time: 5 mins

Khasta puri is an unleavened, traditional, fried, Rajasthani flatbread.

Ingredients for 10 puris

A pinch of salt or to taste
¾ cup refined wheat flour
¼ cup semolina
1 tsp carom seeds (ajwain)
To fry the puris
Oil for deep-frying

Method

Dissolve the salt in 5 tbsp of water.

Mix the flour, semolina and carom seeds in a bowl.

Prepare the dough as given for sada chapatti (p. 66).

Divide the dough into 10 portions and shape them into balls.

Roll out the puris and fry them as given for sada puris (p. 73).

Serve hot with any curry.

Nutritive values for 1 puri: Calories: 82.0kcal; Carbohydrate: 7.5g; Protein: 1.2g;

Fat: 5.2g; Minerals: 0.1g; Fibre: 0.13g.

Healthy modifications: Use wholewheat flour or replace half the refined flour with it.

FLATBREADS MADE WITH RICE FLOUR

Botanically called Oryza sativa, of the family Graminaceae, rice is the staple food for south, east and north-east India. It is available as short-grain, long-grain, parboiled and brown rice and is gluten-free. Hundreds of varieties of rice are cultivated in India, but rice flour is usually made with short-grain rice. Brown rice is unrefined rice and so is rich in minerals, protein and fibre. Its bran is rich in B-complex vitamins and vitamin E. It is available as short and long-grain rice.

Flatbreads made with rice flour are delicious, but not as nutritious as those made with wholewheat flour, millet flours and multigrain flours.

MALABAR ARI PATHIRI

Malabar rice flatbread

Preparation time: 20 mins; Cooking time: 15 mins

Malabar ari pathiri is an unleavened, traditional flatbread. Tandlachi bhakri, chaval bhakri and chaval roti of Maharashtra are similar to ari pathiri.

Ingredients for 5 pathiris

A pinch of salt or to taste
1 cup rice flour
To serve
1 cup thick coconut milk

Method

Boil 1 cup of water in a pan and dissolve the salt in it.

Gradually add the rice flour, stirring vigorously for a minute to prevent lumps from forming. Remove from the heat.

While still warm, knead the rice dough for 10-15 mins.

Cover the dough and leave it aside for about 20 mins.

Knead it again for about 5 mins.

Divide the dough into 5 portions and shape them into balls.

Roll out each portion of dough on a lightly floured board or press them on a greased plastic sheet as thin as possible.

Toast it on a hot pan.

When bubbles appear on the upper surface, flip it over and cook the other side, till light brown.

Press the pathiri with a broad spatula to puff it up.

Repeat with the remaining portions of dough.

Just before serving dip the pathiris in coconut milk.

Serve hot with any curry.

(Recipe Cont.)

Nutritive values for 1 pathiri: Calories: 58.0kcal; Carbohydrate: 13.0g; Protein: 1.1g; Fat: 0.1g; Minerals: 0.1g; Fibre: 0.03g.

Nutritive values for 1 pathiri dipped in coconut milk: Calories: 130.0kcal; Carbohydrate: 15.0g; Protein: 1.7g; Fat: 6.9g; Minerals: 0.25; Fibre: 0.03g.

Healthy modifications: Coconut milk is rich in saturated fat and high in calories. Use the second extract of coconut milk instead of the first.

Dip the flatbreads in sweetened skimmed milk which is low in calories. While 100 ml of coconut milk provides 430kcal, 100 ml of skimmed milk provides only 29kcal.

Use pathiris made with brown rice flour or replace half the white rice flour with brown rice flour.

COCONUT PATHIRI

Rice flatbread with fresh coconut

Preparation time: 20 mins; Cooking time: 15 mins

Coconut pathiri is an unleavened, traditional flatbread made with rice flour and grated fresh coconut in Kerala. Grind 2 tbsp grated fresh grated coconut, 5-6 peeled baby onions and 1 tsp cumin seeds. Add it to 1 cup of boiling water with the salt and make 5 pathiris as given for Malabar ari pathiri (alongside).

Nutritive values for 1 pathiri: Calories: 159.0kcal; Carbohydrate: 17.0g; Protein: 2.2g; Fat: 9.1g; Minerals: 0.55g; Fibre: 0.37g.

Nutritive values for 1 pathiri dipped in coconut milk: Calories: 231.0kcal; Carbohydrate: 19.0g; Protein: 2.8g; Fat: 15.9g; Minerals: 0.7g; Fibre: 0.37g.

Healthy modifications: Limit the use of flesh coconut in the flatbreads.

See Malabari ari pathiri (alongside) for further modifications.

NEY PATHIRI

Fried rice flatbread

Preparation time: 20 mins; Cooking time: 7 mins

Ney pathiri is an unleavened, traditional fried flatbread made with rice flour and grated fresh coconut In Kerala. Make the dough as given for coconut pathiri (p. 97), make 8 pathiris and deep-fry them in oil, till golden brown. Drain on layers of tissue papers and serve hot with any curry.

Nutritive values for 1 pathiri: Calories: 111.0kcal; Carbohydrate: 11.3g; Protein: 1.3g; Fat: 6.7g; Minerals: 0.3g; Fibre: 0.28g.

Healthy modifications: Prepare ney pathiri with brown rice flour or replace half the white rice flour with brown rice flour for a more nutritious pathiri.

See coconut pathiri (p. 101) for further modifications.

MASALA OROTTI

Spicy, thick rice flatbread

Preparation time: 20 mins; Cooking time: 7 mins

Masala orotti is an unleavened, traditional, thick flatbread made with grated fresh coconut and spices in Kerala. Add ½ tsp of garam masala powder and 1 tsp of cumin seeds to 1 cup of boiling water with the grated coconut and make 4 masala orottis as given for orotti (alongside).

Nutritive values for 1 orotti: Calories: 147.0kcal; Carbohydrate: 21.0g; Protein: 2.3g; Fat: 5.9g; Minerals: 0.3g; Fibre: 0.48g.

Healthy modifications: See orotti (alongside).

OROTTI

Thick rice flatbread

Preparation time: 20 mins; Cooking time: 7 mins

Orotti is an unleavened, traditional flatbread similar to pathiri, but is thicker.

Ingredients for 4 orottis

2 tbsp grated fresh coconut

A pinch of salt or to taste

1 cup rice flour

2 tsp oil

Method

Add the coconut and salt to 1 cup of boiling water, simmer for 1-2 mins and make the dough as given for Malabar ari pathiri (p. 97).

Divide the dough into 4 portions and shape them into balls.

Press a dough ball on a greased plastic sheet into a 4" circle.

Smear a pan with ½ tsp oil and put it on low heat. Invert the plastic sheet over it so that the orotti slips on to the pan.

Cook on low heat, till golden brown on both sides.

Repeat with the remaining portions of dough.

Serve hot with any curry.

Nutritive values for 1 orotti: Calories: 142.0kcal; Carbohydrate: 20.5g; Protein: 2.1g; Fat: 5.8g; Minerals: 0.23g; Fibre: 0.33g.

Healthy modifications: Limit the use of fresh coconut.

Toast the orottis in a non-stick pan without oil. This will reduce 2.5g fat and 27kcal from each orotti.

Use orottis made with brown rice flour or replace half the white rice flour with brown rice flour for a more nutritious orotti.

TANDLACHI BHAKRI

Plain rice flatbread

Preparation time: 20 mins; Cooking time: 8 mins

Tandlachi bhakri is an unleavened, traditional, Marathi flatbread.

Ingredients for 4 bhakris

A pinch of salt or to taste

1 cup rice flour

2 tsp home-made white butter

Method

Dissolve the salt in ¾ cup of water in a large pan and bring to a boil.

Prepare the dough as given for Malabar ari pathiri (p. 97).

Divide the dough into 4 portions and shape them into balls.

Roll out a portion of the dough on a lightly floured board into a 4"- 5" circle.

Put a non-stick pan on medium heat and place the rolled out dough over it.

Sprinkle a little water over the surface and cook, till the water evaporates.

Flip it directly over the flame and cook, till it puffs up.

Flip it over again and cook the other side, till it puffs up.

Repeat with the remaining portions of dough.

Smear each bhakri with ½ tsp of butter.

Serve hot with any curry or dal.

Nutritive values for 1 bhakri: Calories: 105.0kcal; Carbohydrates: 19.6g; Protein: 1.7g; Fat: 2.2g; Minerals: 0.21g; Fibre: 0.1g.

Healthy modifications: Replace butter with vegetable oil.
Avoid smearing the bhakris with butter. This will reduce 2g fat and 19kcal from each bhakri.

RICE PURI

Fried rice flatbread

Preparation time: 20 mins; Cooking time: 8 mins

Rice puris are served in Kerala.

Ingredients for 10 puris

A pinch of salt or to taste

1 cup rice flour

Oil for deep-frying

Method

Boil 1 cup of water in a pan and dissolve the salt in it.

Prepare the dough as given for Malabar ari pathiri (p. 97).

Roll out each ball on a lightly floured board or press it on a greased plastic sheet into a 2"- 3" circle.

Heat the oil in a kadhai or wok and fry the puris as given for sada puri (p. 73).

Serve hot with any south Indian chutney.

Nutritive values for 1 puri: Calories: 53.0kcal; Carbohydrate: 6.7g; Protein: 0.64g; Fat: 2.6g; Minerals: 0.1g; Fibre: 0.1g.

BIYYAMU ROTI

Spicy rice flatbread

Preparation time: 20 mins; Cooking time: 8 mins

Biyyamu roti is an unleavened, traditional, Andhra flatbread.

Ingredients for 6 rotis

2 tbsp husked, split Bengal gram (chana dal)
A pinch of salt or to taste
1 cup rice flour
2 tbsp grated fresh coconut
4 green chillies, minced
2 onions, minced
1 tomato, chopped
½ cup coriander leaves, chopped
2 tsp sesame seeds
1 sprig curry leaves
6 tsp oil

Method

Wash the dal and soak it in water for 1 hour. Drain.

Dissolve the salt in 5 tbsp of hot water.

Combine all the ingredients, except the salt water and oil, in a bowl.

Add the salt water gradually and knead it for about 5-10 mins to make a smooth dough.

Divide the dough into 6 portions and shape them into balls.

Press each ball on a greased plastic sheet into a 6" circle.

Put a non-stick pan on medium heat and invert the plastic sheet over it so that the roti slips on to the pan.

Drizzle ½ tsp oil around the edges.

When the base is golden, flip it over, spoon ½ tsp oil over the edges again and cook on medium heat, till the other side is golden.

(Method Cont.)

Repeat with the remaining portions of the dough.

Serve hot with any south Indian curry.

Nutritive values for 1 roti: Calories: 164.0kcal; Carbohydrate: 19.4g; Protein: 3.1g; Fat: 8.2g; Minerals: 0.55g. Fibre: 0.71g.

Healthy modifications: Limit the use of fresh coconut.

Toast the roti in a non-stick pan without oil. This will reduce 5g fat and 45kcal from each flatbread.

Use rotis made with brown rice flour or replace half the white rice flour with brown rice flour.

BROWN RICE ROTI

Brown rice flatbread

Preparation time: 20 mins; Cooking time: 12 mins

Brown rice roti is an unleavened, innovative flatbread made with cooked brown rice and brown rice flour. It is nutritious, but takes longer to cook than refined rice. Cook the rice for 10-15 mins in a pressure cooker on low heat after the cooker reaches full pressure. The roti too, takes longer to cook than those made with white rice.

Use brown rice instead of white rice and prepare 4 rotis as given for akki otti (facing page). Serve them with a peanut or garlic chutney

Nutritive values for 1 roti: Calories: 100.0kcal; Carbohydrates: 20.9g; Protein: 1.9g; Fat: 0.77g; Minerals: 1.0g; Fibre: 1.3g.

AKKI OTTI

Rice flatbread

Preparation time: 20 mins; Cooking time: 8 mins

Akki otti is an unleavened, traditional, Kodava flatbread made with cooked rice and rice flour.

Ingredients for 4 ottis

2 cups cooked rice
½ cup rice flour
A pinch of salt or to taste

Method

Knead the cooked rice, rice flour and salt for 5-10 mins.

Divide the dough into 4 portions and shape them into balls.

Roll out a portion of dough on a lightly floured board into a 4"- 5" circle.

Toast it on a pan, till light brown on both sides. Puff it while toasting, by pressing the otti with the back of the spatula along the edges.

Repeat with the remaining portions of the dough.

Serve hot with any curry or dal.

Nutritive values for 1 otti: Calories: 95.0kcal; Carbohydrates: 21.5g; Protein: 1.7g; Fat: 0.14g; Minerals: 0.17g; Fibre: 0.1g.

FLATBREADS MADE WITH MAIZE FLOUR

The botanical name for maize is Zea mays, of the family Poaceae. It is a whole grain cereal commonly called corn. While preparing the dough with maize flour, hot salt water is added to the flour for binding purposes, as it lacks gluten and is high in fibre. It is not possible to roll maize dough as it sticks to the pin, the edges cracks and the roti breaks while lifting it. So press the dough with your fingertips on a greased plastic sheet. Sprinkle a tablespoon of water on the upper surface of the roti while toasting it on the pan.

A few decades ago, maize flour was available only in winter. Today, it is available throughout the year. Makkai ki roti is served with dollops of fresh, home-made white butter. Maize flour is coarse and yellow and is made from dried yellow corn kernels, whereas cornflour is a very fine, white, refined flour, low in fibre. It is made with white corn and used as a thickening agent.

MAKKAI KI ROTI

Maize flatbread

Preparation time: 20 mins; Cooking time: 6 mins

Makkai ki roti is an unleavened, traditional, Punjabi and Rajasthani flatbread made with maize flour. It is usually served with sarson ka saag (mustard greens).

Ingredients for 2 roti

A pinch of salt or to taste
1 cup maize flour
2 tsp home-made unsalted white butter

Method

Dissolve the salt in 5 tbsp of hot water.

Add hot salted water to the flour and knead it for about 5 mins to make a smooth dough.

Cover the dough with a damp cloth and leave it aside for about 20 mins.

Divide it into 2 portions and shape them into balls.

Flatten each ball between your palms or press them on a greased plastic sheet with your fingertips into a round shape as thin as possible.

Invert the sheet over a hot tava kept on medium heat, so that the roti slips on to it.

When the base is slightly cooked, sprinkle 1 tbsp of water over the surface evenly and wait till the water evaporates.

Flip the roti over carefully and cook the other side.

Press the edges of the roti with a wooden spatula so that the roti is well cooked and puffs up.

Flip the roti and puff up the other side.

Smear each roti with 1 tsp butter.

Serve hot with spicy mustard greens.

Nutritive values for 1 roti: Calories: 216.0kcal; Carbohydrates: 33.2g; Protein: .6g; Fat: 6.8g; Minerals: 0.76g; Fibre: 1.3g.
Healthy modifications: Replace butter with oil.
Avoid smearing the rotis with fat. This will reduce 4g fat and 37kcal from each roti.

MASALA MAKKAI ROTI

Spicy maize flatbread

Preparation time: 20 mins; Cooking time: 6 mins

Masala makkai roti is an unleavened, traditional, Punjabi flatbread made with maize flour and spices. Add 2 chopped onions, 4 chopped green chillies and 1 cup of chopped coriander leaves to the flour and make 2 rotis as given for makkai ki roti (alongside). Serve them with curd and any curry.

Nutritive values for 1 roti: Calories: 238.0kcal; Carbohydrate: 39.3g; Protein: 6.6g; Fat: 5.7g; Minerals: 1.2g; Fibre: 2.3g.

METHI MAKKAI ROTI

Maize flatbread with fenugreek leaves

Preparation time: 30 mins; Cooking time: 12 mins

Methi makkai roti is an unleavened, traditional, Rajasthani flatbread. Rajasthani rotis are thinner than the Punjabi ones and several different vegetables are added to the flour. To make methi makkai roti, add 1 cup of chopped fresh fenugreek leaves, 2 tsp ginger-garlic-green chilli paste and ¼ tsp red chilli powder to the flour. Make 2 rotis as given for makkai ki roti (alongside). Smear them with ghee instead of white butter and serve them with any dal.

Nutritive values for 1 roti: Calories: 118.0kcal; Carbohydrate: 17.9g; Protein: 3.4g; Fat: 3.6g; Minerals: 0.62g; Fibre: 0.93g.

STUFFED CORN ROTI

Corn flatbread wraps

Preparation time: 30 mins; Cooking time: 30 mins

Stuffed corn roti is an unleavened, innovative flatbread made with cornflour, stuffed with spicy corn kernels, legumes and vegetables and topped with grated cheese. They resemble the Mexican fajitas, where a corn tortilla (a thin corn roti) is stuffed with spicy grilled ingredients.

Ingredients for 2 wraps

The marinade
1 cup curd
1 tsp garlic paste
1 onion, puréed
½ tsp garam masala powder
A pinch of salt or to taste
The filling
4 soya chunks
4 baby corns
4 chunks of red capsicum
4 chunks of green capsicums
4 chunks of yellow capsicums
4 tofu cubes
The corn rotis
A pinch of salt or to taste
½ cup corn flour
2 tsp oil
The topping
½ tbsp olive oil
2 tomatoes, finely chopped
1 green chilli, minced
½ tsp cumin-pepper powder
A pinch of salt or to taste
To make the wraps
1 cup shredded lettuce leaves
2 tbsp garlic cheese spread

Method

Combine all the marinade ingredients in a bowl.

Soak the soya chunks in boiling water for 20 mins. Squeeze and rinse it twice in fresh cold water.

Combine all the filling ingredients in a bowl and mix in the marinade. Leave it aside to marinate for 2 hours.

Fix the chunks on to metal skewers and grill them under a medium grill for 10 mins.

Divide them into 2 portions.

Make 2 corn rotis as given for makkai ki roti (p. 102). Sprinkle ½ tsp of oil along with the water, while cooking the rotis.

Keep them warm

Heat the oil for the topping in a pan and sauté the tomatoes and chillies, till the tomatoes soften.

Add the spice powder and the salt and simmer for a few mins.

Divide it into 2 portions.

Divide the lettuce leaves into 2 portions.

Spread 1 tbsp garlic cheese on each corn roti.

Heat the rotis on a pan, till the cheese melts.

Place one lettuce portion in the centre of the roti.

Spoon 1 portion of the filling over the lettuce.

Cover with 1 portion of the topping.

Pull up 2 sides of the roti to cover the filling. Secure it with a clove or a small toothpick.

Make the second wrap in the same way.

Serve immediately.

Nutritive values for 1 corn wrap: Calories: 318.0kcal; Carbohydrate: 25.6g; Protein: 13.1g; Fat: 14.1g; Minerals: 2.5g; Fibre: 2.1g.

TIKKAR

Maize-wheat flour flatbread

Preparation time: 20 mins; Cooking time: 8 mins

Tikkar is an unleavened, traditional, Rajasthani flatbread made with maize flour and wholewheat flour.

Ingredients for 4 tikkars

A pinch of salt or to taste
½ cup maize flour
½ cup wholewheat flour
2 tsp ginger-garlic-green chilli paste
¼ tsp red chilli powder
½ cup coriander leaves, chopped
2 tsp ghee

Method

Dissolve the salt in 5 tbsp of water.

Mix all the remaining ingredients, except the ghee, in a bowl and prepare the dough as given for makkai ki roti (p. 102).

Divide the dough into 4 portions and shape them into balls.

Roll out a portion of the dough on a lightly floured board into a 4"- 5" circle.

Toast it on a hot pan, till golden brown on both sides.

Repeat with the remaining portions of the dough.

Smear each roti with ½ tsp ghee.

Serve hot with any curry of dal.

Nutritive values for 1 tikkar: Calories: 114.0kcal; Carbohydrate: 17.8g; Protein: 3.1g; Fat: 3.3g; Minerals: 0.85g; Fibre: 0.76g.

Healthy modifications: Avoid smearing the tikkars with ghee. This will reduce 2.5g fat and 23kcal from each tikkar.

Smear the tikkars with peanut or hazelnut butter instead of ghee.

FLATBREADS MADE WITH BARLEY FLOUR

Botanically called Hordeum vulgare, of the family Poaceae, barley is a staple food in some parts of rural India. It contains gluten and is high in soluble fibre.

Flatbreads made only from barley flour are slightly crisp, because it contains less gluten than wheat. If it is mixed with wholewheat flour, the flatbreads can be rolled.

JAU ROTI

Barley flatbread

Preparation time: 20 mins; Cooking time: 6 mins

Jau roti is an unleavened, innovative flatbread, rich in soluble fibre. Use 1 cup of barley flour and make 2 rotis in the same way as given for sada chapatti (p. 66), but do not smear them with oil. Serve them hot with onion slices, lime wedges, curd and any curry.

Nutritive values for 1 roti: Calories: 168.0kcal; Carbohydrate: 34.8g; Protein: 5.8g; Fat: 0.65g; Minerals: 0.6g; Fibre: 1.9g.

HERBY BARLEY-PEARL MILLET ROTI

Preparation time: 25 mins; Cooking time: 6 mins

Herby barley-pearl millet roti is an unleavened, innovative flatbread.

Ingredients for 2 rotis

½ cup barley flour
½ cup pearl millet flour
1 cup mixed herbs (parsley, celery, thyme, rosemary, mint, sweet basil and coriander leaves), chopped
A pinch of salt or to taste

Method

Make the dough and roll out the rotis as given for palak paratha (p. 24).

Put a non-stick pan on medium heat and toast the rotis, till golden brown on both sides.

Serve hot with onion slices, lime wedges, curd and any curry or dal.

Nutritive values for 1 roti: Calories: 188.0kcal; Carbohydrate: 36.0g; Protein: 7.1g; Fat: 1.8g; Minerals: 1.5g; Fibre: 1.7g.

JAU PARATHA

Barley flatbread

Preparation time: 20 mins; Cooking time: 6 mins

Jau paratha is an unleavened, innovative flatbread made with barley flour and wheat flour.

Ingredients for 2 parathas

A pinch of salt or to taste
½ cup barley flour
½ cup wholewheat flour

Method

Make the dough as given for sada chapatti (p. 66).

Divide the dough into 2 portions and shape them into balls.

Roll out a portion of the dough on a lightly floured board into a 4"- 5" circle.

Fold it into half and then into a quarter and roll it out again into a 6"- 7" circle.

Put a non-stick pan on medium heat and toast the roti, till golden brown on both sides.

Repeat with the remaining portion of dough.

Serve hot with onion slices, lime wedges, curd and any curry or dal.

Nutritive values for 1 paratha: Calories: 170.0kcal; Carbohydrate: 35.2g; Protein: 5.9g; Fat: 0.7g; Minerals: 0.68g; Fibre: 1.3g.

FLATBREADS MADE WITH OAT FLOUR

The botanical name for oats is Avena sativa, of the family Poaceae. Oats are available as oatmeal or rolled oats from which free flour has been removed. They are high in soluble fibre and contain gluten. Powdered white oats are mixed with the flours of other cereal grains, millet or pulses to make flatbreads.

Dough made only from oat flour are difficult to roll and they are crisp. When mixed with wholewheat flour, it can be rolled.

OATS ROTI

Preparation time: 20 mins; Cooking time: 6 mins

Oats roti is an unleavened, innovative flatbread.

Use 1 cup of powdered oats to make 2 rotis in the same way as given for jau roti (p. 105). Serve them hot with onion slices, lime wedges, curd and any curry.

Nutritive values for 1 roti: Calories: 187.0 kcal; Carbohydrate: 31.4g. Protein: 6.8g; Fat: 3.8g; Minerals: 0.9 g; Fibre: 1.7g.

OATS MISSI ROTI

Oats, wheat and gram flour flatbread

Preparation time: 20 mins; Cooking time: 6 mins

Oats missi roti is an unleavened, innovative flatbread. It is a one-dish meal as it provides good-quality macro and micro nutrients.

Prepare the dough with ¾ cup powdered white oats, ¼ cup wholewheat flour and ¼ cup gram flour, 1 chopped onion and 1 cup of chopped mixed green leafy vegetables and roll out 2 parathas as given for palak paratha (p. 24). Toast them in a non-stick pan on medium heat, till golden brown on both sides. Serve them hot with any curry or dal.

Nutritive values for 1 roti: Calories: 200.0kcal; Carbohydrate: 35.7g; Protein: 8.6g; Fat: 3.0g; Minerals: 1.6g; Fibre: 1.6g.

VEGGIE OATS-BARLEY ROTI

Preparation time: 25 mins; Cooking time: 6 mins

Veggie oats-barley roti is an unleavened, innovative flatbread.

Prepare the dough with ½ cup powdered white oats, ½ cup barley flour and 1 cup grated mixed vegetables and roll out 2 rotis as given for palak paratha (p. 24). Toast them in a non-stick pan on medium heat, till golden brown on both sides. Serve them hot with onion slices, lime wedges, curd and any curry or dal.

Nutritive values for 1 roti: Calories: 202.0 kcal; Carbohydrate: 37.5g; Protein: 7.7g; Fat: 2.3g; Minerals: 1.1 g; Fibre: 2.8g.

FLATBREADS MADE WITH RYE FLOUR

Botanically called Secale cereal, of the family Poaceae, rye flour has a strong flavour and is dark in colour. It is rich in several minerals, protein and insoluble and soluble fibre. It thus helps decrease blood cholesterol, blood sugar and blood pressure levels, thereby reducing the risks of cardiovascular diseases, diabetes, digestive problems and cancer. It contains phytochemicals such as phenolic compounds in the bran. Rye bread is called pumpernickel bread or dark bread in Europe. It contains more protein, fibre, minerals and B-vitamins than wheat. Crisp, rye flatbreads are also popular in some European countries.

RYE ROTI

Rye flatbread

Preparation time: 20 mins; Cooking time: 6 mins

Rye roti is an unleavened, innovative flatbread, which is slightly crisp. Use 1 cup of rye flour and make the dough and roll out the rotis, as given for sada chapatti (p. 66).

Roll the rotis into 4" circles. Toast them in a non-stick pan on medium heat, till golden brown on both sides. Serve them hot with onion slices, lime wedges, curd and any curry.

Nutritive values for 1 roti: Calories: 187.0kcal; Carbohydrate: 40.9g; Protein: 4.3g; Fat: 0.7g; Minerals: 1.0g; Fibre: 7.4g.

RYE PARATHA

Rye-wheat flour flatbread

Preparation time: 20 mins; Cooking time: 6 mins

Rye paratha is an unleavened, innovative flatbread. Use ½ cup rye flour, ½ cup wholewheat flour and salt and make the parathas as given for jau roti (p. 105). Serve them hot with onion slices, lime wedges, curd and any curry.

Nutritive values for 1 paratha: Calories: 180.0kcal; Carbohydrate: 38.3g; Protein: 5.1g; Fat: 0.73g; Minerals: 0.88g; Fibre: 4.0g.

FLATBREADS MADE WITH PEARL MILLET (BAJRA) FLOUR

Botanically called Pennisetum glaucum, of the family Poaceae, pearl millet or bajra is the most popular of the millets. It is a staple in the west Indian states of Rajasthan, Gujarat and Maharashtra and is also consumed in Haryana. In addition to breakfast cereals, puffed grains and porridge, pearl millet is used to make flatbreads called rotis or bhakris. It is used in combination with flours, flatbreads and pancakes. It contains good-quality proteins, iron and vitamin B1. It is gluten-free, high in insoluble fibres and low in saturated fats; hence low in cholesterol.

They are made in the same way as maize flour flatbreads (p. 102).

SADA BAJRA ROTI

Pearl millet flatbread

Preparation time: 20 mins; Cooking time: 6 mins

Sada bajra roti is an unleavened, traditional flatbread in Rajasthan and Maharashtra, where it is called a bhakri. In Gujarat it is called bajri no rotlo and in Karnataka it is sajje roti.

Make the dough, shape the rotis and cook them as given for makkai ki roti (p. 102). Puff the roti, if you like, by putting it directly on the fire, like phulkas. Smear each roti with ½ tsp ghee on both the sides. Serve them hot with a garlic chutney and any curry or dal.

Nutritive values for 1 roti: Calories: 203.0 kcal; Carbohydrates: 33.8 g; Protein: 5.8g; Fat: 5.0 g; Minerals: 1.2g; Fibre: 0.6g.

Healthy modifications: See tikkar (p. 104).

BAJRA-ALOO ROTI

Pearl millet-potato flatbread

Preparation time: 20 mins; Cooking time: 12 mins

Bajra-aloo roti is an unleavened, traditional flatbread in the western states of India, especially Rajasthan and Gujarat. The fasting flatbreads made with buckwheat flour (kuttu atta), amaranth flour (rajgira atta), sago and water chestnut flour (singhada flour) are prepared in a similar way.

Ingredients for 4 rotis

1 cup pearl millet flour

1 cup boiled, mashed potatoes

2 tsp ginger-garlic-green chilli paste

½ cup coriander leaves, chopped

¼ tsp red chilli powder

A pinch of salt or to taste

2 tsp ghee

Method

Mix all the ingredients, except the ghee, in a bowl.

Prepare the dough as given for palak paratha (p. 24).

Divide the dough into 4 portions.

Shape the rotis and cook them as given for makkai ki roti (p. 102).

Smear each roti with ½ tsp ghee.

Serve hot with any curry or dal.

Nutritive values for 1 roti: Calories: 141.0kcal; Carbohydrates: 23.4g; Protein: 3.5g; Fat: 3.9g; Minerals: 0.82g; Fibre: 0.6g.

Healthy modifications: See sada bajra roti (alongside).

SOYA-PANEER-BAJRA ROTI

Pearl millet flatbread with tofu filling

Preparation time: 25 mins; Cooking time: 6 mins

Soya-paneer-bajra roti is an unleavened, innovative flatbread made with pearl millet flour and stuffed with spicy tofu. It is a one-dish meal as it offers good-quality macro and micro nutrients.

Ingredients for 2 rotis

The filling

1 tsp oil

100g tofu, drained and crumbled

1 tsp ginger-garlic-green chilli paste

A pinch of salt or to taste

1 cup mixed herbs (rosemary, thyme, parsley, celery), chopped

The dough

Dough to make 2 sada bajra rotis (alongside)

Method

Heat the oil in a pan and sauté the tofu and ginger-garlic-green chilli paste for 2-3 mins.

Add the salt and the herbs and mix well.

Divide the filling into 2 portions and leave aside, till cool.

Divide the dough into 4 portions and shape them into balls.

Prepare and cook the rotis as given for kela paratha (p. 36).

Serve hot with cucumber raita.

Nutritive value for 1 roti: Calories: 250.0 kcal; Carbohydrates: 36.9 g; Protein: 10.2 g; Fat: 7.2g; Minerals: 1.3 g; Fibre: 0.79g.

FLATBREADS MADE WITH SORGHUM (JOWAR) FLOUR

Botanically called Sorghum vulgare, of the family Poaceae, sorghum is grown in Karnataka, Rajasthan, Maharashtra and Haryana. It is gluten-free, high in insoluble fibres and low in saturated fats; hence low in cholesterol.

They are made in the same way as maize flour flatbreads (p. 105).

JOWAR ROTI

Sorghum flatbread

Preparation time: 20 mins; Cooking time: 6 mins

Jowar roti is an unleavened, traditional flatbread. It is called juvar no rotlo in Gujarat. Jowar roti with pitla curry is a famous dish of rural Maharashtra, while jonna roti with sorrel leaf (gongura) chutney is served in Andhra Pradesh and it is called jolada roti in Karnataka.

Make the dough, shape the rotis and cook them as given for makkai ki roti (p. 102). Puff the roti, if you like, by putting it directly on the fire, like phulkas. Smear each roti with ½ tsp ghee on both the sides. Serve them hot with a gram flour gravy and a green chutney.

Nutritive values for 1 roti: Calories: 197.0kcal; Carbohydrate: 36.3g; Protein: 5.2g; Fat: 3.5g; Minerals: 0.8g; Fibre: 0.8g.

Healthy modifications: See sada bajra roti (p. 108).

JOWAR-BAJRA ROTI

Sorghum-pearl millet flatbread

Preparation time: 20 mins; Cooking time: 6 mins

Jowar bajra roti is an unleavened, innovative flatbread made with sorghum flour and pearl millet flour.

Use ½ cup each of sorghum and pearl millet flours to make 2 rotis, as given for makkai ki roti (p. 102). Serve them with any curry or dal.

Nutritive values for 1 roti: Calories: 89.0kcal; Carbohydrate: 17.5g; Protein: 2.8g; Fat: 0.85g; Minerals: 0.48g; Fibre: 0.35g.

HARA JOWAR-OATS ROTI

Green sorghum oats flatbread

Preparation time: 25 mins; Cooking time: 6 mins

Hara jowar-oats roti is an unleavened, innovative flatbread.

Use ½ cup each of sorghum and oats flours mixed with 1 cup of chopped mixed green leafy vegetables to make 2 rotis. Make the dough as given for palak paratha (p. 24) and cook them as you would makkai ki roti (p. 102). Serve them hot with onion slices, lime wedges, curd and any curry or dal.

Nutritive values for 1 roti: Calories: 200.0kcal; Carbohydrate: 36.1g; Protein: 7.6g; Fat: 2.8g; Minerals: 1.7g; Fibre: 1.7g.

FLATBREADS MADE WITH FINGER MILLET (RAGI/ MANDUA) FLOUR

Botanically known as Eleusine coracana, of the family Poaceae, finger or red millet is available in the rural areas of Karnataka, Andhra Pradesh, Tamil Nadu and Kerala. Several dishes are made with finger millet flour such as ragi mudde (Karnataka), ragi sankati (Andhra Pradesh), ragi sevai (Tamil Nadu) and ragi puttu (Kerala). Finger millet pancakes are served in south and west India. Finger millet bread is dark brown and contains more protein, fibre, minerals and B-vitamins than wheat bread. It Is gluten-free and contains more calcium than other millets. Ragi rotis are known in Karnataka and Maharashtra as nachni bhakri. Crisp flatbreads called khakras made with finger millet flour are popular in Gujarat. They are made in the same way as maize flour flatbreads (p. 102).

RAGI/MANDUA ROTI

Finger millet or red millet flatbread

Preparation time: 20 mins; Cooking time: 6 mins

Ragi roti is an unleavened, traditional flatbread in south Indian, Marathi and Bihari cuisines.

Use 1 cup of finger millet flour and make 2 rotis as given for makkai ki roti (p. 102). Smear them with 1 tsp ghee and serve with curd and any dal.

Nutritive values for 1 roti: Calories: 209.0kcal; Carbohydrate: 36.0g; Protein: 3.7g; Fat: 5.7g; Minerals: 1.4 g; Fibre: 1.8g.

Healthy modifications: See sada bajra roti (p. 108).

MANDUA KI ROTI

Finger millet or red millet flatbread

Preparation time: 20 mins; Cooking time: 6 mins

Mandua ki roti is an unleavened, traditional flatbread served in Uttarakhand, where it is a staple.

Use ¾ cup of finger millet flour and ¼ cup of wholewheat flour and make 2 rotis as given for makkai ki roti (p. 102). Smear them with 1 tsp of home-made white butter and serve with any dal.

Nutritive values for 1 roti: Calories: 202.0kcal; Carbohydrate: 35.7g; Protein: 4.3g; Fat: 4.7g; Minerals: 1.4g; Fibre: 1.6g.

Healthy modifications: See sada bajra roti (p. 108).

TOFU-RAGI/MANDUA ROTI

Tofu finger millet flatbread

Preparation time: 20 mins; Cooking time: 6 mins

Tofu-ragi roti is an unleavened, innovative spicy flatbread made with finger millet and tofu.

Ingredients for 2 rotis

A pinch of salt or to taste

1 cup finger millet flour

1 tsp ginger-garlic paste

1 tsp coriander leaves paste

1 onion, puréed

100g tofu, grated

Method

Dissolve the salt in 5 tbsp of hot water.

Mix the remaining ingredients in a bowl.

Prepare the rotis as given for makkai ki roti (p. 102).

Serve hot with any curry or dal.

Nutritive values for 1 roti: Calories: 212.0 kcal; Carbohydrate: 40.0 g; Protein: 7.8g; Fat: 2.8g; Minerals: 1.5g; Fibre: 2.0g.

GAHAT DAL BHARA MANDUA ROTI

Finger millet flatbread with horse gram filling

Preparation time: 20 mins; Cooking time: 16 mins

Gahat dal bhara mandua roti is an unleavened, traditional flatbread made in the Uttarakhand, where gahat (horse gram) grows plentifully, especially in Garhwal.

Ingredients for 2 rotis

The filling

Gahat ki dal (p. 228)

The dough

A pinch of salt or to taste

¾ cup finger millet flour

¼ cup wholewheat flour

To serve

2 tsp home-made white butter

Method

Cook the dal till nearly dry.

Divide the dal into 2 portions and leave aside, till cool.

Prepare the dough as given for sada chapatti (p. 66) and divide it into 2 portions.

Make the rotis as given for band gobi paratha (p. 25).

Toast them on a hot pan on medium heat, till golden brown on both sides.

Smear each roti with 1 tsp butter.

Serve hot with curd and onion slices.

Nutritive values for 1 roti: Calories: 407.0kcal; Carbohydrate: 62.2g; Protein: 14.2g; Fat: 11.3g; Minerals: 3.2g; Fibre: 5.5g.

Healthy modifications: See sada bajra roti (p. 108).

FLATBREADS MADE WITH LESSER KNOWN MILLET FLOURS

Some of the lesser known millets used to make flatbreads are: Foxtail or Italian millet (Setaria italica, kangni in Hindi, tinai in Tamil, korralu in Telugu); little millet (Panicum sumatrense, kutki in Hindi, samai in Tamil, sama in Telugu); white or proso millet (Panicum millaceum, barri in Hindi, panivaragu in Tamil, varagulu in Telugu); Indian barnyard millet (Echinochloa frumentacea, jhangora or shama in Hindi, odalu in Telugu); and kodo millet (Paspalum scrobiculatum, kodra in Hindi, varagu in Tamil, arikalu in Telugu). Some are consumed in the rural South and others in the North. They are gluten-free and as nutritious as the other millets.

KORRALU ROTI

Foxtail or Italian millet flatbread

Preparation time: 20 mins; Cooking time: 12 mins

Korralu roti is an unleavened, traditional flatbread in rural Andhra Pradesh, Tamil Nadu and Karnataka.

Use 1 cup of foxtail millet flour and make 4 rotis as given for makkai ki roti (p. 102). Smear them with ½ tsp ghee and serve with any dal.

Nutritive values for 1 roti: Calories: 105.0kcal; Carbohydrates: 15.2g; Protein: 3.1g; Fat: 3.6g; Minerals: 0.83g; Fibre: 2.0g.

Healthy modifications: See sada bajra roti (p. 108).

KANGNI-ALOO ROTI

Foxtail millet-potato flatbread

Preparation time: 25 mins; Cooking time: 12 mins

Kangni-aloo roti is an unleavened, innovative flatbread .

Use foxtail millet flour and mashed potatoes in the same way as bajra-aloo roti (p. 109), using 1 cup of foxtail millet flour instead of pearl millet flour. Serve them hot with any curry.

Nutritive values for 1 roti: Calories: 113.0kcal; Carbohydrates: 21.7g; Protein: 3.7g; Fat: 1.3g; Minerals: 1.1g; Fibre: 2.3g.

SAMA ROTI

Little millet flatbread

Preparation time: 20 mins; Cooking time: 12 mins

Sama roti is an unleavened, traditional flatbread in rural Andhra Pradesh, Tamil Nadu and Karnataka.

Use 1 cup of little millet flour and make 4 rotis as given for makkai ki roti (p. 102). Smear them with ½ tsp ghee and serve with a dal.

Nutritive values for 1 roti: Calories: 108.0kcal; Carbohydrates: 16.8g; Protein: 1.9g; Fat: 3.7g; Minerals: 0.38g; Fibre: 1.9g.
Healthy modifications: See sada bajra roti (p. 108).

VARAGULU ROTI

White millet flatbread

Preparation time: 20 mins; Cooking time: 12 mins

Varagulu roti is an unleavened, traditional flatbread in rural Andhra Pradesh, Tamil Nadu and Karnataka.

Use 1 cup of white millet flour and make 4 rotis as given for makkai ki roti (p. 102). Smear them with ½ tsp ghee and serve with any dal.

Nutritive values for 1 roti: Calories: 108.0kcal; Carbohydrates: 17.6g; Protein: 3.1g; Fat: 2.8g; Minerals: 0.48g; Fibre: 0.55g.
Healthy modifications: See sada bajra roti (p. 108).

KUTTI-ALOO ROTI

Little millet-potato flatbread

Preparation time: 25 mins; Cooking time: 12 mins

Kutti-aloo roti is an unleavened, innovative flatbread made with little millet flour and mashed potatoes in the same way as bajra aloo roti (p. 109).

Use 1 cup of little millet flour instead of pearl millet flour and substituting mint leaves for coriander leaves. Serve them hot with any curry or dal.

Nutritive values for 1 roti: Calories: 117.0kcal; Carbohydrates: 23.6g; Protein: 2.8g; Fat: 1.3g; Minerals: 0.71g; Fibre: 2.2g.

BARRI-ALOO ROTI

White millet-potato flatbread

Preparation time: 25 mins; Cooking time: 12 mins

Barri-aloo roti is an unleavened, innovative flatbread made with white millet flour and mashed potatoes in the same way as bajra-aloo roti (p. 109).

Use 1 cup of white millet flour instead of pearl millet flour. Substitute celery leaves for coriander leaves and cumin-pepper powder for red chilli powder. Serve them hot with any dal.

Nutritive values for 1 roti: Calories: 116.0kcal; Carbohydrates: 24.1g; Protein: 3.9g; Fat: 0.46g; Minerals: 0.77g; Fibre: 0.88g.

SHAMA/JHANGORA ROTI

Indian barnyard millet flatbread

Preparation time: 20 mins; Cooking time: 12 mins

Shama/jhangora roti is an unleavened, traditional flatbread in rural north India.

Use 1 cup of Indian barnyard millet flour and make 4 rotis as given for makkai ki roti (p. 102). Smear them with ½ tsp ghee and serve with any curry.

Nutritive values for 1 roti: Calories: 99.0kcal; Carbohydrates: 16.4g; Protein: 1.6g; Fat: 3.1g; Minerals: 1.1g; Fibre: 2.5g.

Healthy modifications: See sada bajra roti (p. 108).

SHAMA/JHANGORA-ALOO ROTI

Indian barnyard millet-potato flatbread

Preparation time: 25 mins; Cooking time: 12 mins

Jhangora aloo-roti is an unleavened, innovative flatbread made with Indian barnyard millet flour and mashed potatoes in the same way as bajra-aloo roti (p. 109).

Use 1 cup of barnyard millet flour instead of pearl millet flour. Substitute parsley leaves for coriander leaves and pav bhaji masala for red chilli powder. Serve them hot with any curry or dal.

Nutritive values for 1 roti: Calories: 109.0kcal; Carbohydrates: 23.2g; Protein: 2.4g; Fat: 0.75g; Minerals: 1.4g; Fibre: 2.8g.

ARIKALU ROTI

Kodo millet flatbread

Preparation time: 20 mins; Cooking time: 12 mins

Arikalu roti is an unleavened, traditional flatbread in rural Andhra Pradesh, Tamil Nadu and Karnataka.

Use 1 cup of kodo millet flour and make 4 rotis as given for makkai ki roti (p. 102). Smear them with ½ tsp ghee and serve with any curry or dal.

Nutritive values for 1 roti: Calories: 100.0kcal; Carbohydrates: 16.5g; Protein: 2.1g; Fat: 2.9g; Minerals: 0.65g; Fibre: 2.3g.

Healthy modifications: See sada bajra roti (p. 108).

KODRA-ALOO ROTI

Kodo millet-potato flatbread

Preparation time: 25 mins; Cooking time: 12 mins

Kodra aloo-roti is an unleavened, innovative flatbread made with kodo millet flour and mashed potatoes in the same way as bajra-aloo roti (p. 109).

Use 1 cup of kodo millet flour instead of pearl millet flour. Substitute basil leaves for coriander leaves and garam masala powder for red chilli powder. Serve them hot with any curry or dal.

Nutritive values for 1 roti: Calories: 108.0kcal; Carbohydrates: 22.9g; Protein: 2.9g; Fat: 0.54g; Minerals: 0.95g; Fibre: 2.6g.

FLATBREADS MADE WITH MULTIGRAIN FLOUR (WHEAT, RICE, SORGHUM, MILLETS, OATS, PULSES AND SOYA BEAN)

Flatbreads made with multigrain flours are more nutritious than those made with a single grain flour, as it contains nutrients from various sources which can meet the RDA requirements of several nutrients. These are one-dish meals as they contain good-quality macro and micro nutrients.

MULTIGRAIN ROTLO

Seven-grain flatbread

Preparation time: 20 mins; Cooking time: 6 mins

Rotlos in Gujarati cuisine and bhakris in Marathi cuisine are similar and are traditionally made with single grain flours. Multigrain rotlos and bhakris are now becoming increasingly popular. The seven-grain flour in this recipe comprises wheat, sorghum (jowar), pearl millet (bajra), finger millet (ragi/ mandua), maize, rice and gram or soya flours.

Ingredients for 2 rotlos

1 cup seven-grain flour

2 tsp ginger-garlic-green chilli paste

½ cup coriander leaves, chopped

½ tsp turmeric powder

A pinch of salt or to taste

To cook the rotlos

4 tsp oil

Method

Prepare the dough and cook the rotlos as given for sada chapatti (p. 66).

Serve hot with curd and any curry or dal.

Nutritive values for 1 rotlo: Calories: 272.0kcal; Carbohydrate: 36.4g; Protein: 6.2g; Fat: 11.2g; Minerals: 1.2g; Fibre: 1.0g.

Healthy modifications: Toast each rotlo with 1 tsp oil instead of 2 tsp. This will reduce 5g fat and 45kcal from each rotlo.

Toast the rotlos in a non-stick pan without oil. This will further reduce 5g fat and 45kcal from each rotlo.

MASALA MULTIGRAIN ROTI

Spicy seven-grain flatbread

Preparation time: 20 mins; Cooking time: 6 mins

Masala multigrain roti is an unleavened, traditional flatbread, which is being increasingly served in Andhra Pradesh.

Use 1 cup of multigrain flour (see rotlo; alongside) and make 2 rotis. Add ½ tsp each of garam masala powder, cumin powder, coriander powder and turmeric powder, and ¼ tsp each of red chilli powder, black pepper powder and aniseed powder. Cook the rotis as given for sada chapatti (p. 66). Serve them hot with curd, a chutney and any curry or dal.

Nutritive values for 1 roti: Calories: 288.0kcal; Carbohydrate: 17.6g; Protein: 6.8g; Fat: 12.0g; Minerals: 1.6g; Fibre: 1.7g.
Healthy modifications: See multigrain rotlo (alongside).

MULTIGRAIN ROTLI/PHULKA

Puffed multigrain flatbread

Preparation time: 15 mins; Cooking time: 8 mins

Multigrain rotlis and phulkas are increasingly in importance in Gujarat and Maharashtra. They are not as soft, thin and fluffy as those made with wholewheat flour.

Use 1 cup of multigrain flour (see rotlos; p. 116) and make 4 rotlis as given for phulkas (p. 69). Serve them hot with any curry or dal.

Nutritive values for 1 rotli: Calories: 91.0kcal; Carbohydrate: 15.1g; Protein: 4.2g; Fat: 1.5g; Minerals: 1.3g; Fibre: 0.57g.

MULTIGRAIN STUFFED PARATHA

Preparation time: 25 mins; Cooking time: 15 mins

Multigrain stuffed paratha is an unleavened, innovative flatbread made with multigrain flour and stuffed with a mixture of multigrain noodles, mixed vegetable and nuts.

Ingredients for 2 parathas

The filling

100g multigrain noodles with taste maker

1 cup grated mixed vegetables (carrot, green pea, cabbage, capsicum, cauliflower)

1 cup chopped mixed leafy green vegetables (fenugreek, dill, sour spinach, mustard greens)

2 tbsp mixed nuts, grated

50g tofu, crumbled

The dough

1 cup multigrain flour

Method

Boil 2 cups of water and add the filling ingredients. Mix well.

Cook till the contents are tender and dry.

Divide the filling into 2 portions and leave aside, till cool.

Make the dough as given for sada chapatti (p. 66) and divide it into 4 portions.

Prepare the parathas as given for kela paratha (p. 36).

Serve hot with onion slices, lemon wedges and a tomato chutney (p. 219).

Nutritive values for 1 paratha: Calories: 337.0kcal; Carbohydrate: 43.3g; Protein: 14.5g; Fat: 11.8g; Minerals: 2.7g; Fibre: 2.9g.

MIXED HARA BHAJI PARATHA

Multigrain flatbread with leafy greens

Preparation time: 25 mins; Cooking time: 5 mins

Mixed hara bhaji paratha is an unleavened, innovative flatbread made with multigrain flour and fresh leafy green vegetables.

Ingredients for 2 parathas

1 cup multigrain flour

2 cups mixed leafy green vegetables, chopped

A pinch of salt or to taste

Method

Make the dough and roll out the parathas as given for palak paratha (p. 24).

Put a non-stick pan on medium heat and toast the parathas, till golden brown on both sides.

Serve hot with curd and any curry or dal.

Nutritive values for 1 paratha: Calories: 192.0kcal; Carbohydrate: 36.9 g; Protein: 7.3 g; Fat: 1.5g; Minerals: 2.0 g; Fibre: 1.4g.

CHOTA BHUTA PARATHA

Multigrain flatbread with baby corn

Preparation time: 25 mins; Cooking time: 5 mins

Chota bhuta paratha is an unleavened, innovative flatbread made in the same way as mixed hara bhaji paratha (alongside).

Use 1 cup of multigrain flour (see rotlo; p. 116), substitute 1 cup grated baby corn for the leafy vegetables and add 2 tsp ginger-garlic-green chilli paste to the flour. Serve them hot with any curry or dal.

Nutritive values for 1 paratha: Calories: 213.0kcal; Carbohydrates: 40.5g; Protein: 8.7g; Fat: 1.8g; Minerals: 2.1g; Fibre: 1.2g.

ALOO-CHEESE PARATHA

Multigrain flatbread with potato and cheese

Preparation time: 25 mins; Cooking time: 5 mins

Aloo-cheese paratha is an unleavened, innovative flatbread made in the same way as multigrain stuffed paratha (p. 117).

Mix 2 boiled, mashed potatoes with 4 tbsp of grated low-fat cheese paneer and 1 tsp of red chilli flakes to make the filling. Serve them hot with any curry or dal.

Nutritive values for 1 paratha: Calories: 262.0kcal; Carbohydrate: 47.4g; Protein: 13.1g; Fat: 2.4g; Minerals: 2.7g; Fibre: 1.8g.

Clockwise from left:

Sabudana Thalipeeth (p. 207)

Chapatti Cone with Brown Rice, Mixed Sprouts and Vegetables (p. 185)

Sada Chapatti (p. 66)

Sada Baida Roti (p. 136)

Biscuit Bhakris Open Sandwich (p. 180, 181)

Biscuit Bhakris (p. 152, 179, 180, 181)

A Platter of Khakras (p. 177, 178, 192, 193, 194)

Chapatti Cone with Spicy Capsicum (p. 184)

Anda Paratha (p. 132)

Bajra Roti (p. 108)

Shahi Murgh Paratha (p. 141)

Roomali Roti (p. 90)

Chapatti Cone with Chopped Fruits (p. 158)

Shimla Mirch Paratha (p. 36)

Puris with Sprouts or Spicy Vegetables (p. 199)

Celery Paratha (p. 40)

Soya-Hara Mattar Paratha (p. 51)

Tofu-Hara Pyaz Paratha (p. 50)

Chapatti Cone with Teekha Paneer (p. 185)

Corn and Chickpea Roll (p. 184)

Tandlachi Bhakri (p. 99)

Chukandar Paratha (p. 29)

Khasta Roti (p. 95)

Sprout Puri (p. 200)

Rajgira Paratha (p. 206)

Kela Paratha (p. 36)

Gajar Halwa Poli (p. 153)

Tandoori Roti (p. 90)

Phulkas (p. 69)

Paratha Pizza with Mixed Sprouts (p. 182)

Vada Pav, Usal Pav and Dabeli (p. 213, 212, 217)

Bandh Gobi Paratha (p. 25)

Mattiris (p. 163, 190, 194)

Kothu Parotta (p. 87)

Mughlai Kheema Paratha (p. 145)

Lassoon Naan (p. 81)

Pav with Mixed Sprouts (p. 212)

Khumb Paratha (p. 51)

Malabar Parotta (p. 88)

Cheese Naan (p. 80)

Makkai Roti (p. 102)

Makkai-Pudina Paratha (p. 54)

Sooji Halwa Poli (p. 156)

Tava Paratha (p. 23)

Missi Roti (p. 122)

Ragi Roti (p. 111)

Methi Thepla (p. 71)

Mixed Dal Poli (p. 152)

Malpuas (p. 167)

Puran Poli (p. 161)

Ragi Khakra (p. 193)

ALOO-GOBI PARATHA

Multigrain flatbread with potato and cauliflower

Preparation time: 25 mins; Cooking time: 5 mins

Aloo-gobi paratha is an unleavened, innovative flatbread made in the same way as mixed hara bhaji paratha (p. 118).

Use 1 cup of multigrain flour (see rotlo; p. 116), substitute 2 boiled and mashed potatoes and 1 cup of boiled and mashed cauliflower florets for the leafy vegetables and add 2 tsp ginger-garlic-green chilli paste and 1 tsp red chilli flakes to the flour. Serve them hot with any curry or dal.

Nutritive values for 1 paratha: Calories: 243.0kcal; Carbohydrates: 49.2g; Protein: 7.8g; Fat: 1.7g; Minerals: 2.0g; Fibre: 2.3g.

TOMATO-PYAZ PARATHA

Multigrain flatbread with tomato and onion

Preparation time: 25 mins; Cooking time: 5 mins

Tomato-pyaz paratha is an unleavened, innovative flatbread in the same way as mixed hara bhaji paratha (p. 118).

Use 1 cup of multigrain flour (see rotlo; p. 116), substitute 2 puréed tomatoes and 2 chopped onions for the leafy vegetables and add 2 tsp ginger-garlic-green chilli paste and 1 tsp red chilli flakes to the flour. Serve them hot with any curry or dal.

Nutritive values for 1 paratha: Calories: 222.0kcal; Carbohydrate: 44.2g; Protein: 7.4g; Fat: 1.7g; Minerals: 2.0g; Fibre: 2.5g.

ALOO-PALAK PARATHA

Multigrain flatbread with potato and spinach

Preparation time: 25 mins; Cooking time: 5 mins

Aloo-palak paratha is an unleavened, innovative flatbread made in the same way as mixed hara bhaji paratha (p. 118)

Use 1 cup of multigrain flour (see rotlo; p. 116), substitute 2 boiled and mashed potatoes and 1 cup of chopped spinach for the leafy vegetables and add 2 tsp ginger-garlic-green chilli paste and 1 tsp red chilli flakes to the flour. Serve them hot with any curry or dal.

Nutritive values for 1 paratha: Calories: 238.0kcal; Carbohydrates: 48.3g; Protein: 7.6g; Fat: 1.7g; Minerals: 2.1g; Fibre: 2.1g.

ALOO-PANEER PARATHA

Multigrain flatbread with potato and paneer

Preparation time: 25 mins; Cooking time: 5 mins

Aloo-paneer paratha is an unleavened, innovative flatbread made in the same way as multigrain stuffed paratha (p. 117).

Mix 2 boiled, mashed potatoes with 4 tbsp of crumbled paneer, ½ tsp garam masala powder and salt to make the filling. Serve them hot with any curry or dal.

Nutritive values for 1 paratha: Calories: 270.0kcal; Carbohydrate: 50.8g; Protein: 13.3g; Fat: 1.5g; Minerals: 1.8g; Fibre: 1.4g.

THALIPEETH

Multigrain flatbread with pulses

Preparation time: 20 mins; Cooking time: 12 mins

Thalipeeth is an unleavened, traditional, spicy Marathi flatbread made with multigrain flour, gram flour and mixed vegetables and is served at breakfast.

Ingredients for 4 thalipeeths

The dough

¼ cup wholewheat flour

¼ cup any millet flour

¼ cup rice flour

¼ cup gram flour (besan)

1 cup grated mixed vegetables (carrot, cabbage, capsicum, cauliflower)

1 onion, minced

2 green chillies, minced

½ cup coriander leaves, minced

A pinch of asafoetida powder

½ tsp red chilli powder

A pinch of salt or to taste

To cook the thalipeeth

8 tsp oil

Method

Make the dough as given for palak paratha (p. 24).

Divide the dough into 4 portions and shape them into balls.

Press a dough ball on a greased plastic sheet with your fingertips into a circle as thin as possible.

Invert the plastic sheet over a hot pan.

Spoon 1 tsp oil along the edges and cook, till the base is crisp and golden.

Flip it over and spoon another 1 tsp oil along the edges and cook, till the other side is crisp and golden brown.

(Method Cont.)

Repeat with the remaining portions of dough.

Serve hot with a dollop of home-made white butter, curd and a green chutney.

Nutritive values for 1 thalipeeth: Calories: 194.0kcal; Carbohydrate: 20.7g; Protein: 3.8g; Fat: 10.7g; Minerals: 0.87g; Fibre: 0.76g.

Healthy modifications: See multigrain rotlo (p. 116).

DHAPATE

Sorghum-gram-rice flatbread

Preparation time: 20 mins; Cooking time: 10 mins

Dhapate is an unleavened, traditional, Marathi flatbread.

Ingredients for 4 dhapate

The dough

A pinch of salt or to taste

1 cup sorghum (jowar) flour

2 tbsp rice flour

2 tbsp gram flour (besan)

2 tbsp sesame seeds

1 cup fenugreek leaves, chopped

2 onions, puréed

2 tsp ginger-garlic-green chilli paste

½ tsp garam masala powder

½ tsp carom seeds (ajwain)

¼ tsp asafoetida powder

¼ tsp turmeric powder

½ tsp red chilli powder

To pan-fry the dhapate

4 tsp oil

(Recipe Cont.)

Method

Dissolve the salt in 3 tbsp of water.

Mix all the dough ingredients in a bowl and prepare the dough as given for palak paratha (p. 24).

Divide the dough into 4 portions and shape them into balls.

Spread a portion of the dough on a greased plastic sheet as thin as possible.

Invert it over a hot pan and spoon 1 tsp oil along its edges. Cook, till golden brown on both sides.

Repeat with the remaining portions of dough.

Serve hot with any chutney.

Nutritive values for 1 dhapate: Calories: 259.0 kcal; Carbohydrates: 33.6g; Protein: 7.7g; Fat: 10.5 g; Minerals: 1.7g; Fibre: 1.3g.

Healthy modifications: Toast the dhapates in a non-stick pan without fat. This will reduce 5g fat and 45kcal from each dhapate.

VADA

Multigrain fried flatbread

Preparation time: 20 mins; Cooking time: 5 mins

Vada is an unleavened, traditional, fried flatbread made with multigrain flour and spices, served in the coastal areas of Maharashtra, especially in Malvani cuisine. The flour used here is a mixture of wheat, rice, sorghum (jowar) and husked, split black gram.

Ingredients for 10 vadas

The dough

A pinch of salt or to taste

1 cup multigrain flour

½ tsp cumin powder

½ tsp coriander powder

To fry the vadas

Oil for deep-frying

Method

Prepare the dough as given for sada chapatti (p. 66).

Divide the dough into 10 portions and shape them into balls.

Press each portion of the dough on a greased plastic sheet into a 2"- 3" circle.

Heat the oil in a kadhai or wok and fry the vadas in batches, till golden on both sides.

Drain them on layers of tissue paper.

Serve hot with any curry.

Nutritive values for 1 vada: Calories: 81.0kcal; Carbohydrate: 7.1g; Protein: 1.2g; Fat: 5.3g; Minerals: 0.26g; Fibre: 0.25.

Healthy modifications: Toast the vadas in a non-stick pan. This will reduce a considerable quantity of fat and calories for each vada.

FLATBREADS MADE WITH WHEAT FLOUR AND LEGUME/PULSE FLOUR

Legumes and pulses are rich sources of proteins in vegetarian diets, and especially so in vegan ones. While animal proteins obtained from fish, meat, poultry and eggs are complete proteins of high quality, plant proteins, except for soya, are incomplete ones. Plant proteins do not contain all the essential amino acids required by the body. Pulses and legumes are deficient in the amino acid, methionine but are rich in lysine, while cereals are rich in methionine and deficient in lysine. Thus the two combine well and contribute to the essential fatty acid requirement of the day.

Legumes lack saturated fats and cholesterol and contain complex carbohydrates, B-vitamins (thiamine, riboflavin, niacin and folic acid) and minerals (calcium, potassium, phosphorus, magnesium, iron, zinc, copper, manganese and selenium). Some legumes (chickpeas, broad beans and soya beans) contain vitamin E. Pulses and legumes lack vitamins A and C and are low in fat except soya, which contain omega-3 fatty acids. Legumes such as soya are rich in phytochemicals which are powerful antioxidants. Sprouted legumes contain vitamin C.

Flatbreads made with wholewheat flour and pulse/legume flour are one-dish meals as they offer good-quality macro and micro nutrients.

MISSI ROTI

Wholewheat, gram flour flatbread

Preparation time: 20 mins; Cooking time: 4 mins

Missi roti is an unleavened, traditional flatbread made with wholewheat flour, gram flour and spices, consumed in Rajasthan and Central and north India.

Ingredients for 2 rotis

The dough

A pinch of salt or to taste

½ cup wholewheat flour

½ cup gram flour (besan)

½ tsp coriander powder

¼ tsp red chilli powder

¼ tsp cumin powder

¼ tsp carom seeds (ajwain)

To serve

2 tsp ghee

Method

Make the dough and roll out the rotis as given for sada chapatti (p. 66).

Put a non-stick pan on medium heat and toast the rotis, till golden on both sides.

Smear the rotis with ghee.

Serve hot with any curry or dal.

Nutritive values for 1 roti: Calories: 232.0kcal; Carbohydrate: 33.2g; Protein: 8.6g; Fat: 7.2g; Minerals: 1.4g; Fibre: 1.0g.

Healthy modifications: See tikkar (p. 104).

RAJMA ROTI

Wholewheat and red kidney bean flatbread

Preparation time: 20 mins; Cooking time: 15 mins

Rajma roti is an unleavened, traditional, Mughlai flatbread made with wholewheat flour and red kidney beans.

Ingredients for 4 rotis

The dough

½ cup rajma, boiled

1 cup wholewheat flour

½ tsp chola masala

A pinch of salt or to taste

To serve

2 tsp ghee or home-made white butter

Method

Drain the rajma and purée it to make a smooth paste.

Make the dough and roll out the rotis as given for palak paratha (p. 24).

Bake them in a clay, gas or electric tandoor, till golden and cooked on both sides.

Smear each roti with ½ tsp ghee or butter.

Serve hot with any chutney, curd and curry.

Nutritive values for 1 roti: Calories: 151.0kcal; Carbohydrate: 24.9g; Protein: 5.9g; Fat: 3.1g; Minerals: 1.1g; Fibre: 1.1g.

Healthy modifications: See tikkar (p. 104).

KABULI CHANA PARATHA

Flatbread with chickpea filling

Preparation time: 25 mins; Cooking time: 20 mins

Kabuli chana paratha is an unleavened, innovative flatbread stuffed with spicy chickpeas.

Ingredients for 2 parathas

The filling

½ cup chickpeas, boiled

2 tsp oil

1 onion, chopped

2 tsp ginger-garlic-green chilli paste

½ cup mixed herbs (mint, coriander, celery and parsley), chopped

A pinch of salt or to taste

The dough

Dough to make 2 sada parathas (p. 22)

Method

Drain the chickpeas and purée them to make a smooth paste.

Heat the oil and sauté the onion for a minute.

Add the ginger-garlic-green chill paste and sauté for a minute longer.

Mix in the chickpea purée and the herbs.

Divide the filling into 2 portions and leave aside, till cool.

Divide the dough into 2 portions and shape them into balls.

Make the parathas as given for band gobi paratha (p. 25).

Put a non-stick pan on medium heat and toast the parathas on both sides, till golden.

Serve hot with curd and any curry.

Nutritive values for 1 paratha: Calories: 373.0kcal; Carbohydrate: 54.4g; Protein: 11.2g; Fat: 12.2g; Minerals: 2.4g; Fibre: 2.2g.

SATTU PARATHA

Flatbread with gram flour filling

Preparation time: 25 mins; Cooking time: 10 mins

Sattu paratha is an unleavened, traditional flatbread stuffed with spicy, moist roasted Bengal gram flour, especially popular in Bihar and eastern Uttar Pradesh.

Ingredients for 2 parathas

The filling

1 cup gram flour (besan), roasted

1 onion, chopped

2 tsp ginger-garlic-green chilli paste

1 tsp nigella seeds

1 tsp carom seeds (ajwain)

2 tbsp coriander leaves, chopped

2 tbsp oil drained from any pickle

2 tbsp lime juice

A pinch of salt or to taste

The dough

Dough for 2 sada parathas (p. 22)

To pan-fry the parathas

2 tsp oil

(Recipe Cont.)

Method

Mix all the filling ingredients in a bowl.

If required, add more pickle oil and lime juice to make the stuffing moist.

Divide the filling into 2 portions.

Divide the dough into 2 portions and shape them into balls.

Make the parathas and pan-fry them as given for band gobi paratha (p. 25).

Serve hot with curd, pickle and any curry.

Nutritive values for 1 paratha: Calories: 577.0kcal; Carbohydrate: 70.4g; Protein: 18.1g; Fat: 24.8g; Minerals: 3.4g; Fibre: 2.9g.

Healthy modifications: Avoid adding pickle oil to the filling. This will reduce 15g fat and 135kcal for each flatbread. It is high in fat, salt and chilli powder. Add more lime juice instead.

CHANA DAL PARATHA
Flatbread with bengal gram filling

Preparation time: 25 mins; Cooking time: 20 mins

Chana dal paratha is an unleavened, traditional flatbread made with refined wheat flour and stuffed with spicy Bengal gram. It is consumed in Gujarat and Rajasthan, though the Rajasthani parathas are thinner than the Gujarati ones.

Ingredients for 4 parathas

The filling

1 cup Bengal gram (chana dal), boiled

2 tsp ghee

1 tsp ginger-garlic-green chilli paste

½ tsp garam masala powder

¼ tsp red chilli powder

½ tsp cumin powder

½ tsp coriander powder

A pinch of salt or to taste

The dough

A pinch of salt or to taste

1 cup refined wheat flour

½ tsp red chilli powder

1 tbsp oil

To pan-fry the parathas

2 tsp ghee

(Recipe Cont.)

Method

Purée the dal to make a smooth paste.

Heat the ghee and sauté the dal paste and the ginger-garlic-green chilli paste for a few mins, till dry.

Add the spice powders and salt and mix well.

Divide the filling into 4 portions and leave aside, till cool.

Prepare the dough as given for sada chapatti (p. 66).

Divide it into 4 portions and shape them into balls.

Make the parathas and pan-fry them as given for band gobi paratha (p. 25).

Serve hot with curd, pickle and any curry.

Nutritive values for 1 paratha: Calories: 262.0kcal; Carbohydrate: 33.8g; Protein: 8.2g; Fat: 10.5g; Minerals: 0.9g; Fibre: 0.75g.
Healthy modifications: Replace refined flour with wholewheat flour.

Avoid adding oil to the flour while making the dough. This will reduce 7.5g fat and 68kcal from each paratha.

Replace ghee with oil.

Toast the parathas in a non-stick pan. This will further reduce 2.5g fat and 23kcal for each paratha.

MUNG DAL PARATHA

Flatbread with husked, split mung filling

Preparation time: 25 mins; Cooking time: 20 mins

Mung dal paratha is an unleavened, traditional flatbread made with wholewheat flour and stuffed with boiled, spiced husked, split mung. It is consumed in Gujarat and Rajasthan, while the Sindhi dal jololo, is similar to this paratha.

Ingredients for 2 parathas

The seasoning

2 tsp oil

½ tsp cumin-mustard seeds

The filling

½ cup husked, split mung, roasted and boiled

2 tsp ginger-garlic-green chilli paste

A pinch of red chilli powder

A pinch of turmeric powder

½ tsp garam masala powder

½ tsp dried mango powder

2 tbsp coriander leaves, chopped

A pinch of asafoetida powder

The dough

Dough to make sada paratha (p. 22)

To pan-fry the paratha

2 tsp oil or ghee

(Recipe Cont.)

Method

Heat 2 tsp of oil and sauté the seasoning ingredients, till fragrant.

Add the filling ingredients and sauté, till dry.

Divide the filling into 2 portions and leave aside, till cool.

Divide the dough into 2 portions and shape them into balls.

Make the parathas and pan-fry them as given for band gobi paratha (p. 25).

Serve hot with any curry.

Nutritive values for 1 paratha: Calories: 364.0kcal; Carbohydrate: 52.6g; Protein: 12.8g; Fat: 6.4g; Minerals: 2.5g; Fibre: 1.5g.

Healthy modifications: Toast the parathas in a non-stick pan without oil. This will reduce 5g fat and 45kcal from each paratha.

CHOORI KA PARATHA

Flatbread with husked, split mung

Preparation time: 20 mins; Cooking time: 12 mins

Choori ka paratha is an unleavened, traditional, Rajasthani flatbread, where mung dal is mixed into the dough.

Ingredients for 4 parathas

2 tbsp husked, split mung, soaked in water for 1 hour

1 tbsp ghee

1 cup wholewheat flour

¼ tsp red chilli powder

A pinch of asafoetida powder

A pinch of salt or to taste

To pan-fry the parathas

4 tsp oil

Method

Drain the dal and grind it to make a smooth paste.

Rub the ghee into the flour.

Mix in all the remaining ingredients, except the oil.

Make the parathas and pan-fry them as given for palak paratha (p. 24).

Serve hot with a tomato chutney (p. 219).

Nutritive values for 1 paratha: Calories: 190.0kcal; Carbohydrate: 21.9g; Protein: 4.9g; Fat: 9.3g; Minerals: 0.95g; Fibre: 0.54g.

Healthy modifications: Avoid adding ghee to the flour while making the dough. This will reduce 15g fat and 135kcal from the dough.

Replace ghee with oil.

Toast the paratha in a non-stick pan. This will further reduce 5g fat and 45kcal from each paratha.

URAD DAL PARATHA

Flatbread with black gram filling

Preparation time: 25 mins; Cooking time: 15 mins

Urad dal paratha is a well-known, stuffed, unleavened, traditional flatbread from Uttar Pradesh and Rajasthan.

Ingredients for 4 parathas

The filling

4 tbsp husked, split black gram (urad dal), soaked in water for a few hours

¼ tsp red chilli powder

A pinch of asafoetida powder

1 tsp aniseed powder

A pinch of salt or to taste

2 tsp ghee

The dough

Dough to make 2 sada parathas (p. 22)

To pan-fry the paratha

4 tsp

Method

Drain the gram and grind it to make a smooth paste.

Mix all the filling ingredients together, except ghee.

Heat the ghee in a pan and sauté the paste for a few mins, till just dry.

Divide the filling into 4 portions and leave aside, till cool.

Divide the dough into 4 portions.

Make the parathas and pan-fry them as given for band gobi paratha (p. 25).

Serve hot with a curd curry.

Nutritive values for 1 paratha: Calories: 221.0kcal; Carbohydrate: 26.8g; Protein: 6.9g; Fat: 9.6g; Minerals: 1.2g; Fibre: 0.76g.

Healthy modifications: Replace ghee with oil.

Toast the parathas in a non-stick pan. This will reduce 5g fat and 45kcal from each paratha.

DAL DHOKLI

Flatbread in lentil gravy

Preparation time: 20 mins; Cooking time: 20 mins

Dhokli is an unleavened, traditional flatbread made with wholewheat flour, where the dough is cooked in a sweetened, spicy dal. Dal dhokli is a traditional Gujarati dish.

Ingredients for 2 servings

The dough

A pinch of salt or to taste

1 cup wholewheat flour

¼ tsp of turmeric powder

½ tsp red chilli powder

1 tsp coriander powder

The dal

4 tbsp red gram (arhar/tuvar dal)

¼ tsp turmeric powder

½ tsp red chilli powder

½ tsp cumin powder

½ tsp coriander powder

¼ tsp black pepper powder

¼ tsp dried mango powder or kokum

¼ tsp aniseed powder

½ tsp garam masala powder (clove, cinnamon, black cardamom, caraway seeds, bay leaf)

1 tsp grated jaggery or sugar

A pinch of salt or to taste

The seasoning

2 tsp ghee

½ tsp mustard seeds

½ tsp cumin seeds

1 sprig curry leaves

2 green chillies, chopped

A pinch of asafoetida powder

(Recipe Cont.)

The garnish

2 tsp coriander leaves, chopped

Method

The dough: Dissolve the salt in 5 tbsp of water.

Prepare the dough as given for sada chapatti (p. 66).

Divide it into 2 portions.

Roll out a portion of the dough on a lightly floured board into a 6″ circle.

Cut it into square pieces. Sprinkle a little flour on the pieces to prevent them from sticking to each other during cooking.

Repeat with the remaining portion of the dough.

The dal: Wash the dal and drain.

Pressure-cook the dal with ½ cup of water on low heat for 5 mins after the cooker reaches full pressure.

Heat the ghee for the seasoning in a pan and sauté the seasoning ingredients, till fragrant.

Add all the spice powders, except the garam masala powder, and sauté for a second.

Mix in the cooked dal, garam masala powder, jaggery or sugar and the salt and bring to a boil.

Add the dough pieces and continue to boil on high heat for about 5 mins, stirring continuously to prevent the dough pieces from sticking to each other.

Reduce the heat and simmer for 10 mins longer.

Serve hot, garnished with coriander leaves.

Nutritive values for 1 serving: Calories: 343.0kcal; Carbohydrate: 55.3g; Protein: 12.6g; Fat: 2.9g; Minerals: 3.4g; Fibre: 3.5g.

Healthy modifications: Replace ghee with oil.

PANEER-CHEESE PARATHA

Flatbread with paneer-cheese filling

Preparation time: 25 mins; Cooking time: 4 mins

Paneer-cheese paratha is an unleavened, innovative flatbread made with wholewheat and gram flour and stuffed with paneer and cheese.

Ingredients for 2 parathas

The filling

2 tbsp grated low-fat cheese

2 tbsp grated paneer (made with skimmed milk)

2 onions, finely chopped

1 tsp ginger-garlic-green chilli paste

The dough

A pinch of salt or to taste

½ cup wholewheat flour

½ cup gram flour (besan)

Method

Mix the filling ingredients in a bowl.

Divide the filling into 2 portions.

Dissolve the salt in 5 tbsp of water.

Prepare the dough and make the parathas as given for band gobi paratha (p. 25).

Put a non-stick pan on medium heat and toast the parathas, till golden brown on both sides.

Serve hot with curd and any curry or dal.

Nutritive values for 1 paratha: Calories: 270.0kcal; Carbohydrate: 39.8g; Protein: 16.7g; Fat: 3.4g; Minerals: 2.9g; Fibre: 1.3g.

HERB PARATHA

Herb flatbread

Preparation time: 20 mins; Cooking time: 4 mins

Herb paratha is an unleavened, innovative flatbread made with wholewheat flour, gram flour and fresh herbs.

Ingredients for 2 parathas

A pinch of salt or to taste

¾ cup wholewheat flour

¼ cup gram flour (besan)

2 cups mixed herbs (rosemary, sage, sweet basil, thyme, celery, parsley, coriander, mint), chopped

1 onion, puréed

Method

Dissolve the salt in 5 tbsp of water.

Prepare the dough and roll out the parathas as given for palak paratha (p. 24).

Put a non-stick pan on medium heat and toast the parathas, till golden brown on both sides.

Serve hot with curd and any curry or dal.

Nutritive values for 1 paratha: Calories: 194.0kcal; Carbohydrate: 37.0g; Protein: 7.9g; Fat: 1.4g; Minerals: 1.7g; Fibre: 1.2g.

MIXED ROOT VEGETABLE PARATHA

Flatbread with mixed root vegetables

Preparation time: 25 mins; Cooking time: 4 mins

Mixed root vegetables paratha is an unleavened, innovative flatbread made with wholewheat flour, soya flour and mixed root vegetables.

Ingredients for 4 parathas

¾ cup wholewheat flour

¼ cup soya flour

2 cups grated mixed root vegetables (carrot, beetroot, radish, turnip)

A pinch of salt or to taste

Method

Mix all the ingredients in a bowl.

Prepare the dough and roll out the parathas as given for palak paratha (p. 24).

Put a non-stick pan on medium heat and toast the parathas, till golden brown on both sides.

Serve hot with a salad and chutney.

Nutritive values for 1 paratha: Calories: 117.0kcal; Carbohydrates: 20.1g; Protein: 5.5g; Fat: 1.6g; Minerals: 1.2g; Fibre: 1.1g.

MIXED STEM VEGETABLE PARATHA

Flatbread with mixed stem vegetables

Preparation time: 25 mins; Cooking time: 4 mins

Mixed stem vegetable paratha is an unleavened, innovative flatbread made with wholewheat flour, soya flour and fresh stem vegetables.

Ingredients for 4 parathas

4 baby potatoes

1 sweet potato

4 colocasia

100g yam

A pinch of salt or to taste

¼ tsp turmeric powder

¾ cup wholewheat flour

¼ cup soya flour

Method

Wash all the vegetables and boil them separately in salted water with turmeric powder, till tender. Peel and mash them.

Mix all the ingredients in a bowl.

Prepare the dough and roll out the parathas as given for palak paratha (p. 24).

Put a non-stick pan on medium heat and toast the parathas, till golden brown on both sides.

Serve hot with a salad and chutney.

Nutritive values for 1 paratha: Calories: 197.0kcal; Carbohydrates: 38.8g; Protein: 1.7g; Fat: 6.7g; Minerals: 2.0g; Fibre: 1.4g.

NON-VEGETARIAN FLATBREADS

Egg is the most nutritious food in our diet as it is rich in protein, minerals and vitamins. Egg protein has high biological value as it provides most of the essential amino acids. They are rich in vitamins such as B vitamins, especially B12, vitamins A, D, E and K. Calcium, phosphorus, zinc, iron and iodine are the other important nutrients found in eggs. However, they are also high in cholesterol-rich fat. People with metabolic problems such as hypercholesterolemia (increased bad cholesterol levels) should avoid the cholesterol-rich egg yolks. Serve egg flatbreads with plenty of coloured vegetables and unstrained, unsweetened fruit juices to reduce health risks. Each egg provides 75-80kcal of energy. Choose chicken eggs over duck and cook them thoroughly to avoid the risk of bacterial contamination.

Egg flatbreads of Mughlai and Punjabi cuisines are made with wholewheat or refined flour. They are one-dish meals as they offer good-quality macro and micro nutrients.

EGG FLATBREADS

ANDA PARATHA

Egg flatbread

Preparation time: 30 mins; Cooking time: 10 mins

Anda paratha is an unleavened, traditional flatbread.

Ingredients for 2 parathas

2 eggs, beaten

½ tsp cumin-pepper powder

A pinch of salt or to taste

2 tbsp mixed herbs, chopped

Dough to make 2 sada parathas (p. 22)

2 tsp ghee

Method

Mix the eggs with the spice powder and salt.

Divide the eggs and herbs into 2 portions.

(Method Cont.)

Divide the dough into 2 portions and shape them into balls.

Roll out a portion of dough on a lightly floured board as thin as possible into a circle.

Pan-fry it on a hot pan with ½ tsp ghee.

When the base is golden brown, flip it over and transfer it to a plate.

Spread a portion of egg evenly over it and sprinkle a portion of chopped herbs on top.

For the inverted triangle egg paratha

Fold the dough on 2 sides to form an inverted 'V' at the top, in the centre. Fold the bottom of the dough upwards to form a triangle. Press the edges carefully to seal.

For the rectangle egg paratha

Fold 2 sides of the paratha towards the centre. Fold the top and bottom towards the centre again to form a rectangle.

To complete the cooking

Pan-fry the paratha with ½ tsp ghee. Cook on low heat, till the base is golden brown.

Flip it over and cook, till the other side is golden brown.

Allow it remain on low heat for a minute longer, to ensure that the egg is thoroughly cooked.

Serve hot with a tomato pickle and green chutney or a sweet and hot tomato sauce.

Nutritive values for 1 paratha: Calories: 285.0kcal; Carbohydrate: 35.2g; Protein: 13.0g; Fat: 10.3g; Minerals: 2.5g; Fibre: 1.1g.

ANDA NAAN

Egg flatbread

Preparation time: 20 mins; Cooking time: 2 mins

Anda naan is a leavened, traditional, Punjabi flatbread made with refined wheat flour, beaten egg and butter. It is made in the same way as sada naan (p. 81).

Add 1 whisked egg to the dough ingredients. Before baking the naans, gently press 1 tsp of nigella or sesames seeds into each naan. Serve hot with any curry or dal.

Nutritive values for 1 naan: Calories: 394.0kcal; Carbohydrate: 59.9g; Protein: 13.1g; Fat: 11.2g; Minerals: 1.1g; Fibre: 0.4g.
Healthy modifications: See sada naan (p. 81).

ANDA ROLL

Egg roll

Preparation time: 25 mins; Cooking time: 8 mins

Cook an omelette with 2 chopped onions, 2 minced green chillies and salt and wrap it in a hot sada chapatti (p. 66) to make an anda roll.

Nutritive values for 1 roll: Calories: 310.0kcal; Carbohydrate: 27.4g; Protein: 11.2g; Fat: 17.2g; Minerals: 2.5g; Fibre: 1.2g.

EGG CONE

Preparation time: 25 mins; Cooking time: 24 mins

Egg cone is an unleavened, innovative flatbread made with wholewheat flour, shaped in a cone, filled with egg and topped with a sweet and sour chutney.

Ingredients for 2 cones

The sweet-n-sour chutney

6 dates, soaked in water for a few hours

2 tbsp tamarind pulp

A pinch of salt or to taste

The cones

2 eggs

1 tsp salt

1 cup shredded lettuce

2 hot phulkas (p. 69)

Method

Remove and discard the seeds from the dates.

Grind the chutney ingredients to make a smooth paste.

Hard-boil the eggs in salted water for about 20 mins.

Peel the eggs and separate the yolks from the whites, keeping the yolks whole.

Chop the egg whites and mix it into the shredded lettuce.

Shape a phulka into a cone and fill it with half the egg white and lettuce mix.

Drop an egg yolk into the centre and spoon half the chutney on top.

Repeat with the remaining phulka.

Serve immediately.

Nutritive values for 1 cone: Calories: 214.0kcal; Carbohydrate: 22.5g; Protein: 9.5g; Fat: 9.6g; Minerals: 0.95 g; Fibre: 0.5g.

EGG WRAPS

Preparation time: 20 mins; Cooking time: 20 mins

Egg wraps are unleavened, innovative flatbreads made with cornflour. They are used to wrap spicy scrambled eggs and vegetables and resemble the Mexican quesadillas.

Ingredients for 2 wraps

The filling

1 cup diced mixed vegetables (carrot, green pea, cabbage, capsicum, cauliflower)

A pinch of salt or to taste

2 eggs, beaten

½ tsp cumin-pepper powder

2 tsp oil

1 cup mixed herbs, chopped

The wraps

A pinch of salt or to taste

½ cup cornflour

2 tsp oil

The topping

½ cup yogurt

½ tsp garam masala powder

A pinch of salt or to taste

(Recipe Cont.)

Method

Boil the vegetables with salt, till just tender.

Mix the eggs, spice powder and salt in a bowl.

Heat 2 tsp oil in a pan. Add the eggs and scramble them.

Mix in the boiled vegetables and herbs.

Divide the filling into 2 portions and leave aside, till cool.

Make 2 corn rotis as given for makkai ki roti (p. 102). Sprinkle ½ tsp of oil along with the water, while cooking the rotis.

Keep them warm

Mix the topping ingredients in another bowl. Divide it into 2 portions.

Spread a portion of the filling on to one half of a roti. Spoon a portion of the topping over the filling. Fold the other half of the roti to cover the filling.

Repeat with the remaining corn roti, filling and topping.

Serve immediately.

Nutritive values for 1 egg wrap: Calories: 265.0kcal; Carbohydrate: 22.6g; Protein: 12.0g; Fat: 14.0g; Minerals: 2.1g; Fibre: 2.0g.

BIHARI KABAB ROLL

Preparation time: 20 mins; Cooking time: 4 mins

A Bihari kabab roll comprises a Bihari kabab wrapped in an unleavened, traditional flatbread made with refined flour and egg (tava anda paratha).

Ingredients for 2 rolls

The dough for tava anda paratha

1 cup refined flour

2 tsp home-made white butter, melted

1 egg, beaten

A pinch of salt or to taste

To cook the paratha

2 tsp butter

To serve

2 Bihari kababs

Method

Prepare the dough and cook the parathas as given for palak paratha (p. 24).

Roll a kabab in the paratha and serve immediately.

Nutritive values for 1 paratha: Calories: 254.0kcal; Carbohydrate: 37.0g; Protein: 8.8g; Fat: 7.8g; Minerals: 0.8g; Fibre: 0.2g.

Healthy modifications: Use wholewheat flour or replace half the refined flour with it.

Replace butter with oil.

Toast the paratha in a non-stick pan without butter. This will reduce 4g fat and 37kcal from each paratha.

MUGHLAI ANDA LACHHA PARATHA

Multilayered flatbread with egg

Preparation time: 30 mins; Cooking time: 4 mins

Mughlai anda lachha paratha is a leavened, traditional flatbread made with refined wheat flour and egg.

Ingredients for 2 parathas

The dough

1½ cups refined flour

A pinch of salt or to taste

1 tbsp ghee

½ tsp baking powder

1 egg, beaten

1 tsp sugar

½ cup milk

To make the parathas

1 tbsp ghee

2 tsp oil

Method

Prepare the dough and make the parathas as given for sada Mughlai lachha paratha (p. 91). Whisk the egg with the sugar into the milk before adding it to the dry ingredients.

Serve hot with curd and any curry or dal.

Nutritive values for 1 paratha: Calories: 519.0kcal; Carbohydrate: 59.2g; Protein: 12.7g; Fat: 25.6g; Minerals: 0.9g; Fibre: 0.23g.

Healthy modifications: See sada Mughlai lachha paratha (p. 91).

SADA BAIDA ROTI

Plain egg flatbread

Preparation time: 25 mins; Cooking time: 8 mins

Baida rotis are leavened, traditional, Mughlai flatbreads, served as street food in Mumbai. Refined wheat flour parathas are stuffed with dairy products, chicken or minced mutton. The parathas are then coated with egg and toasted on a pan, till golden brown on both sides.

Ingredients for 2 rotis

The dough

A pinch of salt or to taste

1 cup refined wheat flour

½ tsp baking powder

1 tbsp oil

To cook the roti

2 eggs, beaten separately

½ tsp cumin-pepper powder

A pinch of salt or to taste

4 tsp oil

Method

The dough

Dissolve the salt in 4 tbsp of water.

Prepare the dough as given for sada chapatti (p. 66).

Divide the dough into 2 portions and shape them into balls.

Roll out the dough on a lightly floured board into 5"- 6" circles.

To cook the rotis

Put a non-stick pan on medium heat and toast the roti, till golden brown on both sides.

(Method Cont.)

Mix one egg with half the cumin-pepper powder and a pinch of salt.

Pour half the egg on a pan and spread it as thin as possible.

Pour 1 tsp oil along its edges.

Place a roti over the egg and pour the remaining egg evenly over the roti.

When the egg appears slightly set on top, flip it over and spoon 1 tsp oil along the edges. Cook till the base is golden brown.

Repeat with the remaining roti and egg.

Serve hot with a lettuce salad, red chutney and any curry.

Nutritive values for 1 roti: Calories: 423.0kcal; Carbohydrate: 37.4g; Protein: 12.4g; Fat: 24.8g; Minerals: 0.87g; Fibre: 0.3g.

Healthy modifications: Avoid adding fat to the dough. This will reduce 15g fat and 135kcal from the dough.

Toast the rotis in a non-stick pan without oil. This will further reduce 10g fat and 90kcal from each roti.

Use wholewheat flour or replace half the refined flour with it.

CHEESE BAIDA ROTI

Egg flatbread with cheese filling

Preparation time: 30 mins; Cooking time: 8 mins

Cheese baida roti is a leavened, traditional, Mughlai flatbread, where the baida roti is stuffed with cheese.

Prepare the dough for sada baida roti (p. 136). Stuff each roti with 2 tbsp of grated cheese and roll them out as given for band gobi paratha (p. 25). Cook the rotis as given for sada baida roti. Serve hot with curd or a mixed vegetable raita, coriander coconut chutney and a hot tomato sauce.

Nutritive values for 1 roti: Calories: 527.0kcal; Carbohydrate: 39.4g; Protein: 19.6g; Fat: 32.4g; Minerals: 2.1g; Fibre: 0.3g.

Healthy modifications: Use low-fat cheese.

See sada baida roti (p. 136) for further modifications.

PANEER BAIDA ROTI

Egg flatbread with paneer filling

Preparation time: 30 mins; Cooking time: 8 mins

Paneer baida roti is a leavened, traditional, Mughlai flatbread where the baida roti is stuffed with paneer.

Sauté 2 minced onions in 1 tsp of oil, till light brown. Add 4 tbsp grated paneer, ½ tsp garam masala powder and salt to make the filling. Prepare the rotis as given for cheese baida roti (above). Serve hot with curd or a mixed vegetable raita, pudina coconut chutney and a hot tomato sauce.

Nutritive values for 1 roti: Calories: 554.0kcal; Carbohydrate: 43.7g; Protein: 18.7g; Fat: 33.8g; Minerals: 1.9g; Fibre: 0.75g.

Healthy modifications: Use low-fat paneer.

See sada baida roti (p. 136) for further modifications.

SEAFOOD FLATBREADS

Seafood flatbreads are consumed in the coastal regions of India, especially Kerala, where they are made with wholewheat, refined wheat or rice flour and stuffed with seafood. They are one-dish meals as they offer good-quality macro and micro nutrients.

Fish and shellfish are important in a healthy non-vegetarian diet as they contain essential nutrients. Fish has high protein and provides most of the essential fatty acids. Oily fish are a good source of omega-3 fatty acids and contain vitamins A, D and B (thiamine, riboflavin and niacin). Phosphorus, magnesium, calcium, potassium, iodine, fluoride, iron, zinc and selenium are the minerals found in fish. Take care to consume fish from unpolluted sources of water.

Shellfish includes clams, oysters, mussels and scallops. Prawns, shrimps, crabs and lobsters are crustaceans as their bodies have segmented shells. Shellfish and crustaceans are low in fat, high in protein, vitamins and minerals. People with metabolic problems such as hypercholesterolemia should avoid the cholesterol-rich shrimps and prawns.

CHEMEEN PARATHA

Flatbread with prawn filling

Preparation time: 20 mins; Cooking time: 20 mins

Chemeen paratha is an unleavened, traditional flatbread made with wholewheat flour and stuffed with prawns and egg in the coastal regions of Kerala.

Ingredients for 2 parathas

The filling

1 egg, beaten

2 tsp herbs, chopped

¼ tsp cumin-pepper powder

A pinch of salt or to taste

2 tbsp coconut oil

2 tsp ginger-garlic-green chilli paste

2 tbsp grated fresh coconut

1 onion, chopped

100g prawns, peeled and deveined

½ tsp turmeric powder

The dough

Dough to make 2 sada parathas (p. 22)

4 tsp oil

Method

Mix the egg, herbs, spice powder and salt in a bowl. Divide it into 2 portions.

Heat the coconut oil in a pan and add the ginger-garlic-green chilli paste, coconut and onion and sauté for a few seconds.

Mix in the prawns, turmeric powder and salt to taste and cook on medium heat, till the prawns just turn pink.

Divide the filling into 2 portions and leave aside, till cool.

Divide the dough into 2 portions and shape them into balls.

(Method Cont.)

Roll out a portion of the dough on a lightly floured board into a 6"- 7" circle.

Put a non-stick pan on medium heat and put the paratha on it.

Spread a portion of the prawn filling evenly over the paratha and then a portion of the eggs.

Spoon 1 tsp oil along the edges.

Cook the paratha on high heat for 1 minute.

Reduce the heat and cook, till the egg is set and the base is golden brown.

Flip it over carefully, spoon 1 tsp oil along the edges and cook till it is done.

Repeat with the remaining portions of dough and filling.

Serve hot with a dry vegetable curry.

Nutritive values for 1 paratha: Calories: 570.0kcal; Carbohydrate: 41.4g; Protein: 20.3g; Fat: 36.0g; Minerals: 2.8g; Fibre: 1.7g.

Healthy modifications: Limit the use of coconut oil.

Replace coconut oil with any vegetable oil.

Toast the flatbreads in a non-stick pan without fat. This will reduce 10g fat and 90kcal from each flatbread.

MEEN PATHIRI

Thin rice flatbread with fish filling

Preparation time: 30 mins; Cooking time: 30 mins

Meen pathiri is an unleavened, traditional, thin flatbread made with rice flour and grated fresh coconut and stuffed with an oily fish in the coastal regions of Kerala. It is a one-dish meal, as it offers good-quality macro and micro nutrients.

Ingredients for 5 pathiri

The marinade

2 tbsp lime juice

2 tsp ginger-garlic-green chilli paste

2 tsp red chilli powder

1 tsp turmeric powder

A pinch of salt or to taste

The filling

1 cup filleted fish pieces

1 tbsp + 1 tbsp coconut oil

2 tbsp grated fresh coconut

5-6 shallots, peeled

1 tsp aniseed

2 large onions, chopped

2 green chillies, minced

3 cloves garlic, chopped

2" piece ginger, grated

1 sprig curry leaves

½ tsp red chilli powder

½ tsp turmeric powder

1 tsp garam masala powder

2 tomatoes, chopped

A pinch of salt or to taste

The dough

Dough for 5 coconut pathiris (p. 97)

(Recipe Cont.)

Method

Mix the marinade ingredients in a bowl. Rub it into the fish and leave aside to marinate for 1 hour.

Heat 1 tbsp oil and sauté the fish till tender. Shred the fish and leave it aside.

Roast the coconut, shallots and aniseed in a pan on low heat for a few mins, till fragrant.

Leave aside, till cool. Grind to make a paste.

Heat 1 tbsp of coconut oil in a pan on medium heat and sauté the onions, green chillies, garlic, ginger and curry leaves for a few mins.

Add the spice powders and sauté for a second.

Stir in the tomatoes and salt. Sauté for a few mins, till the contents leaves the sides of the pan and the oil rises to the surface.

Mix in the shredded fish and simmer for about 10 mins.

Divide the filling into 5 portions and leave aside, till cool.

Divide the dough into 10 portions and shape them into balls.

Roll out 2 portions of the dough balls on a lightly floured board into 5" circles or press them on a greased plastic sheet with your fingertips.

Spread a portion of the fish filling on one pathiri.

Cover the filling with the second pathiri and press the edges gently with moist fingertips to seal the edges. Repeat with the remaining dough and the filling portions.

Steam the pathiris in a steamer or rice cooker for 15 mins.

Alternatively, pack each pathiri in a banana leaf packet and steam them.

Serve hot with any curry.

Nutritive values for 1 pathiri: Calories: 262.0kcal; Carbohydrates: 29.6g; Protein: 8.3g; Fat: 12.3g; Minerals: 1.5g; Fibre: 2.1g.

Healthy modifications: Limit the use of coconut and fat.

Replace coconut oil with any vegetable oil.

MEEN OROTTI

Thick rice flatbread with fish filling

Preparation time: 30 mins; Cooking time: 30 mins

Meen orotti is an unleavened, traditional thick flatbread made with rice flour and fresh coconut and stuffed with fish. It is consumed in the coastal regions of Kerala. It is cooked on low heat, as it is thick. It is a one-dish meal as it offers good-quality macro and micro nutrients.

Ingredients for 4 orottis

The marinade

A pinch of turmeric powder

1 tsp red chilli powder

1 tsp garam masala powder

2 tsp ginger-garlic-green chilli paste

A pinch of salt or to taste

The fish curry

1 cup oily fish flakes

1 cup thick coconut milk

1 tbsp coconut oil

1 tsp cumin seeds

2 onions, minced

½ cup mixed herbs, chopped

The dough

½ cup grated fresh coconut

1 tsp cumin seeds

1 cup rice flour

To cook the orottis

2 tsp coconut oil

Method

Mix the marinade ingredients in a bowl.

Rub it into the fish flakes and leave it aside to marinate for 1 hour.

(Method Cont.)

Put the fish with its marinade in a pan and add the coconut milk. Cover and simmer on low to medium heat, till the fish is tender and dry.

Heat the oil in another pan and sauté the cumin seeds and onions for a minute.

Add the cooked fish and herbs. Mix well and simmer for 10-15 mins.

To make the orottis

Boil ¾ cup of water in a pan and add the coconut, cumin seeds and fish curry.

Bring to a boil, reduce the heat and add the rice flour, stirring vigorously to prevent lumps from forming.

Leave it aside, till cool enough to handle.

Knead the dough, till smooth.

Divide the dough into 4 portions and shape them into balls.

Grease a plastic sheet and press a ball of dough on it with your fingertips into a 3"- 4" circle.

To cook the orottis

Put a pan on medium heat and grease it with ½ tsp oil.

Invert the plastic sheet over it and slip the orotti into the pan. Cook, till golden brown on both sides.

Repeat with the remaining portions of dough.

Serve hot with any curry.

Nutritive values for 1 orotti: Calories: 253.0kcal; Carbohydrate: 26.5g; Protein: 8.4g; Fat: 12.5g; Minerals: 1.1g; Fibre: 1.1g.

Healthy modifications: Limit the use of coconut, coconut milk and coconut oil.

Replace coconut oil with any vegetable oil.

Use the second extract of the coconut milk instead of the first.

Toast the orotti in a non-stick pan without fat. This will reduce 2.5g fat and 23kcal from each orotti.

CHICKEN FLATBREADS

Chicken flatbreads are traditional to Punjabi, Mughlai and Kerala cuisines. In Punjabi cuisine, they are made with wholewheat flour, whereas Mughlai cuisine uses refined flour. In Kerala they are made with rice flour and refined wheat flour.

The fat in chicken is concentrated in the skin which is however a good source of MUFA and PUFA. So consume chicken without skin and use chicken breast, as it is the leanest part. Chicken flatbreads are one-dish meals as they offer good-quality macro and micro nutrients. Chicken is considered highly nutritious. Chicken protein provides all essential amino acids, vitamins A, E and B (thiamine, niacin and folate) and minerals (calcium, magnesium, potassium, phosphorus, iron, copper, manganese, selenium and zinc).

SHAHI MURGH PARATHA

Flatbread with chicken filling

Preparation time: 25 mins; Cooking time: 30 mins

Shahi murgh paratha is an unleavened, traditional, north Indian and Mughlai flatbread made with wholewheat flour and stuffed with spicy chicken.

Ingredients for 2 parathas

The filling

2 tbsp cashew nuts, soaked in water for 1 hour

2 tsp ginger-garlic-green chilli paste

1 tbsp oil

1 spring onion, minced

100g chicken, boiled and shredded

1 tsp garam masala powder

¼ tsp red chilli powder

¼ tsp dried mango powder

1 cup mixed herbs (sweet basil, thyme, rosemary, mint), chopped

A pinch of salt or to taste

The dough

Dough to make 4 sada parathas (p. 22)

To cook the parathas

4 tsp ghee

Method

Drain the cashew nuts and grind them with a little water to make a smooth paste.

Mix the cashewnut paste with the ginger-garlic-green chilli paste in a bowl.

Heat the oil in a pan and sauté the cashew nut paste mins, till fragrant.

Add the spring onion and sauté for a minute.

Mix in the chicken, spice powders, herbs and salt and simmer for about 10 mins.

(Method Cont.)

Divide the filling into 2 portions and leave aside, till cool.

Divide the dough into 4 portions and shape them into balls.

To make the stuffed parathas and cook them

Roll out 2 portions of the dough on a lightly floured board into 6" circles.

Cook 1 side of both parathas on a pan on medium heat. Spoon ½ tsp ghee around the edges.

Put a paratha on the hot pan, uncooked side down. Spread a portion of the filling evenly over it.

Cover with the other paratha, cooked side down. Press gently with moist fingertips to seal.

Spoon ½ tsp ghee around the edges.

When the base is golden, flip it over carefully.

Spoon ½ tsp ghee around the edges and cook, till the other side is golden.

Repeat with the remaining portions of dough and filling.

Transfer the stuffed parathas to a serving plate. Cut them into 2 pieces.

Serve with lime pickle, carrot strips, lime wedges and any curry.

Nutritive values for 1 paratha: Calories: 463.0kcal; Carbohydrate: 49.8g; Protein: 24.0g; Fat: 18.6g; Minerals: 3.1g; Fibre: 2.3g.

Healthy modifications: Replace ghee with oil.

Toast the parathas in a non-stick pan without fat. This will reduce 10g fat and 90kcal from each flatbread.

MURGH BAIDA ROTI

Egg flatbread with chicken filling

Preparation time: 25 mins; Cooking time: 40 mins

Murgh baida roti is a leavened, traditional, Mughlai flatbread.

Ingredients for 2 rotis

The filling

1 tbsp oil

1 onion, minced

100g chicken, boiled and shredded

2 tsp ginger-garlic-green chilli paste

A pinch of salt or to taste

1 tsp garam masala powder

The rotis

Dough to make 2 sada baida rotis (p. 136)

2 eggs, beaten separately

½ tsp cumin-pepper powder

A pinch of salt or to taste

4 tsp oil

Method

Heat the oil in a pan and sauté the onion, till light brown. Add the chicken, ginger-garlic-green chilli paste and salt and cook, till dry.

Mix in the garam masala powder.

Divide the filling into 2 portions and leave side, till cool.

Divide the dough into 2 portions and shape them into balls. Roll out and stuff the rotis as given for band gobi paratha (p. 25).

Cook the rotis as given for sada baida roti (p. 136).

Serve hot with curd or vegetable raita, pudina coconut chutney and a hot tomato sauce.

Nutritive values for 1 roti: Calories: 569.0kcal; Carbohydrate: 41.8g; Protein: 26.1g; Fat: 1.8g; Minerals: 0.69g; Fibre: 0.6g

Healthy modifications: See sada baida roti (p. 136).

CHICKEN OROTTI

Thick rice flatbread with spicy chicken

Preparation time: 25 mins; Cooking time: 30 mins

Chicken orotti is an unleavened, traditional, thick flatbread made with a mixture of rice flour, grated fresh coconut and chicken curry.

Ingredients for 4 orottis

The marinade

A pinch of turmeric powder

A pinch of red chilli powder

1 tsp garam masala powder

2 tsp ginger-garlic-green chilli paste

A pinch of salt or to taste

The chicken curry

1 chicken breast, cut into pieces

1 cup thick coconut milk

1 tbsp coconut oil

1 tsp cumin seeds

2 onions, minced

½ cup mixed herbs (mint, coriander, celery and parsley), chopped

The dough

½ cup grated fresh coconut

1 tsp cumin seeds

1 cup rice flour

2 tsp oil

(Recipe Cont.)

Method

Mix the marinade ingredients in a bowl.

Rub it into the chicken and leave it aside for 1 hour to marinate.

Place the chicken with its marinade in a pan with the coconut milk. Cover and cook on low heat, till the chicken is tender and dry. Shred the chicken.

Heat the oil in a pan and sauté the cumin seeds and onions for a few mins.

Add the cooked chicken and the herbs. Mix well and simmer for 10-15 mins.

Make the orottis and cook them as given for meen orotti (p. 140).

Serve hot with any curry.

Nutritive values for 1 orotti: Calories: 221.0kcal; Carbohydrate: 26.5g; Protein: 3.2g; Fat: 12.0g; Minerals: 0.65g; Fibre: 1.1g.

Healthy modifications: See meen orotti (p. 140).

MUTTON FLATBREADS

Mutton flatbreads are popular in Punjabi, Mughlai and Kerala cuisines. In Punjab, they are made with wholewheat flour, whereas Mughlai cuisine uses refined flour. In Kerala, they are made with rice flour and refined wheat flour.

Mutton flatbreads can be one-dish meals, as they offers good-quality macro and micro nutrients. It provides calories, fats, protein, phosphorus, potassium, chloride, sodium, iron, zinc, iodine and various other essential trace minerals, along with the vitamins thiamine, riboflavin, niacin, vitamin B6 and vitamin B12.

Select lean meat cuts (tenderloin, chump chops and leg) rather than those high in saturated fat and cholesterol. The loin is above the belly and the chump is before the hind leg.

KHEEMA NAAN

Baked flatbread with mince filling

Preparation time: 25 mins; Cooking time: 40 mins

Kheema naan is an unleavened, traditional flatbread made with refined wheat flour and stuffed with spicy minced mutton.

Prepare the filling as given for mutton baida roti (p. 147), adding 1 cup of chopped leafy green vegetables (spinach, fenugreek, mustard) before the tomatoes. Prepare the dough for 2 naans as given for sada naan (p. 81). Stuff them as given for band gobi paratha (p. 25) and bake them in a clay, electric or gas tandoor, till golden on both sides. Serve them hot with curd, onion slices, lime wedges and any dal.

Nutritive values for 1 naan: Calories: 487.0kcal; Carbohydrate: 49.1g; Protein: 17.9g; Fat: 24.6g; Minerals: 2.0g; Fibre: 1.5g.

Healthy modifications: See sada naan (p. 81).

MUGHLAI KHEEMA PARATHA

Mughlai flatbread with mince filling

Preparation time: 25 mins; Cooking time: 30-40 mins

Mughlai kheema paratha is a leavened, traditional flatbread made with refined wheat flour and stuffed with spicy minced mutton. Mutton Mughlai porotha, similar to Mughlai kheema paratha is served during Durga pujo celebrations in Bengal.

Ingredients for 2 parathas

The filling

1 tbsp cashew nuts

2 tsp poppy seeds

2 onions, roughly chopped

1 tbsp + 1 tbsp oil

100g lean mutton, minced

1 tbsp ginger-garlic-green chilli paste

1 tsp garam masala powder

½ cup tomato purée

A pinch of salt or to taste

1 egg, beaten

¼ tsp cumin-pepper powder

The parathas

Dough to make 2 sada Mughlai lachha parathas (p. 91)

2 tsp oil

Method

Grind the cashew nuts, poppy seeds and onions to make a paste.

Heat 1 tbsp oil in a pan and sauté the mince for 4-5 mins on medium heat.

Add the ginger-garlic-green chilli paste, cashew nut paste, garam masala powder, tomato purée and salt. Mix well and cook on high heat for a minute.

(Method Cont.)

Reduce heat and simmer for 10-15 mins, till dry.

Mix the beaten egg with the spice powder and a pinch of salt.

Heat the remaining oil and add the beaten egg. Scramble till done.

Mix the minced curry and the scrambled egg in a bowl.

Divide the filling into 2 portions and leave aside, till cool.

Divide the dough into 2 portions and shape them into balls.

Make the parathas and pan-fry them as given for band gobi paratha (p. 25).

Pat the parathas on the sides with the palms to make them more flaky.

Serve hot with a green chutney, curd, onion slices, lime wedges and a dry vegetable curry.

Nutritive values for 1 paratha: Calories: 919.0kcal; Carbohydrate: 73.0g; Protein: 30.1g; Fat: 55.9g; Minerals: 2.9g; Fibre: 2.0g.

Healthy modifications: See sada Mughlai lachha paratha (p. 91).

PUNJABI KHEEMA PARATHA

Punjabi flatbread with mince filling

Preparation time: 25 mins; Cooking time: 30-40 mins

Punjabi kheema paratha is an unleavened, traditional flatbread made with wholewheat flour and stuffed with spicy minced mutton.

Ingredients for 2 parathas

The filling

1 tbsp oil

100g lean mutton, minced

2 onions, puréed

2 tsp ginger-garlic-green chilli paste

2 tomatoes, chopped

2 tsp dried fenugreek leaves

A pinch of salt or to taste

1 tsp garam masala powder

½ tsp red chilli powder

The parathas

Dough to make 2 sada parathas (p. 22)

2 tsp oil

(Recipe Cont.)

Method

Heat the oil in a pressure cooker and sauté the mince for a minute.

Add the onion purée and the ginger-garlic-green chilli paste and continue to sauté for a minute.

Stir in the tomatoes, fenugreek leaves and salt.

Add 1 cup of water and pressure-cook the mince on low heat for 20 mins after the cooker reaches full pressure.

Open the cooker when it returns to normal pressure. Add the spice powders and cook, till the contents are dry.

Divide the mince into 2 portions and leave aside, till cool.

Divide the dough into 4 portions and shape into balls.

Make the stuffed parathas and cook them as given in shahi murgh paratha (p. 141).

Transfer the stuffed parathas to a serving plate. Cut them into 2 pieces.

Serve hot with lime pickle, carrot strips, lime wedges and a dry vegetable curry.

Nutritive values for 1 paratha: Calories: 408.0kcal; Carbohydrate: 43.2g; Protein: 18.3g; Fat: 17.9g; Minerals: 2.1g; Fibre: 2.2g.

Healthy modifications: Toast the flatbread in a non-stick pan without fat. This will reduce 5g fat and 45kcal from each flatbread.

MUTTON BAIDA ROTI

Flatbread with mince filling and egg coating

Preparation time: 25 mins; Cooking time: 40 mins

Mutton baida roti is a leavened, traditional flatbread, stuffed with minced mutton and coated with egg.

Ingredients for 2 rotis

The filling

1 tbsp oil

100g lean mutton, minced

1 onion, minced

2 tsp ginger-garlic-green chilli paste

1 tsp garam masala powder

A pinch of salt or to taste

The parathas

Dough to make 2 sada baida rotis (p. 136)

2 eggs, beaten separately

½ tsp cumin-pepper powder

4 tsp oil

A pinch of salt or to taste

(Recipe Cont.)

Method

Heat the oil in a pressure cooker and sauté the minced mutton for a few mins.

Add the onion, ginger-garlic-green chilli paste and sauté for a minute.

Add 1 cup of water and pressure-cook on low heat for 20 mins after the cooker reaches full pressure.

Open the cooker when it returns to normal pressure. Add the garam masala powder and salt and cook, till the contents are dry.

Divide the filling into 2 portions and leave aside, till cool.

Divide the dough into 2 portions and shape them into balls.

Roll out and stuff the rotis as given for band gobi paratha (p. 25).

Cook the rotis as given for sada baida roti (p. 136).

Serve hot with curd or vegetable raita, coriander coconut chutney and a hot tomato sauce.

Nutritive values for 1 roti: Calories: 573.0kcal; Carbohydrate: 41.8g; Protein: 23.8g; Fat: 34.4g; Minerals: 1.7g; Fibre: 0.84g.

Healthy modifications: See sada baida roti (p. 136).

ERACHI PATHIRI

Thin rice flatbread with mince filling

Preparation time: 30 mins; Cooking time: 30 mins

Erachi pathiri is an unleavened, traditional, thin flatbread made with rice flour and grated fresh coconut and stuffed with spicy minced meat. It is served in Kerala.

Make it in the same way as meen pathiri (p. 139). Use 100g of mince instead of the fish and pressure-cook it for 20 mins.

Nutritive values for 1 pathiri: Calories: 328.0 kcal; Carbohydrates: 28.3 g; Protein: 7.5g; Fat: 20.5g; Minerals: 1.2g; Fibre: 2.1g.

Healthy modifications: Use lean meat cuts.

See meen pathiri (p. 139) for further modifications.

ERACHI OROTTI

Thick rice flatbread with spicy mince

Preparation time: 30 mins; Cooking time: 30 mins

Erachi orotti is an unleavened, traditional thick flatbread made with rice flour and grated fresh coconut and curried minced meat.

Make it in the same way as chicken orotti (p. 143). Use 100g of mince instead of the chicken and pressure-cook it for 20 mins.

Nutritive values for 1 orotti: Calories: 253.0kcal; Carbohydrate: 26.5g; Protein: 7.8g; Fat: 15.4g; Minerals: 0.98g; Fibre: 1.1g.

Healthy modifications: Use lean meat cuts.

See chicken orotti (p. 143) for further modifications.

SWEET FLATBREADS

Sweets and desserts are very important in Indian culture. Every happy occasion is celebrated with sweets which are high in fat, sugar and calories. Indians have a sweet tooth and it is difficult to resist Indian sweets and desserts. Meals usually end with a dessert.

Whole grain cereals, millets, pulses and legume flours are used to make sweet flatbreads. They can be prepared with plenty of vegetables, sprouts, fruits, nuts and low-fat dairy products and are healthier if jaggery is used instead of sugar, as the latter has no nutritive value. A sweet flatbread can be a small nutritious meal if it is low in calories and fat and high in vitamins, minerals and fibre. It can provide good-quality protein, complex carbohydrates and fats. A small, healthy sweet dish boosts metabolism, helps lose weight, enhances the mood, induces good sleep and improves overall physical and mental health.

Sweet flatbreads are usually prepared during festivals and weddings. They are prepared at home with refined wheat flour and rice flour and are not nutritious, but are preferable to packaged sweets, which are high in fat. Most flatbreads are toasted, though some are fried. Some are stuffed with cereals, pulses and vegetables. Nuts, cardamom, saffron and ghee are used liberally while making traditional sweet flatbreads.

SWEET FLATBREADS MADE WITH WHOLEWHEAT FLOUR

Sweet flatbreads made with wholewheat flour are one-dish meals as they offer good-quality macro and micro nutrients. Take care not to over-sweeten them with jaggery or sugar and avoid loading them with too much saturated or hydrogenated fats (dalda), high-fat dairy products, nuts and oilseeds.

MEETHI ROTI

Sweet flatbread

Preparation time: 20 mins; Cooking time: 8 mins

Meethi roti is a sweet, soft, unleavened, Punjabi flatbread made with wholewheat flour and evaporated milk.

Ingredients for 4 rotis

1 cup wholewheat flour

½ cup sweetened evaporated or condensed milk

2 tsp ghee

Method

Mix the flour and milk in a large bowl.

Knead it for about 5-10 mins to make a smooth dough.

Cover the dough with a damp cloth and leave it aside for about 20 mins.

Divide the dough into 4 portions and shape them into balls.

Roll them on a lightly floured board into 3"- 4" circles.

Put a non-stick pan on medium heat and toast the rotis, till golden brown on both sides.

Smear each roti with ½ tsp ghee.

Serve hot.

Nutritive values for 1 roti: Calories: 168.0kcal; Carbohydrate: 20.5g; Protein: 5.7g; Fat: 7.0g; Minerals: 1.2g; Fibre: 0.95g.

Healthy modifications: Replace ghee with oil.

Avoid smearing the rotis with fat. This will reduce 2.5g fat and 23kcal from each roti.

VEDMI

Flatbread with sweetened red gram filling

Preparation time: 25 mins; Cooking time: 15 mins

Vedmi is an unleavened, traditional, Gujarati flatbread made with wholewheat flour and stuffed with sweetened red gram.

Ingredients for 4 vedmis

The filling

4 tbsp red gram (arhar/tuvar dal)

2 tsp ghee

1 cup grated jaggery or sugar

½ tsp green cardamom powder

½ tsp saffron strands, dissolved in 2 tbsp hot milk

A pinch of nutmeg powder

The dough

1 cup wholewheat flour

1 tbsp oil

To cook the vedmis

2 tsp ghee

Method

Soak the dal for a few hours. Pressure cook it in fresh water, till tender.

Drain the dal and mash it well.

Heat the ghee in a pan and fry the ground dal on low heat, stirring continuously, till golden.

Mix in the jaggery or sugar, cardamom powder, saffron milk and nutmeg and simmer for about 5 mins, till dry.

Divide the filling into 4 portions and leave aside, till cool.

Put the flour in a bowl and rub in the oil.

Use 4 tbsp of water, without salt, and make the dough as given for sada chapatti (p. 66).

(Method Cont.)

Divide the dough into 4 portions and shape them into balls.

Roll the dough and prepare the stuffed vedmis as given for band gobi paratha (p. 25)

Put a non-stick pan on medium heat and toast the rotis, till golden brown on both sides.

Alternatively, divide the dough into 8 portions and prepare them as given for kela paratha (p. 36).

Smear both sides of the vedmis with ½ tsp ghee and serve hot.

Nutritive values for 1 vedmi: Calories: 309.0kcal; Carbohydrate: 47.8g; Protein: 7.0g; Fat: 9.7g; Minerals: 2.2g; Fibre: 1.4g.

Healthy modifications: Avoid adding fat to the flour while making the dough. This will reduce 3.75g fat and 33.75kcal from each vedmi.

Avoid frying the dal paste in ghee. This will further reduce 2.5g fat and 22.5kcal from each vedmi.

Avoid smearing the vedmis with ghee. This will also reduce 2.5g fat and 23kcal from each vedmi.

SWEET BISCUIT BHAKRI

Sweet crisp flatbread

Preparation time: 20 mins; Cooking time: 18 mins

Sweet biscuit bhakri is an unleavened, traditional, Gujarati and Rajasthani flatbread made with wholewheat flour and sugar.

Ingredients for 6 bhakris

2 tbsp sugar

¼ tsp saffron strands

½ cup warm milk

1 cup wholewheat flour

2 tbsp ghee

To cook the bhakris

2 tbsp ghee

Method

Dissolve the sugar and saffron in the milk.

Put the flour in a bowl and rub in 2 tbsp ghee.

Use the flavoured milk, without salt, and make the dough as given for sada chapatti (p. 66).

Divide the dough into 6 portions and shape them into balls.

Roll out a dough ball into a 2½" circle.

Toast it on a pan smeared with ½ tsp ghee on low heat, pressing down on the bhakri to prevent it from puffing up.

When the base is firm and golden brown, raise it off the pan with a spatula, sprinkle ½ tsp ghee on the pan and cook the other side, till golden brown.

Repeat with the remaining portions of dough.

When cool, store them in an airtight container.

Nutritive values for 1 bhakri: Calories: 175.0kcal; Carbohydrate: 17.0g; Protein: 2.4g; Fat: 10.8g; Minerals: 0.52g; Fibre: 0.32g.

Healthy modifications: Avoid adding ghee to the flour while making the dough. This will reduce 5g fat and 45kcal.

Toast the bhakris on a non-stick pan without fat. This will further reduce 5g fat and 45kcal for each bhakri.

MIXED DAL POLI

Flatbread with sweetened mixed pulse filling

Preparation time: 25 mins; Cooking time: 18 mins

Mixed dal poli is an unleavened, innovative, sweet flatbread made with wholewheat flour and stuffed with cooked mixed pulses. Use a mixture of husked, split mung, Bengal gram (chana dal), red gram (arhar/ tuvar dal), Egyptian lentils (masoor dal) and black gram (urad dal).

Ingredients for 4 polis

The filling

1 cup mixed dals

½ cup grated jaggery

¼ tsp green cardamom powder

The dough

Dough to make 2 sada parathas, without salt (p. 22)

Method

Soak the dals in water for a few hours.

Drain and cook the dal in fresh water, till just tender and dry.

Mix in the jaggery and cardamom powder.

When it cools a little, grind it to make a paste.

Divide the filling into 4 portions.

Divide the dough into 4 portions and shape them into balls.

Prepare the polis and cook them as given for vedmi (p. 151).

Serve hot.

Nutritive values for 1 poli: Calories: 228.0kcal; Carbohydrate: 45.4g; Protein: 8.8g; Fat: 1.3g; Minerals: 1.5g; Fibre: 0.73g.

MUNG DAL HALWA POLI

Flatbread with sweetened mung filling

Preparation time: 25 mins; Cooking time: 20 mins

Mung dal halwa poli is an unleavened, innovative flatbread made with wholewheat flour and stuffed with sweetened husked, split mung.

Ingredients for 4 polis

The filling

1 cup husked, split mung

½ cup unrefined brown sugar, powdered

¼ tsp green cardamom powder

¼ tsp saffron strands, dissolved in 2 tbsp hot milk

2 tbsp grated mawa/khoya (milk solids), made with skimmed buffalo milk

2 tbsp mixed nuts, chopped

1 tbsp seedless raisins

The dough

Dough to make 2 sada parathas, without salt (p. 22)

Method

Soak the dal in water for a few hours.

Drain the dal and grind it to make a smooth paste.

Mix the paste with all the remaining filling ingredients in a heavy-bottomed pan.

Cook on low heat, stirring continuously, till dry.

Divide the filling into 4 portions and leave aside, till cool.

Divide the dough into 4 portions and shape them into balls.

Prepare the polis and cook them as given for vedmi (p. 151).

Serve hot.

Nutritive values for 1 poli: Calories: 336.0kcal; Carbohydrates: 51.1g; Protein: 12.5g; Fat: 9.0g; Minerals: 2.2g; Fibre: 0.86g.

GAJAR HALWA POLI

Flatbread with carrot halwa filling

Preparation time: 25 mins; Cooking time: 20 mins

Gajar halwa poli is an unleavened, innovative flatbread made with wholewheat flour and stuffed with cooked sweet carrots.

Ingredients for 4 polis

The filling

2 large, sweet carrots

2 tbsp grated jaggery or unrefined brown sugar

½ cup grated mawa/khoya (milk solids), made with skimmed buffalo milk

¼ tsp green cardamom powder

2 tbsp mixed nuts, chopped

1 tbsp seedless raisins

The dough

Dough to make 2 sada parathas, without salt (p. 22)

Method

Wash the carrots, peel and grate them.

Combine all the filling ingredients in a heavy-bottomed pan and cook with ½ cup of water, till tender and dry.

Divide the filling into 4 portions and leave aside, till cool.

Divide the dough into 4 portions and shape them into balls.

Prepare the polis and cook them as given for vedmi (p. 151).

Serve hot.

Nutritive values for 1 poli: Calories: 249.0 kcal; Carbohydrates: 40.0g; Protein: 8.1g; Fat: 6.4g; Minerals: 2.3g; Fibre: 1.6g.

MASOOR DAL HALWA POLI

Flatbread with sweetened split Egyptian lentil filling

Preparation time: 25 mins; Cooking time: 20 mins

Masoor dal halwa poli is an unleavened, innovative flatbread made with wholewheat flour and stuffed with sweetened masoor dal.

Ingredients for 4 polis

The filling

1 cup husked, split Egyptian lentils (masoor dal)

2 tsp ghee

2 tbsp mixed nuts, chopped

1 tbsp seedless raisins

½ cup grated jaggery

2 tbsp grated fresh coconut

¼ tsp green cardamom powder

¼ tsp saffron strands, dissolved in 2 tbsp hot milk

The dough

Dough to make 2 sada parathas, without salt (p. 22)

Method

Soak the dal in water for a few hours.

Boil it in fresh water, till tender and dry.

When cool, grind it to make a smooth paste.

Heat the ghee in a heavy-bottomed pan and fry the nuts and raisins, till golden. Drain.

Add the ground dal to the same pan and fry on low heat, stirring continuously, till golden.

Mix in the fried nuts and raisins and the remaining filling ingredients. Simmer for about 5 mins, till dry.

Divide the filling into 4 portions and leave aside, till cool.

(Method Cont.)

Divide the dough into 4 portions and shape them into balls.

Prepare the polis and cook them as given for vedmi (p. 151).

Serve hot.

Nutritive values for 1 poli: Calories: 347.0kcal; Carbohydrates: 49.3g; Protein: 10.2g; Fat: 11.8g; Minerals: 1.8g; Fibre: 1.2g.

CHUKANDAR HALWA POLI

Flatbread with beetroot filling

Preparation time: 25 mins; Cooking time: 20 mins

Chukandar halwa poli is an unleavened, innovative flatbread made with wholewheat flour and stuffed with cooked sweet beetroots.

Make them in the same way as the gajar halwa poli (p. 153), substituting beetroots for the carrots.

Nutritive values for 1 poli: Calories: 248.0kcal; Carbohydrates: 34.7g; Protein: 7.2g; Fat: 8.7g; Minerals: 1.7g; Fibre: 1.1g.

SHAKHARKAND HALWA POLI

Flatbread with sweet potato filling

Preparation time: 25 mins; Cooking time: 20 mins

Shakharkand halwa poli is an unleavened, innovative flatbread made with wholewheat flour and stuffed with cooked sweet potato.

Ingredients for 4 polis

The filling

2 sweet potatoes

½ cup mawa/khoya (milk solids), made with skimmed buffalo milk

2 tbsp grated jaggery or unrefined brown sugar

¼ tsp saffron strands

2 tbsp mixed nuts, chopped and roasted

The dough

Dough to make 2 sada parathas, without salt (p. 22)

Method

Wash the sweet potatoes, peel and boil them, till tender.

Mash them well.

Mix all the filling ingredients in a heavy-bottomed pan and cook on medium heat, till the contents are dry.

Divide the filling into 4 portions and leave aside, till cool.

Divide the dough into 4 portions and shape them into balls.

Prepare the polis and cook them as given for vedmi (p. 151).

Serve hot.

Nutritive values for 1 poli: Calories: 277.0kcal; Carbohydrates: 37.5g; Protein: 6.9g; Fat: 8.9g; Minerals: 1.7g; Fibre: 1.1g.

CORN HALWA POLI

Flatbread with sweet corn filling

Preparation time: 25 mins; Cooking time: 20 mins

Corn halwa poli is an unleavened, innovative sweet flatbread made with wholewheat flour and stuffed with corn halwa.

Ingredients for 4 polis

The filling

2 cups sweet corn kernels

2 tbsp grated jaggery

¼ tsp green cardamom powder

¼ tsp saffron, dissolved in 2 tbsp hot milk

2 tbsp mawa/khoya (milk solids), made with skimmed buffalo milk

2 tbsp mixed nuts, chopped

1 tbsp seedless raisins

The dough

Dough to make 2 sada parathas, without salt (p. 22)

Method

Grind the corn kernels to make a smooth paste.

Mix the corn paste with the remaining filling ingredients in a heavy-bottomed pan and cook on medium heat, till the contents are dry.

Divide the filling into 4 portions and leave aside, till cool.

Divide the dough into 4 portions and shape them into balls.

Prepare the polis and cook them as given for vedmi (p. 151).

Serve hot.

Nutritive values for 1 poli: Calories: 216.0kcal; Carbohydrates: 29.2g; Protein: 5.7g; Fat: 8.5g; Minerals: 1.8g; Fibre: 0.66g.

SOOJI HALWA POLI

Flatbread with sweet semolina filling

Preparation time: 25 mins; Cooking time: 20 mins

Sooji halwa poli is an unleavened, traditional Andhra flatbread made with wholewheat flour and stuffed with sweet semolina.

Make a dough for 2 sada parathas (p. 22), without salt, and stuff them with sooji halwa (p. 218). Toast each poli with 1 tsp ghee and serve hot.

Nutritive values for 1 poli: Calories: 339.0kcal; Carbohydrates: 52.5g; Protein: 7.2g; Fat: 11.2g; Minerals: 0.94g; Fibre: 0.71g;

Healthy modifications: Limit the use of fat in the dish.

GUD POLI

Flatbread with jaggery filling

Preparation time: 25 mins; Cooking time: 10 mins

Gud poli is an unleavened, traditional, Marathi flatbread.

Roast 2 tbsp each of sesame seeds, poppy seeds, gram flour (besan) and mix them with 1 cup grated jaggery, ¼ tsp green cardamom powder and a pinch of nutmeg powder to make the filling. Make a dough for 2 sada parathas (p. 22), without salt, and make the polis as given for vedmi (p. 151).

Nutritive value for 1 poli: Calories: 304 kcal; Carbohydrates: 50.2g; Protein: 7.7g; Fat: 8.1g; Minerals: 2.2 g; Fibre: 1.4 g.

Healthy modifications: Limit the use of jaggery in the dish. Avoid smearing the polis with ghee.

CHINI PARATHA

Caramelized sugar flatbread

Preparation time: 20 mins; Cooking time: 8 mins

Chini paratha is an unleavened, innovative flatbread made with wholewheat flour and caramelized sugar.

To make caramelized sugar, dissolve 1 cup of sugar in ¼ cup of water in a heavy-bottomed metal pan. Boil, till it turns brown. Mix a few drops of lemon juice with 1 tsp of water and add it just before removing the pan from the heat, to prevent re-crystallization. Mix 2 tbsp of caramelized sugar with ¼ tsp of green cardamom powder to make the filling. Make a dough for 2 sada parathas (p. 22), without salt, and make the polis as given for vedmi (p. 151).

Nutritive values for 1 paratha: Calories: 116.0kcal; Carbohydrate: 24.8g; Protein: 3.0g; Fat: 0.4g; Minerals: 0.68g; Fibre: 0.48g.

MEETHA NUT PARATHA

Flatbread with sweetened nut filling

Preparation time: 25 mins; Cooking time: 8 mins

Meetha nut paratha is an unleavened, innovative sweet flatbread made with wholewheat flour and stuffed with sweetened nuts.

Combine 4 tbsp of mixed nuts (almonds, walnuts, cashew nuts, pistachios) with 2 tbsp grated jaggery, 2 tbsp milk and ½ tsp green cardamom powder to make the filling. Make a dough for 2 sada parathas (p. 22), without salt, and make the polis as given for vedmi (p. 151).

Nutritive values for 1 paratha: Calories: 188.0kcal; Carbohydrate: 26.5g; Protein: 5.2g; Fat: 6.7g; Minerals: 0.96g; Fibre: 0.69g.

MEETHA BEEJ PARATHA

Flatbread with sweetened seed filling

Preparation time: 25 mins; Cooking time: 8 mins

Meetha beej paratha is an unleavened, innovative sweet flatbread made with wholewheat flour and stuffed with sweetened seeds.

Replace the nuts in meetha nut paratha (p. 156) with powdered mixed seeds (sesame, poppy, water melon and pumpkin) and proceed as given.

Nutritive values for 1 paratha: Calories: 205.0kcal; Carbohydrate: 28.1g; Protein: 7.0g; Fat: 6.9g; Minerals: 1.6g; Fibre: 0.9g.

MEETHA PANEER PARATHA

Flatbread with sweetened paneer filling

Preparation time: 25 mins; Cooking time: 8 mins

Meetha paneer paratha is an unleavened, innovative flatbread made with wholewheat flour and stuffed with sweetened paneer.

Combine 1 cup grated paneer (made with skimmed milk) with 2 tbsp grated jaggery, ½ tsp green cardamom powder, 2 tbsp warm milk and ½ tsp saffron strands, dissolved in warm milk to make the filling. Make a dough for 2 sada parathas (p. 22), without salt, and make the polis as given for vedmi (p. 151).

Nutritive values for 1 paratha: Calories: 154.0kcal; Carbohydrate: 27.7g; Protein: 8.3g; Fat: 0.93g; Minerals: 1.4g; Fibre: 0.48g.

MEETHA NARIAL PARATHA

Flatbread with sweetened fresh coconut filling

Preparation time: 25 mins; Cooking time: 8 mins

Meetha narial paratha is an unleavened, traditional, sweet flatbread made with wholewheat flour and stuffed with coconut and jaggery in coastal cuisines.

Combine 1 cup of grated fresh coconut with 4 tbsp grated jaggery or unrefined brown sugar and 1 tsp aniseed powder to make the filling. Make a dough for 2 sada parathas (p. 22), without salt, and make the polis as given for vedmi (p. 151).

Nutritive values for 1 paratha: Calories: 261.0kcal; Carbohydrate: 36.0g; Protein: 4.4g; Fat: 11.0g; Minerals: 1.0g; Fibre: 1.5g.

Healthy modifications: Limit the use of jaggery

Limit the use of fresh coconut.

TIL-GUD KI ROTI

Jaggery and sesame flatbread

Preparation time: 20 mins; Cooking time: 8 mins

Til-gud ki roti is an unleavened, traditional, Gujarati flatbread, served for breakfast.

Make it in the same way as sada gud ki roti (p. 158), adding 2 tbsp of sesame seeds to the dough.

Nutritive values for 1 roti: Calories: 201.0kcal; Carbohydrate: 26.4g; Protein: 4.4g; Fat: 8.7g; Minerals: 1.1g; Fibre: 0.69g.

Healthy modifications: See sada gud ki roti (p. 158).

SADA GUD KI ROTI

Plain jaggery flatbread

Preparation time: 20 mins; Cooking time: 8 mins

Sada gud ki roti is an unleavened, traditional, Gujarati flatbread made with wholewheat flour and jaggery and served for breakfast.

Ingredients for 4 rotis

The dough

2 tbsp grated jaggery

1 cup wholewheat flour

A pinch of salt

2 tsp ghee

To serve

2 tsp ghee

Method

Dissolve the jaggery in 4½ tbsp of water.

Mix the remaining dough ingredients in a bowl.

Gradually mix in the jaggery syrup.

Knead the dough and roll out the rotis as given for sada chapatti (p. 66).

Put a non-stick pan on medium heat and toast the rotis, till golden brown on both sides.

Smear the rotis with ghee and serve hot.

Nutritive values for 1 roti: Calories: 149.0kcal; Carbohydrate: 22.1g; Protein: 3.1g; Fat: 5.4g; Minerals: 0.71g; Fibre: 0.95g.

Healthy modifications: Avoid adding ghee to the dough. This will reduce 2.5g fat and 22kcal from each roti.

Avoid smearing the rotis with ghee. This will further reduce 2.5g fat and 23kcal from each roti.

KUTTI

Crumbled flatbread with sugar and ghee

Preparation time: 20 mins; Cooking time: 8 mins

Kutti is a unleavened, traditional, Sindhi flatbread, prepared on religious occasions and served with papad. Make 4 sada parathas (p. 22), crumble them and mix with 2 tbsp of sugar and 2 tbsp of hot ghee.

Nutritive values for 1 serving: Calories: 195.0kcal; Carbohydrate: 24.9g; Protein: 3.1g; Fat: 9.2g; Minerals: 0.7g; Fibre: 0.48g.

Healthy modifications: Use half the quantity of ghee. This will reduce 20g fat and 180kcal from the dish.

Omit the ghee. This will further reduce 10g fat and 90kcal from the dish.

See sada gud ki roti (alongside) for further modifications.

CHAPATTI CONE WITH CHOPPED FRUITS

Preparation time: 25 mins; Cooking time: 8 mins

Chapatti cone with chopped fruits is an innovative dish.

Shape 2 sada chapattis (p. 66) into cones. Fill the cones with 2 cups of chopped mixed fruits (orange, pomegranate, apples, bananas) and serve immediately.

Nutritive values for 1 cone: Calories: 219.0kcal; Carbohydrate: 36.7g; Protein: 4.6g; Fat: 5.8g; Minerals: 2.3g; Fibre: 1.5g.

MITHO LOLI

Sweet Flatbread

Preparation time: 20 mins; Cooking time: 8 mins

Mitho loli is an unleavened, traditional, Sindhi flatbread. It is prepared with wholewheat flour and a thick jaggery and sugar syrup and is served at festivals.

Ingredients for 2 lolis

1 tbsp sugar

1 tbsp grated jaggery

¼ tsp green cardamom powder

4 tsp oil

1 cup wholewheat flour

To cook the lolis

4 tsp oil

Method

Bring 1 cup of water to a boil in a pan.

Add the sugar, jaggery and cardamom powder and continue to boil, till it reaches a one-thread consistency. (When a few drops of cooled syrup is stretched between the thumb and forefinger, a single thread is formed.)

Remove the pan from the heat and leave aside, till cool.

Rub the oil into the flour.

Gradually stir in the syrup.

Knead the dough and cook it as given for sada chapatti (p. 66).

Alternatively, roll the dough into 2" circles, prick them with a fork and deep-fry them in oil.

Serve with curd.

(Method Cont.)

Nutritive values for 1 loli: Calories: 407.0kcal; Carbohydrate: 48.7g; Protein: 6.2g; Fat: 20.9g; Minerals: 1.2g; Fibre: 0.95g.

Healthy modifications: Avoid adding fat to the flour. This will reduce 10g fat and 90kcal from each loli.

Toast the lolis in a non-stick pan without fat. This will further reduce 10g fat and 90kcal from each loli.

CHAPATTI CONE WITH FRUIT YOGURT

Preparation time: 25 mins; Cooking time: 8 mins

Chapatti cone with fruit yogurt is an innovative dish.

Shape 2 sada chapattis (p. 66) into cones. Blend 1 cup of mixed berries with 1 cup of thick yogurt, fill the cones and serve immediately.

Nutritive values for 1 cone: Calories: 216.0kcal; Carbohydrate: 30.7g; Protein: 5.7g; Fat: 7.7g; Minerals: 2.4g; Fibre: 1.0g.

CHURMA

Flatbread with jaggery

Preparation time: 25 mins; Cooking time: 8 mins

Churma is a sweet dish, served with baati (p. 188) and panchmel dal (p. 233) as a one-dish meal in Rajasthan.

Ingredients for 2 servings

2 leftover parathas or rotis made with wholewheat flour

2 tbsp ghee

2 tbsp mixed nuts, chopped

4 tbsp grated jaggery

½ tsp green cardamom powder

Method

Break the parathas or rotis into small pieces.

Heat the ghee and sauté them with the nuts.

Mix in the jaggery and cardamom powder and stir for 5 mins on low heat.

Serve with dal baati.

Alternatively, make a dough of wholewheat flour and shape them into balls. Deep-fry them in ghee and crush them. Mix with grated mawa/khoya and jaggery, dried fruits, nuts and cardamom powder.

Nutritive values for 1 serving: Calories: 578.0kcal; Carbohydrate: 62.8g; Protein: 9.5g; Fat: 32.0g; Minerals: 2.5g; Fibre: 1.2g.

Healthy modifications: Limit the use of ghee to 2 tsp. This will reduce 20g fat and 180kcal from the dish.

Replace ghee with oil.

SWEET EGG TOAST

Preparation time: 20 mins; Cooking time: 16 mins

Sweet egg toast is an unleavened, innovative flatbread made with wholewheat flour and toasted with egg.

Ingredients for 8 egg toasts

Dough to make 2 sada parathas (p. 22)

1 tsp ghee

2 eggs, beaten

½ cup milk

A few drops of vanilla essence

1 tbsp unrefined brown sugar, powdered

The garnish

1 tbsp nuts, grated

Method

Divide the dough into 8 portions and shape them into balls.

Roll out each portion of dough into a 3″ circle.

Put a non-stick pan on medium heat and toast the rotis with a few drops of ghee, till light gold on both sides.

Mix the eggs with the milk, vanilla essence and sugar.

Dip the rotis in the egg mixture and toast them on the same pan till golden brown on both sides.

Garnish with nuts and serve hot.

Nutritive values for 1 egg toast: Calories: 383.0kcal; Carbohydrate: 44.6g; Protein: 15.4g; Fat: 15.8g; Minerals: 2.3g; Fibre: 1.1g.

SWEET FLATBREADS MADE WITH REFINED WHEAT FLOUR

PURAN POLI

Flatbread with sweetened Bengal gram filling

Preparation time: 25 mins; Cooking time: 20 mins

Puran poli is an unleavened, traditional, Marathi flatbread made with refined wheat flour and stuffed with sweetened Bengal gram. It is called bobatlu in Andhra Pradesh and obbattu in Karnataka.

Ingredients for 4 polis

The filling

1 cup husked, split Bengal gram (chana dal)

1 cup grated jaggery

A pinch of green cardamom powder

The dough

2 tsp ghee

1 cup refined wheat flour

To cook the polis

2 tsp ghee

(Recipe Cont.)

Method

Soak the dal in water for a few hours.

Drain the dal and cook it in fresh water, till just tender and dry.

Mix in the jaggery and cardamom powder.

Leave aside, till cool. Grind it to make a paste.

Rub the ghee into the flour.

Gradually add 4 tbsp of water to the flour and knead it for about 5-10 mins to make a smooth dough.

Cover the dough and leave it aside for about 20 mins.

Knead it again for a few mins.

Divide the filling into 4 portions.

Divide the dough into 4 portions and shape them into balls.

Prepare the polis as given for band gobi paratha (p. 25).

Toast each poli on a hot pan with ½ tsp ghee, till golden on both sides.

Serve hot.

Nutritive values for 1 poli: Calories: 294.0kcal; Carbohydrate: 56.1g; Protein: 8.8g; Fat: 3.8g; Minerals: 1.5g; Fibre: 0.73g.

Healthy modifications: Avoid adding fat to the flour while making the dough. This will reduce 2.5g fat and 23kcal from each poli.

Toast the polis in a non-stick pan without fat. This will further reduce 2.5g fat and 23kcal from each poli.

Use wholewheat flour or replace half the refined flour with it.

Limit the use of jaggery.

PURAN PURI

Fried flatbread with sweetened Bengal gram filling

Preparation time: 25 mins; Cooking time: 25 mins

Puran puri is an unleavened, traditional fried flatbread made with refined wheat flour and stuffed with sweetened split Bengal gram. It is served in some south Indian states.

Ingredients for 8 puris

The filling

4 tbsp husked, split Bengal gram (chana dal)

1 tsp ghee

2 tbsp mixed nuts, chopped

1 tbsp seedless raisins

2 tbsp grated fresh coconut

1 cup grated jaggery

¼ tsp green cardamom powder

¼ tsp saffron strands dissolved in 2 tbsp hot milk

The dough

1 cup refined wheat flour

To cook the puris

Ghee for deep-frying

(Recipe Cont.)

Method

Soak the dal in water for a few hours.

Drain the dal and boil it in fresh water, till tender and dry.

When cool, grind it to make a smooth paste.

Heat the ghee in a pan and fry the nuts and raisins, till golden.

Mix in the ground dal paste and the remaining filling ingredients.

Divide the filling into 8 portions and leave aside, till cool.

Prepare the dough as given for sada puri (p. 73).

Divide the dough into 8 portions and shape them into balls.

Make the puris and fry them as given for bedmi puri (p. 76).

Nutritive values for 1 puri: Calories: 243.0kcal; Carbohydrate: 30.0g; Protein: 5.1g; Fat: 11.5g; Minerals: 0.9g; Fibre: 0.41g.

Healthy modifications: Replace ghee with oil for frying.

Limit the use of jaggery.

SWEET MATTIRI

Sweet fried flatbread

Preparation time: 25 mins; Cooking time: 15 mins

Sweet mattiri is a leavened, traditional, Punjabi flatbread made with refined wheat flour and dipped in sugar syrup. It is served during festivals.

Ingredients for 8 mattiris

The sugar syrup

1 cup sugar

The dough

1 cup refined wheat flour

½ tsp baking soda

1 tbsp ghee

2 tbsp curd

To fry the mattiris

Ghee for deep-frying

(Recipe Cont.)

Method

Bring ½ cup of water to a boil in a pan. Add the sugar and stir, till it dissolves. Continue to boil, till it reaches a hard-ball consistency. (When ¼ tsp of the syrup is dropped into a cup of cold water, it becomes a hard ball.)

Remove the pan from the heat and keep warm.

Mix the flour and baking soda in a bowl. Stir in the ghee and curd.

Gradually add 2 tbsp of water and knead to make a dough as given for sada chapatti (p. 66).

Divide the dough into 8 portions and shape them into balls.

Roll out each portion of dough into a 2"- 3" circle And prick them all over with a fork.

Heat the ghee in a kadhai or wok and deep-fry the mattiris, till crisp and light brown.

Drain them on layers of tissue paper.

Dip them into the warm sugar syrup for a few mins.

Remove and put them on a plate, till dry.

When cool, store them in an airtight container.

Nutritive values for 1 mattiri: Calories: 135.0kcal; Carbohydrates: 21.8g; Protein: 1.5g; Fat: 4.7g; Minerals: 0.12g; Fibre: 0.1g.

Healthy modifications: Replace ghee with oil for frying.

Omit the fat from the dough.

Limit the use of sugar.

SHAHI MEETHA PARATHA

Flatbread with sweetened milk solid filling

Preparation time: 25 mins; Cooking time: 8 mins

Shahi meetha paratha is a leavened, traditional, Mughlai flatbread stuffed with sweetened milk solids.

Ingredients for 4 parathas

The dough

1 cup refined wheat flour

2 tsp ghee

½ cup milk

1 tsp yeast

2 tsp sugar

The filling

1 cup grated mawa/khoya (milk solids)

1 tbsp powdered cashew nuts

2 tbsp sugar, powdered

¼ tsp green cardamom powder

¼ tsp saffron strands, dissolved in 2 tbsp warm milk

To cook the parathas

4 tsp ghee

(Recipe Cont.)

Method

Put the flour in a bowl and rub in the ghee.

Dissolve the sugar in 2 tbsp of warm milk and add the yeast. Leave it aside for 10 mins to froth up.

Add the yeast mixture to the flour.

Gradually add the remaining milk and prepare the dough as given for sada naan (p. 81)

Divide the dough into 4 portions.

Mix all the filling ingredients in a bowl.

Divide the filling into 4 portions.

Roll out the parathas, stuff them and pan-fry them with ghee as given for band gobi paratha (p. 25).

Serve hot.

Nutritive values for 1 paratha: Calories: 340.0kcal; Carbohydrates: 27.9g; Protein: 8.0g; Fat: 18.5g; Minerals: 0.2g; Fibre: 0.12g.

Healthy modifications: Replace ghee with oil.

Avoid adding ghee to the dough. This will reduce 2.5g fat and 23kcal from each paratha.

Use milk solids made with skimmed buffalo milk. This will reduce 54kcal from each paratha.

Toast the paratha in a non-stick pan without ghee. This will further reduce 5g fat and 45kcal from each paratha.

Use wholewheat flour or replace half the refined flour with it.

BAKAR KHANI

Layered sweet flatbread

Preparation time: 25 mins; Cooking time: 2 mins

Bakar khani is a leavened, traditional, Mughlai, sweet flatbread made with refined wheat flour and served with milk pudding.

Ingredients for 4 bakar khanis

2 tbsp sugar

½ cup warm milk

½ tsp active dried yeast

1 cup refined flour

A few drops of rose essence

2 tbsp mixed nuts, chopped or flaked

1 tbsp seedless raisins, chopped

1 tbsp home-made white butter

A pinch of salt or to taste

4 tsp ghee

(Recipe Cont.)

Method

Dissolve the sugar in warm milk and add the yeast. Leave it aside for about 10 mins to froth up.

Mix all the remaining ingredients, except the ghee, in a bowl.

Gradually add the milk mixture and prepare the dough as given for sada naan (p. 81)

Divide the dough into 4 portions and shape them into balls.

Roll out a portion of dough into a 4″ circle.

Apply ½ tsp ghee over it and fold it into half. Apply another ½ tsp ghee and then fold it into a quarter.

Shape it into a ball again and roll it out into a 4″ circle.

Repeat with the remaining portions of the dough.

Bake the bakar khanis in a clay, gas or electric tandoor, till golden on both sides.

Alternatively, bake them in an electric or gas oven, preheated to 180°C; toast them on a non-stick pan on medium heat; or deep-fry them in ghee.

Serve hot with a kheer poured over them or dip them in the kheer and eat.

Nutritive values for 1 bakar khani: Calories: 262.0kcal; Carbohydrate: 30.5g; Protein: 4.8g; Fat: 13.3g; Minerals: 0.6g; Fibre: 0.26g.

Healthy modifications: Avoid adding butter to the dough. This will reduce 12g fat and 110kcal from the dough.

Avoid the ghee while rolling the dough. This will further reduce 5g fat and 45kcal from each bakar khani.

Use wholewheat flour or replace half the refined flour with it.

MAWA KACHORI

Fried flatbread with sweetened milk solid filling

Preparation time: 20 mins; Cooking time: 8 mins

Mawa kachori is a leavened, traditional, flatbread made with refined wheat flour, stuffed with sweetened milk solids and fried. They are served in Rajasthan and Uttar Pradesh, plain or with sugar syrup spooned over them.

Ingredients for 8 kachoris

The dough

1 cup refined wheat flour

½ tsp baking powder

2 tbsp ghee

The filling

1 cup grated mawa/khoya (milk solids)

3 tbsp sugar, powdered

2 tbsp mixed nuts, coarsely powdered

¼ tsp green cardamom powder

To cook the kachoris

Oil for deep-frying

(Recipe Cont.)

Method

Mix the flour and the baking powder in a bowl.

Rub the ghee into the flour.

Gradually add 5 tbsp of water to the flour and knead it to make a slightly firm dough.

Cover the dough and leave it aside for 20 mins.

Knead it again for a few mins.

Divide the dough into 8 portions.

Mix all the filling ingredients in a bowl.

Divide the filling into 8 portions.

Roll out the kachoris and stuff them as given for bedmi puri (p. 76).

Heat the oil in a kadhai or wok and deep-fry the kachoris, till crisp and golden.

Drain them on layers of tissue paper.

Serve hot.

Nutritive values for 1 kachori: Calories: 222.0kcal; Carbohydrate: 18.0g; Protein: 3.9g; Fat: 14.9g; Minerals: 0.55g; Fibre: 0.11g.

Healthy modifications: Avoid adding fat to the dough.

Use wholewheat flour or replace half the refined flour with it.

Use milk solids prepared from skimmed milk. 100g milk solids prepared from skimmed milk provides 1.6g fat and 206kcal, whereas that prepared from full-cream buffalo milk provides 31.2g fat and 421 calories.

Bake instead of frying.

MALPUAS

Flatbread in milk pudding

Preparation time: 25 mins; Cooking time: 20 mins

Malpuas are unleavened, traditional flatbreads made with refined wheat flour and served with a milk pudding. It is a famous dessert of Uttar Pradesh, Bihar and Rajasthan. Malpuas are made differently in each of the states.

Ingredients for 4 servings

The milk pudding

1 litre full-cream milk

2 tbsp mixed nuts, powdered

4 tbsp sugar

1 tbsp seedless raisins, chopped

½ tsp green cardamom powder

½ tsp saffron strands

The dough

1 cup refined wheat flour

To fry the malpuas

Ghee for deep-frying

(Recipe Cont.)

Method

Boil the milk on medium heat, till it is reduced to half its original quantity.

Add the remaining pudding ingredients, mix well and simmer for 10 mins.

Divide the pudding into 4 portions.

Put the flour in a bowl.

Gradually add 5 tbsp of water and make the dough as given for sada chapatti (p. 66) and divide it into 4 portions.

Roll out each portion of dough into a 3" circle.

Heat the ghee in a kadhai or wok and fry the malpuas, till light brown on both sides.

Drain them on layers of tissue paper.

Place 2 fried malpuas in a serving plate.

Pour a portion of the milk pudding over them and toss the malpuas, till they are soaked through.

Nutritive values for 1 serving: Calories: 490.0kcal; Carbohydrate: 48.6g; Protein: 15.4g; Fat: 26.0g; Minerals: 3.0g; Fibre: 0.66g.

Healthy modifications: Use oil instead of ghee for frying.

Use wholewheat flour instead of refined flour.

Toast the malpuas on a pan instead of deep-frying them.

KHAJOOR NI GHARI

Fried flatbread with date filling

Preparation time: 25 mins; Cooking time: 10 mins

Khajoor ni ghari is part of Parsi cuisine.

Ingredients for 12 gharis

The filling

200g dates, seeded

1 tbsp ghee or home-made white butter or hydrogenated fat

1 tbsp sugar

½ tsp green cardamom powder

¼ tsp nutmeg powder

½ tsp vanilla essence

The dough

A pinch of salt or to taste

2 cups refined wheat flour

1 tbsp ghee or white butter or hydrogenated fat

½ tsp baking powder

To fry the gharis

Oil for deep-frying

(Recipe Cont.)

Method

Blend the dates to make a coarse paste.

Heat the ghee, butter or fat in a pan on low heat and add the sugar. Stir, till the sugar melts.

Add the dates and sauté for a few mins.

Stir in the remaining filling ingredients.

Leave aside till cool and divide into 12 portions.

Dissolve the salt in 150 ml of water.

Mix the flour, baking powder and the fat in a bowl.

Gradually add the salt water and knead the dough and prepare the stuffed gharis as given for bedmi puri (p. 76).

Heat the oil in a kadhai or wok and fry the gharis, till golden brown.

Drain on layers of tissue paper.

Serve hot or store in an airtight container when cool.

Nutritive values for 1 ghari: Calories: 182.0kcal; Carbohydrates: 26.1g; Protein: 2.1g; Fat: 6.4g; Minerals: 0.4g; Fibre: 0.1g.

Healthy modifications: Avoid adding fat to the dough. This will reduce 15g of fat and 135kcal from the dish.

Avoid adding sugar, since dates are sweet. This will reduce 15g of carbohydrates and 60kcal from the dish.

Avoid frying the filling. This will further reduce 15g fat and 135kcal from the dish.

Toast the gharis in a non-stick pan instead of frying them.

SWEET PURIS

Sweet fried flatbread

Preparation time: 25 mins; Cooking time: 20 mins

Malpuas in some north Indian states and Rajasthan are made traditionally in the form of puris dipped in flavoured sugar syrup and served with rabri.

Ingredients for 8 puris

The syrup

1 cup sugar

¼ tsp saffron strands

The puris

½ cup refined wheat flour

½ cup semolina

To fry the puris

Oil for frying

Method

Bring 1 cup of water to a boil in a pan on medium heat and dissolve the sugar in it.

Continue boiling, till it attains a soft-ball consistency. (When ¼ tsp of the syrup is dropped into a cup of cold water, it becomes a soft ball.)

Add the saffron and stir, till it is dissolved.

Keep the syrup warm.

Make 8 puris as given for sada puris (p. 73), without salt.

Drain them on layers of tissue paper.

Dip the fried puris in the sugar syrup for a few mins, drain and arrange on a serving dish.

Serve them hot with rabri.

Nutritive values for 1 puri: Calories: 138kcal; Carbohydrate: 21.7g; Protein: 1.4g; Fat: 5.1g; Minerals: 0.1g; and Fibre: 0.03g

SWEET FLATBREADS MADE WITH RICE FLOUR

TAFTAN

Sweet rice flatbread

Preparation time: 25 mins; Cooking time: 10 mins

Taftan is a leavened, traditional, sweet Mughlai flatbread made with rice flour. It is always served with a non-vegetarian dish.

Ingredients for 4 taftans

The dough

1 tsp + 2 tsp sugar

½ tsp active dried yeast

¼ cup warm milk

1 cup rice flour

2 tbsp curd

1 tbsp ghee

A pinch of salt or to taste

The topping

2 tsp poppy seeds or nigella seeds

2 tsp ghee

(Recipe Cont.)

Method

Add 1 tsp sugar and the yeast to the warm milk and leave it aside for 10 mins to froth up.

Mix 2 tsp sugar with the rice flour, curd, ghee and salt in a bowl.

Stir in the yeast mixture.

Prepare the dough as given for sada naan (p. 81).

Divide the dough into 4 portions and shape them into balls.

Roll out each portion of dough on a lightly floured board into a thick, 3" circle.

Make grooves with your fingertips all over the rolled out dough.

Sprinkle poppy seeds or nigella seeds over it and press them in with a spatula.

Place the taftans on a baking sheet and bake them in an oven preheated to 180°C-190°C for about 5 mins.

Remove them from the oven and smear each taftan with ¼ tsp ghee.

Return to the oven and bake for another 5 mins, till they are golden.

Serve hot with a Mughlai chicken dish.

Nutritive values for 1 taftan: Calories: 177.0kcal; Carbohydrate: 24.7g; Protein: 2.7g; Fat: 7.5g; Minerals: 0.51g; Fibre: 0.25g.

Healthy modifications: Avoid adding ghee to the dough. This will reduce 15g fat and 135kcal from the taftans.

Avoid smearing the taftans with ghee. This will further reduce 2.5g fat and 23kcal from each taftan.

CHATTI PATHIRI

Baked layered flatbread with a sweet filling

Preparation time: 30-40 mins; Cooking time: 25 mins

Chatti pathiri is an unleavened, traditional flatbread made with rice flour in Kerala.

Ingredients for 8 servings

The filling

5 eggs, beaten

5 tbsp sugar, powdered

½ tsp green cardamom powder

2 tsp ghee

½ cup grated fresh coconut

2 tbsp mixed nuts, chopped

2 tbsp seedless raisins, chopped

2 tbsp poppy seeds

The topping

5 eggs, beaten

5 tbsp powdered sugar

½ tsp green cardamom powder

The pathiris

2 tsp ghee

9 Malabar ari pathiris (p. 97)

(Recipe Cont.)

Method

Mix the eggs, sugar and cardamom powder in a bowl.

Heat the ghee and sauté the coconut, nuts, raisins and poppy seeds for a minute.

Add the egg mixture and stir continuously, till the eggs are thoroughly scrambled.

Divide it into 8 portions.

Mix all the topping ingredients in a bowl.

Spread 2 tsp ghee over a baking tray.

Dip a pathiri in the topping and place it on the baking tray.

Sprinkle one portion of the filling on top.

Continue layering the pathiris and filling, ending with a pathiri.

Pour the remaining topping over it.

Bake in an oven preheated to 170°C-180°C, till golden brown on top.

Slice and serve hot.

Nutritive values for 1 serving: Calories: 448.0kcal; Carbohydrate: 59.9g; Protein: 12.2g; Fat: 17.7g; Minerals: 1.8g; Fibre: 1.2g.

Healthy modifications: Reduce all the quantities by half so that there are only 4 layers. This will reduce the number of eggs and the amount of sugar and coconut used.

CHURUTTU

Rice flatbread cone

Preparation time: 20 mins; Cooking time: 20 mins

Churuttu is an unleavened, traditional flatbread made with rice flour and a sweetened rice flour and coconut filling, commonly consumed in Kerala.

Ingredients for 4 cones

The filling

1 cup rice flour

½ fresh coconut, grated

½ tsp cumin seeds

1 cup sugar

The dough

1 cup rice flour

The topping

4 tsp ghee

(Recipe Cont.)

Method

Roast the rice flour for the filling, till light brown.

Mix the roasted rice flour, grated coconut and the cumin seeds in a bowl.

Mix the sugar with 1 cup of water in a pan on medium heat and stir, till dissolved. Bring it to a boil and continue boiling, till it reaches a soft-ball consistency. (When ¼ tsp of the syrup is dropped into a cup of cold water, it becomes a soft ball.)

Mix in the remaining filling ingredients.

Divide the filling into 4 portions and leave aside, till cool.

Make the dough, roll out the rotis and toast them as given for Malabar ari pathiri (p. 97).

Shape each roti into a cone and fill it with the prepared filling.

Spoon 1 tsp ghee over each cone and serve.

Nutritive values for 1 churuttu: Calories: 428.0kcal; Carbohydrate: 67.2g; Protein: 4.6g; Fat: 15.7g; Minerals: 0.58g; Fibre: 1.0g.

Healthy modifications: Avoid spooning ghee over the rice cone. This will reduce 5g fat and 45kcal from each churuttu.

ELLADA

Rice flatbread with fresh coconut filling

Preparation time: 20 mins; Cooking time: 20 mins

Ellada is an unleavened flatbread made with rice flour and stuffed with sweetened coconut. The stuffed flatbreads are steamed in banana leaves in Kerala.

Ingredients for 4 ellada

The filling

1 cup grated jaggery

1 cup grated fresh coconut

2 tbsp mixed nuts, powdered

½ tsp green cardamom powder

A pinch of salt

The dough

1 cup rice flour

A pinch of salt or to taste

To steam the elladas

4 pieces of banana leaf

The topping

4 tsp ghee or 4 tbsp coconut milk

Method

Dissolve the jaggery in 1 cup of water and boil on low heat for about 5 mins.

Add the coconut, nuts, cardamom powder and salt. Boil on high heat, till the contents are thick and nearly dry.

Divide the filling into 4 portions and leave aside, till cool.

(Method Cont.)

Roast the rice flour for the dough lightly on a pan and allow it to cool.

Mix the rice flour and the salt in a bowl.

Add ½ cup of hot water. Mix the contents well and knead it for about 5-10 mins to make a smooth dough.

Cover the dough with a damp cloth and leave it aside for about 20 mins.

Knead it again for a few mins.

Divide the dough into 4 portions.

Press a portion of the dough on a piece of greased banana leaf into a circle, as thin as possible.

Place the filling along one half of the circle and gently fold other half, along with the banana leaf over it. Press the edges of the dough gently to seal.

Repeat with the remaining portions of dough and filling.

Steam the elladas in the banana leaves for 10 mins.

Spoon 1 tsp ghee or 1 tbsp coconut milk over each ellada and serve immediately.

Nutritive values for 1 ellada: Calories: 387.0kcal; Carbohydrate: 47.7g; Protein: 4.4g; Fat: 19.8g; Minerals: 0.73g; Fibre: 1.1g.

Healthy modifications: Avoid spooning ghee over the elladas. This will reduce 5g fat and 45kcal from each ellada.

ARISELU

Sweet fried rice flatbread

Preparation time: 20 mins; Cooking time: 14 mins

Ariselu is an unleavened, traditional, fried Andhra flatbread made with rice flour and jaggery and sprinkled with sesame seeds.

Ingredients for 4 ariselus

1 cup rice

1 cup grated jaggery

4 tsp sesame seeds

Oil for deep-frying

Method

Soak the rice in water for a few hours and drain.

Dry the rice thoroughly on a towel and powder it.

Heat ½ cup of water in a pan and dissolve the jaggery in it. Bring it to a boil and continue boiling, till it reaches a soft-ball consistency. (When ¼ tsp of the syrup is dropped into a cup of cold water, it becomes a soft ball.)

Add the rice powder gradually, stirring vigorously to avoid lumps and make a smooth dough.

Remove from heat and leave aside, till cool enough to handle.

Divide the dough into 4 portions and shape them into balls

Sprinkle ½ tsp sesame seeds on a greased plastic sheet.

Press a portion of the dough over it with your fingertips and make a 3" circle.

Sprinkle ½ tsp sesame seeds on top of the roti and press them into the dough with the back of a spatula.

Repeat with the remaining portions of dough.

(Method Cont.)

Heat the oil in a kadhai or wok. Fry the ariselu in hot oil, till dark brown.

Drain on layers of tissue paper and serve.

Nutritive values for 1 ariselu: Calories: 248.0kcal; Carbohydrate: 42.3g; Protein: 3.0g; Fat: 7.4g; Minerals: 1.1g; Fibre: 0.2g.

Healthy modifications: Toast the ariselus in a non-stick pan instead of frying them.

KEMENYA ROTI

Sweet fried rice flatbread

Preparation time: 15 mins; Cooking time: 4 mins

Kemenya roti is an unleavened sweet flatbread made with red sticky rice and sugar. It is served during festivals in Nagaland.

Ingredients for 8 rotis

1 cup red sticky rice flour

½ cup sugar

Oil for deep-frying

Method

Mix the rice flour and sugar in a bowl.

Divide the mixture into 8 portions and shape them into balls.

Press the balls with greased palm into 3" circles.

Heat the oil in a kadhai or wok and fry the rotis, till golden brown.

Serve hot.

Nutritive values for 1 roti: Calories: 113.0kcal; Carbohydrate: 16.0g; Protein: 0.85g; Fat: 5.1g; Minerals: 0.1g; Fibre: 0.03g.

Healthy modifications: Toast the rotis in a non-stick pan instead of frying them.

MEETHA PITHA

Sweet steamed flatbread

Preparation time: 30 mins; Cooking time: 30 mins

Meetha pitha is an unleavened, traditional flatbread made with rice flour and stuffed with a sweet filling. They are called pithe in Bengali and served during festivals. Doodhi pithas are made by boiling meetha pithas in water for 5-10 mins and serving them in a milk pudding.

Ingredients for 8 pithas

The filling

1 tsp ghee

1 cup grated fresh coconut

2 tbsp poppy seeds

2 tbsp grated jaggery or sugar

¼ tsp green cardamom powder

The dough

1 cup rice flour

To cook the pithas

½ tsp ghee

(Recipe Cont.)

Method

Heat the ghee in a pan and mix in all the filling ingredients.

Simmer for a few mins and leave aside, till cool.

Gradually add 5 tbsp of hot water to the flour and stir it well.

Knead it for about 5 mins to make a firm dough.

Cover the dough and leave it aside for 20 mins.

Knead it again for a few mins.

Divide the dough and filling into 8 portions.

Roll out a portion of the dough on a lightly floured board into a 4″ circle.

Place a portion of the filling along one half and fold the other half of the dough over it. Gently seal the edges with moist fingertips.

Repeat with the remaining portions of dough and filling.

Boil water in a large pan with the ghee and carefully drop in the pithas.

Boil them for 15 mins.

Drain thoroughly and serve immediately.

Nutritive values for 1 pitha: Calories: 113.0kcal; Carbohydrates: 15.4g; Protein: 2.1g; Fat: 4.9g; Minerals: 0.61g; Fibre: 0.6g.

175

FLATBREADS AS SNACKS

Teatime snacks are an important aspect of Indian culture. They are usually fried, crisp items such as samosas, kachoris, vadas, mixtures, bhajjias, pakoras, chaklis, puris, tikkis, sev, etc.

Flatbread snacks can be prepared from whole grain cereals, millets, pulses and legume flours and served with plenty of vegetables, sprouts, fruits, nuts and low-fat dairy products. These are low in calories, fat and sodium and high in vitamins, minerals and fibre. They provide good-quality protein, complex carbohydrates and fats. Small healthy snacks boost metabolism and help lose weight; they enhance mood, induce good sleep and improve overall physical and mental health.

Flatbread snacks are wholesome and nutritious. They are prepared with only one type of flour or with combinations, similar to other flatbreads.

FLATBREAD SNACKS MADE WITH WHOLEWHEAT FLOUR

KHAKRA (CRISP, THIN FLATBREAD)

SADA KHAKRA

Plain crisp, thin flatbread

Preparation time: 30 mins; Cooking time: 24 mins

Sada khakra is a thin, unleavened, traditional, thin, crisp, Gujarati snack made with wholewheat flour. Each khakra requires 20-25g of dough. They can be stored in an airtight containers for a week to 10 days.

Ingredients for 8 khakras

A pinch of salt or to taste

1 cup wholewheat flour

1 tsp oil

To cook the khakras

8 tsp oil

(Recipe Cont.)

Method

Prepare the dough as given for sada paratha (p. 22).

Divide the dough into 8 portions and shape them into balls.

Roll out each portion of dough on a lightly floured board into a circle, as thin as possible.

Grease a pan with ½ tsp oil and put it on medium heat.

Place a khakra on it.

When the base is slightly cooked, flip it over.

Press it down with a cloth, using a circular motion to make the base crisp and to prevent it from puffing up.

Pick it off the pan and sprinkle ½ tsp oil.

Return the khakra to the pan and press it down again, till the other side is crisp and golden brown.

Place it on a serving plate.

Repeat with the remaining portions of dough.

When cool, store them in an airtight container.

Serve as a teatime snack.

Nutritive values for 1 khakra: Calories: 105.0kcal; Carbohydrate: 8.7g; Protein: 1.5g; Fat: 7.1g; Minerals: 0.34g; Fibre: 0.24g.

Healthy modifications: Avoid adding fat to the dough.

Toast the khakras in a non-stick pan without oil. This will reduce 5g fat and 45kcal from each khakra.

MASALA KHAKRA

Spicy, crisp, thin flatbread

Preparation time: 30 mins; Cooking time: 24 mins

Masala khakra is made in the same way as sada khakra (p. 177).

Add 1 tsp ginger-garlic-green chilli paste, ¼ tsp turmeric powder, ¼ tsp red chilli powder and ¼ tsp cumin powder to the flour with the oil and mix well before adding the salt water.

Nutritive values for 1 khakra: Calories: 96.0kcal; Carbohydrate: 9.0g; Protein: 1.6g; Fat: 5.9g; Minerals: 0.38g; Fibre: 0.33g.

Healthy modifications: See sada khakra (p. 177).

METHI KHAKRA

Crisp, thin flatbread with fresh fenugreek leaves

Preparation time: 30 mins; Cooking time: 24 mins

Methi khakra is made in the same way as sada khakra (p. 177).

Add ½ cup minced fresh fenugreek leaves, 1 tsp carom seeds, 1 tsp sesame seeds, ¼ tsp turmeric powder and ¼ tsp red chilli powder to the flour with the oil and mix well before adding 2 tbsp of salt water.

Nutritive values for 1 khakra: Calories: 102.0kcal; Carbohydrate: 9.3g; Protein: 1.9g; Fat: 6.2g; Minerals: 0.48g; Fibre: 0.45g.

Healthy modifications: See sada khakra (p. 177).

KASOORI METHI KHAKRAS

Crisp, thin, flatbread with dried fenugreek leaves

Preparation time: 30 mins; Cooking time: 24 mins

Kasoori methi khakra is made in the same way as sada khakra (p. 177).

Add ½ cup dried fenugreek leaves, ¼ tsp turmeric powder and ¼ tsp red chilli powder to the flour with the oil and mix well before adding the salt water.

Nutritive values for 1 khakra: Calories: 98.0kcal; Carbohydrate: 9.0g; Protein: 1.7g; Fat: 5.9g; Minerals: 0.4g; Fibre: 0.31g.

Healthy modifications: See sada khakra (p. 177).

PUDINA KHAKRA

Crisp, thin flatbread with mint leaves

Preparation time: 30 mins; Cooking time: 24 mins

Pudina khakra is made in the same way as sada khakra (p. 177).

Add ½ cup minced mint leaves, ¼ tsp turmeric powder and ¼ tsp red chilli powder to the flour, with the oil and mix well before adding 2 tbsp of salt water.

Nutritive values for 1 khakra: Calories: 95.0kcal; Carbohydrate: 8.9g; Protein: 1.7g; Fat: 5.8g; Minerals: 0.34g; Fibre: 0.30g.

Healthy modifications: See sada khakra (p. 177).

SAVOURY BISCUIT BHAKRIS (THICK, SMALL BISCUITS)

JEERA BISCUIT BHAKRI

Flatbread with cumin seeds

Preparation time: 20 mins; Cooking time: 24 mins

Jeera bhakri is an unleavened, traditional, Gujarati and Rajasthani snack made with wholewheat flour and cumin seeds. Biscuit bhakris belong to Gujarati and Rajasthani cuisines. They are pressed while being cooked to prevent them from puffing up, which makes them crunchy, as against puffed bhakris which are soft. Biscuit bhakris are also shallow-fried.

Ingredients for 6 bhakris

A pinch of salt or to taste

1 cup wholewheat flour

2 tsp cumin seeds

4 tbsp oil

To cook the bhakri

6 tsp ghee

Method

Dissolve the salt in 1 tbsp of water.

Mix the flour and cumin seeds in a bowl.

Rub the oil into the flour.

Prepare the dough as given for sada paratha (p. 22).

Divide the dough into 6 portions and roll them out into 2½" circles.

Cook them in the same way as given for sada khakra (p. 177).

When cool, store them in an airtight container.

Nutritive values for 1 bhakri: Calories: 215.0kcal; Carbohydrate: 12.2g; Protein: 2.3g; Fat: 15.5g; Minerals: 0.55g; Fibre: 0.52g.

Healthy modifications: See sada khakra (p. 177).

JEERA BISCUIT BHAKRI OPEN SANDWICH

Preparation time: 25 mins; Cooking time: 8 mins

Jeera biscuit bhakri open sandwich is a traditional snack in which the bhakri is topped with mint chutney and grated carrot.

Ingredients for 2 sandwiches

The mint chutney

100g mint leaves

A pinch of salt or to taste

1 tbsp tamarind pulp

The seasoning

1 tsp oil

½ tsp mustard-cumin seeds

A few fenugreek seeds

1 green chilli, roughly chopped

1 dried red chilli

The sandwich

2 jeera biscuit bhakris (p. 179)

4 tsp grated carrot

(Recipe Cont.)

Method

Pluck out the mint leaves, wash and drain them thoroughly.

Roast the mint leaves lightly or a tava or griddle for a few mins.

Heat the oil for the seasoning and sauté the seasoning ingredients, till fragrant. Leave aside, till cool.

Grind the seasoning ingredients, mint leaves, salt and tamarind to a smooth paste.

Apply 2 tsp of chutney on each bhakri. Sprinkle 2 tsp grated carrot on top and serve immediately.

Nutritive values for 1 sandwich: Calories: 290.0 kcal; Carbohydrate: 20.5g; Protein: 5.2g; Fat: 18.8g; Minerals: 1.8g; Fibre: 1.9g.

Healthy modifications: See sada khakra (p. 177).

KASOORI METHI BISCUIT BHAKRI

Flatbread with dried fenugreek leaves

Preparation time: 20 mins; Cooking time: 24 mins

Kasoori methi biscuit bhakri is made in the same way as jeera biscuit bhakri (p. 179). Use 2 tsp dried fenugreek leaves instead of the cumin seeds.

Nutritive values for 1 bhakri: Calories: 193.0kcal; Carbohydrate: 11.7g; Protein: 2.1g; Fat: 15.3g; Minerals: 0.48g; Fibre: 0.34g.

Healthy modifications: See sada khakra (p. 177).

KASOORI METHI BISCUIT BHAKRI OPEN SANDWICH

Preparation time: 25 mins; Cooking time: 8 mins

Kasoori methi biscuit bhakri open sandwich is a traditional snack in which each bhakri is topped with 2 tsp thick curd and 1 tsp chopped capsicum.

Nutritive values for 1 sandwich: Calories: 200.0kcal; Carbohydrate: 12.2g; Protein: 2.5g; Fat: 15.7g; Minerals: 0.6g; Fibre: 0.39g.

Healthy modifications: See sada khakra (p. 177).

KALONJI BISCUIT BHAKRI

Flatbread with nigella seeds

Preparation time: 20 mins; Cooking time: 24 mins

Kalonji biscuit bhakri is made in the same way as jeera biscuit bhakri (p. 179). Use 2 tsp nigella seeds instead of the cumin seeds.

Nutritive values for 1 bhakri: Calories: 198.0kcal; Carbohydrate: 12.0g; Protein: 2.3g; Fat: 15.7g; Minerals: 0.58g; Fibre: 0.67g.

Healthy modifications: See sada khakra (p. 177).

KALONJI BISCUIT BHAKRI OPEN SANDWICH

Preparation time: 25 mins; Cooking time: 24 mins

Kalonji biscuit bhakri open sandwich is a traditional snack in which each bhakri is topped with 2 tsp garlic chutney (p. 66) and 1 tsp shredded cabbage.

Nutritive values for 1 sandwich: Calories: 219.0kcal; Carbohydrate: 16.2g; Protein: 3.3g; Fat: 15.8g; Minerals: 0.8g; Fibre: 1.1g.

Healthy modifications: See sada khakra (p. 177).

PARATHA SANDWICH

Preparation time: 30 mins; Cooking time: 30 mins

Parathas are coated with different chutneys and stuffed with mixed sprouts or vegetables.

Ingredients for 2 sandwiches

The filling

2 cups mixed sprouts, boiled

1 tsp oil

2 tsp ginger-garlic-green chilli paste

1 tbsp lime juice

A pinch of salt or to taste

The sandwich

Tomato chutney (p.219)

Mint chutney (p.180)

4 sada parathas (p. 22)

Method

Boil the sprouts in salt water, till tender. Mash well.

Heat the oil and sauté the ginger-garlic-green chilli paste for a minute.

Mix all the filling ingredients together and divide into 2 portions.

Mix the tomato and the mint chutneys and spread it over the parathas.

Spread a portion of the filling evenly on 2 parathas and cover them with the remaining. Press down gently.

Serve immediately.

Nutritive values for 1 sandwich: Calories: 541.0kcal; Carbohydrate: 82.1g; Protein: 17.7g; Fat: 16.2g; Minerals: 4.8g; Fibre: 7.1g.

PARATHA PIZZA WITH MIXED SPROUTS

Preparation time: 30 mins; Cooking time: 30 mins

Paratha pizza is an unleavened, innovative snack, topped with a spicy sprout curry and garnished with grated cheese and mixed capsicums. Crisp parathas made with wholewheat flour are used as the base. It is a one-dish meal, as it offers good-quality macro and micro nutrients.

Ingredients for 1 pizza

Dough to make 1 sada paratha (p. 22)

The topping

3 tomatoes, roughly chopped

1 onion, roughly chopped

3 cloves garlic, roughly chopped

2 green chillies, roughly chopped

1" piece ginger, roughly chopped

1 cup mixed sprouts

½ tsp garam masala powder

A pinch of salt or to taste

The garnish

Red, yellow and green capsicum chunks

1 tsp oil

1 tbsp grated cheese, grated

A few strips of red, yellow and green capsicum

A few parsley leaves

Method

Knead the dough and shape it into a ball.

Roll out the dough on a lightly floured board into a 6" circle.

Put a non-stick pan on medium heat and toast the paratha, till golden brown at the base. Keep it aside.

(Method Cont.)

Blend the tomatoes, onion, garlic, green chillies and ginger to make a smooth paste.

Pour it into a pan and bring it a boil.

Mix in the sprouts, garam masala powder and the salt and cook till the contents are tender and dry.

Roast the capsicum chunks in a non-stick pan for a minute.

Place the uncooked surface of the flatbread on a hot pan on low heat.

Spread the sprout topping evenly over the cooked surface.

Pour 1 tsp oil over its edges.

Sprinkle grated cheese over the topping.

Arrange the capsicum chunks around the edges and decorate the centre with the strips.

Cover the pizza with a plate and allow it to cook, till the base is golden brown.

Garnish with parsley leaves and serve hot with sweet-hot tomato sauce.

Nutritive values for 1 paratha pizza: Calories: 542.0kcal; Carbohydrate: 99.2g; Protein: 23.6g; Fat: 5.4g; Minerals: 5.6g; Fibre: 5.0g.

SOYA CUTLET CHAPATTI WRAP

Preparation time: 30 mins; Cooking time: 30 mins

Soya cutlet chapatti wrap is an unleavened, innovative flatbread snack.

Ingredients for 4 wraps

The filling

1 cup soya granules

2 potatoes

A pinch of salt

1 tsp ginger-garlic-green chilli paste

½ cup mixed herbs, chopped

The batter

½ cup gram flour (besan)

2 tbsp semolina

A pinch of salt or to taste

To cook the cutlets

4 tsp oil

The wraps

4 hot sada chapattis, toasted without oil (p. 66)

The topping

4 tsp shredded lettuce, shredded

4 tsp sweet-n-sour tomato sauce or any chutney

Method

Soak the soya granules in boiling hot water for 10 mins and squeeze. Rinse them with fresh water twice and squeeze again.

Wash the potatoes, peel and boil them with a pinch of salt. Mash well.

Mix all the filling ingredients in a bowl.

Divide the filling into 4 portions and shape them into cutlets.

(Method Cont.)

Mix all the batter ingredients in a bowl.

Gradually add a little water at a time and mix to form a thick, coating batter.

Put a non-stick pan on medium heat and smear it with 1 tsp oil.

Dip a soya cutlet in the batter and pan-fry it, till golden and crisp on both sides.

Repeat with the remaining soya cutlets.

Shape each chapatti into a cone.

Place a soya cutlet in it with 1 tsp shredded lettuce.

Top with 1 tsp sauce or chutney and serve immediately.

Nutritive values for 1 wrap: Calories: 218.0kcal; Carbohydrates: 41.6g; Protein: 9.6g; Fat: 1.4g; Minerals: 1.7g; Fibre: 1.2g.

PARATHA PIZZA WITH MIXED VEGETABLES

Preparation time: 30 mins; Cooking time: 30 mins

This paratha pizza is made in the same way as the one with mixed sprouts (p. 182).

Substitute grated mixed vegetables for the sprouts and pav bhaji masala for the garam masala powder. Garnish with grated cheese, a few strips of carrots and a few celery leaves.

Nutritive values for 1 paratha pizza: Calories: 472.0kcal; Carbohydrate: 91.6g; Protein: 19.8g; Fat: 5.0g; Minerals: 5.4g; Fibre: 4.3g.

CORN AND CHICKPEA ROLL

Preparation time: 20 mins; Cooking time: 30 mins

Corn and chickpea roll is an unleavened, innovative flatbread snack.

Ingredients for 2 rolls

The coriander chutney

100g fresh coriander leaves

2 green chillies

A pinch of salt or to taste

The filling

4 tbsp chickpeas, boiled

2 cups corn kernels, boiled

1 tbsp fresh rosemary leaves

1 tsp oil

½ tsp mustard-cumin seeds

2 tsp ginger-garlic-green chilli paste

The rolls

2 hot sada chapattis, toasted without oil (p. 66)

Method

Blend the chutney ingredients to make a smooth paste.

Divide it into 2 portions.

Blend the chickpeas to make a paste.

Mix the chick pea paste with the corn and rosemary leaves in a bowl.

Heat the oil in a pan and sauté the mustard-cumin seeds, till they splutter.

Add the ginger-garlic-green chilli paste and sauté for a minute.

Stir in the chickpea paste and simmer for a few mins.

Divide the filling into 2 portions and shape each portion into a cylinder.

Spread a layer of coriander chutney over each chapatti.

(Method Cont.)

Put the filling along one side of the chapatti and roll it gently.

Serve hot with sweet-n-hot sauce.

Nutritive values for 1 roll: Calories: 400.0kcal; Carbohydrates: 69.8g; Protein: 16.0g; Fat: 6.3g; Minerals: 4.8g; Fibre 4.7g.

CHAPATTI CONE WITH SPICY CAPSICUM

Preparation time: 20 mins; Cooking time: 15 mins

Chapatti cones stuffed with spicy capsicum.

Ingredients for 2 cones

The seasoning

2 tsp oil

½ tsp mustard-cumin seeds

The filling

1 green capsicum, cut into juliennes

1 red capsicum, cut into juliennes

1 yellow capsicum, cut into juliennes

2 tsp dry garlic chutney powder

A pinch of salt or to taste

The cones

2 hot chapattis toasted without oil (p. 66)

Method

Heat the oil and sauté the mustard-cumin seeds, till they splutter.

Add the filling ingredients and sauté on high heat for a few mins.

Divide the filling into 2 portions.

Shape each chapatti into a cone and fill with one portion of filling.

Serve immediately.

Nutritive values for 1 cone: Calories: 188.0kcal; Carbohydrates: 28.0g; Protein: 5.6g; Fat: 6.0g; Minerals: 2.5g; Fibre: 1.7g.

CHAPATTI CONE WITH TEEKHA PANEER

Preparation time: 20 mins; Cooking time: 20 mins

Chapatti cone with teekha paneer is an unleavened, traditional flatbread and a popular street food made with wholewheat flour and stuffed with spicy paneer.

Ingredients for 2 cones

The seasoning

1 tsp sesame oil

½ tsp mustard seeds

¼ tsp fenugreek seeds

¼ tsp asafoetida powder

1 dried red chilli

The onion chutney

4 onions, sliced

1 tbsp tamarind pulp

A pinch of salt or to taste

The filling

2 tbsp dried fenugreek leaves

100g paneer, cubed

Tomato chutney (p. 219)

A pinch of salt or to taste

The cones

2 hot chapattis toasted without oil (p. 66)

Method

Heat the oil for the seasoning and sauté the seasoning ingredients for a minute.

Add the onions and sauté for 2-3 mins.

Remove from heat and leave aside, till cool.

Grind the onions with the tamarind pulp and salt to make a smooth paste. (Store it in an airtight jar and place it in the refrigerator, till ready to use.)

(Method Cont.)

Soak the fenugreek leaves in hot water for 10 mins. Drain.

Put a non-stick pan on medium heat and toast the paneer cubes for a few mins.

Mix in the fenugreek leaves, onion chutney, tomato chutney and salt and simmer for a few mins, till the contents are dry.

Divide the filling into 2 portions.

Shape each chapatti into a cone and fill with one portion of filling.

Serve immediately.

Nutritive values for 1 cone: Calories: 535.0kcal; Carbohydrates: 43.8g; Protein: 16.6g; Fat: 32.4g; Minerals: 4.5g; Fibre: 2.7g.

CHAPATTI CONE WITH BROWN RICE, MIXED SPROUTS AND VEGETABLES

Preparation time: 25 mins; Cooking time: 30 mins

Smear 2 sada chapattis with mint chutney (p. 180) and stuff them with a mixture of 1 cup each of cooked brown rice, mixed sprouts and shredded cabbage, 1 grated carrot 1 chopped tomato shell and salt. Top with tomato chutney (p. 219), garnish with sweet basil and serve immediately.

Nutritive values for 1 cone: Calories: 406.0kcal; Carbohydrates: 60.2g; Protein: 13.4g; Fat: 12.4g; Minerals: 5.0g; Fibre: 4.5g.

NAMKEEN PITHA

Spicy steamed flatbread

Preparation time: 20 mins; Cooking time: 30 mins

Namkeen pitha is an unleavened, traditional snack made with wholewheat flour, stuffed with a spicy filling and boiled in water. They are known in Bengal as pithe and as fara in Uttar Pradesh. They can also be made with rice flour.

Ingredients for 8 pithas

The filling

1 cup husked, split Bengal gram (chana dal)

A pinch of salt or to taste

2 tsp oil

2 tsp ginger-green chilli paste

¼ tsp turmeric powder

¼ tsp red chilli powder

¼ tsp asafoetida powder

¼ tsp dried mango powder

¼ tsp aniseed powder

1 tsp garam masala powder

The dough

A pinch of salt or to taste

1 cup wholewheat flour

½ tsp oil

(Recipe Cont.)

Method

Wash the dal and soak it in water for a few hours.

Drain and grind it with the salt to make a smooth paste.

Heat the oil and sauté the ginger–green chilli paste for a minute.

Mix in the dal paste and the spice powders.

Dissolve the salt for the dough in 5 tbsp of water.

Prepare the dough as given for sada chapatti (p. 66).

Divide the dough and filling into 8 portions.

Roll out a portion of dough on a lightly floured board into a 4″ circle.

Spread a portion of filling on half the roti and fold the other half over it. Gently seal the edges with moist fingertips.

Repeat with the remaining dough and filling portions.

Boil water in a large pan with ½ tsp oil.

Carefully drop in the pithas.

Boil them for 15-20 mins.

Drain thoroughly.

Serve hot with any chutney.

Nutritive values for 1 pitha: Calories: 110.0kcal; Carbohydrates: 16.9g; Protein: 4.4g; Fat: 2.7g; Minerals: 3.1g; Fibre: 0.6g.

LITTIS

Hard bread balls

Preparation time: 20 mins; Cooking time: 20 mins

Litti is a hard, fried, unleavened, traditional bread made with wholewheat flour and stuffed with a sattu mixture. It is served in winter with an aubergine curry, choka in Bihar as a breakfast dish and as an evening snack with ghee.

Ingredients for 4 littis

The sattu filling

4 tbsp gram flour (besan)

1 tsp cumin seeds, roasted

½ tsp carom seeds (ajwain)

½ tsp red chilli powder

1 tsp dried mango powder

1 onion, chopped

2 tsp ginger-garlic-green chilli paste

2 tbsp coriander leaves

1 tbsp lime juice

The dough

A pinch of salt or to taste

1 cup wholewheat flour

½ tsp carom seeds (ajwain)

½ tsp nigella seeds

To cook the littis

Oil for deep-frying

To serve

2 tsp ghee

(Recipe Cont.)

Method

Roast the gram flour in a pan on medium heat, till golden brown.

Mix the roasted gram flour with the remaining filling ingredients in a bowl.

Divide the filling into 4 portions.

Dissolve the salt for the dough in 5 tbsp of water.

Mix the flour with the carom and nigella seeds in a bowl.

Prepare the dough as given for sada chapatti (p. 66).

Divide the dough into 4 portions.

Prepare the littis as given for bedmi puri (p. 76) and shape them into balls.

Heat the oil in a kadhai or wok and fry the littis, till crisp and light brown.

Drain on layers of tissue paper.

Spoon ½ tsp ghee over each litti.

Serve with a hot aubergine curry.

Nutritive values for 1 litti: Calories: 242.0kcal; Carbohydrates: 31.3g; Protein: 7.2g; Fat: 9.6g; Minerals: 1.6g; Fibre: 1.9g.

Healthy modifications: Avoid frying the littis. Bake them in an oven.

Replace ghee with oil.

Avoid spooning ghee over the littis.

BAATI

Hard bread

Preparation time: 20 mins; Cooking time: 20 mins

Baati is a hard, unleavened, traditional snack made with wholewheat flour which is crushed and added to a spicy dal called panchmel dal (p. 233). It is a delicacy served during festivals and weddings with churma (p. 160), which is also made with crushed baatis mixed with jaggery. This one-dish meal is called dal baati churma and is famous in Rajasthani cuisine.

Ingredients for 4 baati

The dough

1 cup wholewheat flour

A pinch of salt or to taste

2 tbsp ghee

½ cup curd

The topping

2 tsp ghee

(Recipe Cont.)

Method

Mix the flour, salt, ghee and curd in a bowl and prepare a dough as given for palak paratha (p. 24).

Divide the dough into 4 portions and shape them into balls.

Traditionally the balls are roasted on hot coals, till they puff up and turn golden.

Alternatively, bake them in an oven preheated to 180°C, till crisp and golden. Turn them occasionally, to ensure even cooking.

Spoon ½ tsp ghee over each baati to keep it moist.

Break them into pieces in a serving plate and pour panchmel dal over it.

Serve with churma.

Nutritive values for 1 baati: Calories: 183.0kcal; Carbohydrates: 17.7g; Protein: 3.4g; Fat: 10.9g; Minerals: 0.78g; Fibre: 0.48g.

Healthy modifications: Avoid roasting the baatis on charcoal as it is harmful for health.

Avoid frying the baatis. Bake them in an oven.

Replace ghee with oil.

Avoid topping the baatis with ghee.

MATTAR BAATI

Hard bread with green pea filling

Preparation time: 20 mins; Cooking time: 20 mins

Mattar baati is a hard unleavened, traditional Rajasthani snack stuffed with green peas.

Ingredients for 4 baatis

The filling

1 cup shelled green peas

A pinch of salt or to taste

2 tsp ginger-garlic-green chilli paste

¼ tsp red chilli powder

The dough

Dough to make 4 baatis (p. 188)

The topping

2 tsp ghee

Method

Boil the green peas with salt till tender. Mash well.

Mix the mashed green peas with the remaining filling ingredients.

Divide the filling and dough into 4 portions.

Make the baatis as given for bedmi puri (p. 76) and shape them into balls.

Cook them as given for baatis (p. 188).

Alternatively, boil them for 10-15 mins, drain and then deep-fry them in oil.

Spoon ½ tsp of ghee over each baati to keep them moist.

Nutritive values for 1 baati: Calories: 210.0kcal; Carbohydrates: 22.3g; Protein: 5.3g; Fat: 11.0g; Minerals: 1.0g; Fibre: 1.6g.

Healthy modifications: See baati (p. 188).

BAFLA

Soft bread balls

Preparation time: 20 mins; Cooking time: 20 mins

Bafla is a soft baati, first boiled in water, drained and then fried. It is served with panchmel dal (p. 233). This one-dish meal is popular in Rajasthan.

Ingredients for 4 baflas

Dough to make baatis (p. 188)

Oil for deep-frying

Method

Divide the dough into 2 portions and shape them into balls.

Put the balls into a pan of boiling water and boil for a few mins, till soft. Drain thoroughly.

Alternatively, steam the balls for a few mins.

Heat the oil in a kadhai or wok and fry the baflas, till crisp and golden.

Drain them on layers of tissue paper.

Break a bafla to pieces in a serving plate.

Pour panchmel dal over it.

Nutritive values for 1 bafla: Calories: 205.0kcal; Carbohydrate: 17.7g; Protein: 3.4g; Fat: 13.4g; Minerals: 0.78g; Fibre: 0.48g.

Healthy modifications: Avoid frying the dough balls. Bake them in an oven preheated to 180°C.

FLATBREAD SNACKS MADE WITH REFINED WHEAT FLOUR

JEERA MATTIRI

Fried flatbread with cumin

Preparation time: 15 mins; Cooking time: 4 mins

Jeera mattiri is a leavened, traditional, fried, Punjabi flatbread made with refined wheat flour and cumin seeds.

Ingredients for 4 mattiris

A pinch of salt or to taste

1 cup refined wheat flour

2 tsp cumin seeds

½ tsp baking soda

1 tbsp ghee

2 tbsp curd

Oil for deep-frying

(Recipe Cont.)

Method

Dissolve the salt in 2 tbsp of water.

Mix the flour, cumin seeds and baking soda in a bowl.

Stir in the ghee and curd.

Gradually add the salt water and prepare the dough as given for sada paratha (p. 22).

Divide the dough into 4 portions and shape them into balls.

Roll out each portion of dough on a lightly floured board into a 2"- 3" circle.

Prick them evenly all over with a fork.

Heat the oil in a kadhai or wok and fry the mattiris, till crisp and golden.

Drain them on layers of tissue paper.

When cool, store them in an airtight container.

Nutritive values for 1 mattiri: Calories: 179.0kcal; Carbohydrate: 19.6g; Protein: 3.5g; Fat: 9.7g; Minerals: 0.36g; Fibre: 0.38g.

Healthy modifications: Avoid adding ghee to the dough. This will reduce 15g fat and 135kcal in the dough.

Use wholewheat flour or replace half the refined flour with it.

Bake the mattiris instead of deep-frying them.

KHASTA KACHORI

Fried flatbread with mung filling

Preparation time: 30 mins; Cooking time: 8 mins

Khasta kachori is a leavened, traditional, fried flatbread made with refined wheat flour and stuffed with husked, split mung, served in Rajasthan and Uttar Pradesh.

Ingredients for 8 kachoris

The filling

4 tbsp husked, split mung

2 tsp ghee

1 tsp cumin seeds

2 tsp ginger-garlic-green chilli paste

1 tsp aniseed, coarsely powdered

1 tsp coriander seeds, coarsely powdered

1 tsp cumin seeds, coarsely powdered

¼ tsp asafoetida powder

½ tsp dried mango powder

½ tsp red chilli powder

½ tsp garam masala powder (clove, cinnamon, black cardamom, caraway seeds, bay leaf)

2 tbsp gram flour (besan), roasted

A pinch of salt or to taste

Coriander-mint-tamarind chutney

2 cups coriander leaves

1 cup mint leaves

2 tbsp tamarind pulp

2 small green chillies

A pinch of salt or to taste

The dough

A pinch of salt or to taste

1 cup refined wheat flour

½ tsp baking powder

(Recipe Cont.)

2 tbsp ghee

To fry the kachoris

Oil for deep-frying

The topping

2 onions, chopped

½ cup coriander leaves, chopped

½ cup sev

Method

Wash the dal and soak it in water for a few hours. Drain and grind to make a coarse paste.

Heat the ghee in a pan and sauté the cumin seeds, till they splutter.

Add the ginger-garlic-green chilli paste and sauté for a minute.

Add the dal paste and sauté for a few mins.

Mix in all the spice powders, roasted gram flour and the salt.

Divide the filling into 8 portions and leave aside, till cool.

Grind all the chutney ingredients and leave aside.

Dissolve the salt for the dough in 50 ml of water.

Mix the flour and the baking powder in a bowl.

Prepare the dough as given for sada paratha (p. 22).

Divide the dough into 8 portions.

Make the kachoris and fry them as given for bedmi puri (p. 76).

Sprinkle the toppings and chutney over them and serve immediately.

Nutritive values for 1 kachori: Calories: 213.0kcal; Carbohydrate: 23.0g; Protein: 5.4g; Fat: 11.0g; Minerals: 0.97g; Fibre: .2g.

Healthy modifications: Avoid adding fat to the dough.

Use wholewheat flour instead of refined wheat flour.

Bake instead of frying.

MASALA MATTIRI

Spicy fried flatbread

Preparation time: 15 mins; Cooking time: 4 mins

Masala mattiri is made in the same way as jeera mattiri (p. 190).

Replace the cumin seeds with 1 tsp garam masala powder.

Nutritive values for 1 mattiri: Calories: 174.0kcal; Carbohydrate: 19.3g; Protein: 3.1g; Fat: 9.4g; Minerals: 0.28g; Fibre: 0.19g.

Healthy modifications: See jeera mattiri (p. 190).

KASOORI METHI MATTIRI

Fried flatbread with dried fenugreek leaves

Preparation time: 15 mins; Cooking time: 4 mins

Kasoori methi mattiri is made in the same way as jeera mattiri (p. 190).

Replace the cumin seeds with 1 tbsp dried fenugreek leaves soaked in water for 10 mins.

Nutritive values for 1 mattiri: Calories: 171.0kcal; Carbohydrate: 18.8g; Protein: 3.0g; Fat: 9.3g; Minerals: 0.23g; Fibre: 0.01g.

Healthy modifications: See jeera mattiri (p. 190).

FLATBREAD SNACKS MADE WITH OTHER FLOURS

BAJRA KHAKRA

Crisp, toasted pearl millet flatbread

Preparation time: 30 mins; Cooking time: 24 mins

Bajra khakra is an unleavened, traditional, thin, crisp Gujarati flatbread made in the same way as sada khakra (p. 177).

Make the dough with ½ cup pearl millet flour, ½ cup wholewheat flour, 2 tbsp roasted sesame seeds, ¼ tsp turmeric powder and ¼ tsp red chilli powder. Cook them as given for sada khakra and garnish with curd and chaat masala before serving them.

Nutritive values for 1 khakra: Calories: 110.0kcal; Carbohydrate: 9.5g; Protein: 2.1g; Fat: 7.0g; Minerals: 0.5g; Fibre: 0.3g.

Healthy modifications: Toast the khakra in a non-stick pan without fat. This will reduce 5g fat and 45kcal for each khakra.

MAKKAI MATHRI

Maize flatbread

Preparation time: 15 mins; Cooking time: 3 mins

Makkai mathri is an unleavened, traditional, fried snack made with maize flour in Rajasthan and refined wheat flour in Punjab.

Ingredients for 6 mathris

A pinch of salt or to taste

1 cup maize flour

2 tsp garlic paste

¼ tsp red chilli powder

Oil for deep-frying

Method

Dissolve the salt in 4½ tbsp of water.

Mix the maize flour, garlic paste and chilli powder in a bowl.

Prepare the dough as given for sada paratha (p. 22).

Divide the dough into 6 portions and shape them into balls.

Press a dough ball on a greased plastic sheet into a 3" circle.

Pinch the edges of the mathri and prick the surface evenly with a fork.

Repeat with the remaining portions of dough.

Heat the oil in a kadhai or wok and fry the mathris, till crisp and golden.

Drain on layers of tissue paper.

When cool, store in an airtight container.

Nutritive values for 1 mathri: Calories: 105.0kcal; Carbohydrate: 11.5g; Protein: 2.0g; Fat: 5.6g; Minerals: 0.27g; Fibre: 0.46g.

Healthy modifications: Bake the mathris instead of deep-frying them.

SOYA KHAKRA

Crispy soya flatbread

Preparation time: 30 mins; Cooking time: 24 mins

Soya khakra is an unleavened, traditional, Gujarati snack made in the same way as bajra khakra (p. 192). Replace the pearl millet flour with soya flour.

Nutritive values for 1 khakra: Calories: 115.0kcal; Carbohydrate: 6.6g; Protein: 4.1g; Fat: 8.0g; Minerals: 0.52g; Fibre: 0.36g.

Healthy modifications: See bajra khakra (p. 192).

RAGI/MANDUA KHAKRA

Crispy finger millet flatbread

Preparation time: 30 mins; Cooking time: 24 mins

Ragi/mandua khakra is an traditional Gujarati snack made in the same way as bajra khakra (p. 192). Replace the pearl millet with finger millet.

Nutritive values for 1 khakra: Calories: 108.0kcal; Carbohydrate: 9.8g; Protein: 1.9g; Fat: 6.9g; Minerals: 0.53g; Fibre: 0.45g.

Healthy modifications: See bajra khakra (p. 192).

MULTIGRAIN KHAKRA

Crisp multi grain toasted flatbread

Preparation time: 30 mins; Cooking time: 24 mins

Multigrain khakra is a crisp unleavened, traditional Gujarati snack made in the same way as bajra khakra (p. 192). Replace the pearl millet and wheat flours with 1 cup of multigrain flour and omit the sesame seeds.

Nutritive values for 1 khakra: Calories: 89.0kcal; Carbohydrate: 6.9g; Protein: 1.1g; Fat: 5.3g; Minerals: 0.23g; Fibre: 0.19g.

Healthy modifications: See bajra khakra (p. 192).

JOWAR BAATI

Hard sorghum flatbread

Preparation time: 20 mins; Cooking time: 10 mins

Jowar baati is a hard, unleavened, traditional snack made with sorghum flour in the tribal communities of Andhra Pradesh. They are harder than wheat baatis.

Ingredients for 2 baatis

1 cup sorghum (jowar) flour

A pinch of salt or to taste

Method

Prepare the dough as given for sada chapatti (p. 66).

Divide it into 2 portions and shape them into balls.

Traditionally, baatis are roasted on hot coals, till they puff up and turn golden. Bake them in an oven preheated to 180°C for about 5 mins on each side.

Serve with onion slices, a pickle and a pachadi.

Nutritive values for 1 baati: Calories: 175.0kcal; Carbohydrate: 36.3g; Protein: 5.2g; Fat: 1.0g; Minerals: 0.8g; Fibre: 0.8g.

BESAN MATHRI

Fried gram flour flatbread

Preparation time: 20 mins; Cooking time: 4 mins

Besan mathris are unleavened, traditional, Rajasthani snacks made with gram flour. They are similar to the Punjabi mattiris, which are made with refined wheat flour.

Ingredients for 8 mathris

A pinch of salt or to taste

1 cup gram flour (besan)

2 tsp garlic paste

¼ tsp red chilli powder

Oil for frying

Method

Dissolve the salt in 50 ml of water.

Mix the gram flour, garlic paste and the chilli powder in a bowl.

Prepare the dough and fry the mattiris as given for makkai mathri (p. 193).

Serve with a pickle.

Nutritive values for 1 mattiri: Calories: 93.0kcal; Carbohydrates: 7.8g; Protein: 2.7g; Fat: 5.7g; Minerals: 0.35g; Fibre: 0.2g.

Healthy modifications: Toast the mathris on a pan or bake them in an oven preheated to 180°C.

SOYA-PANEER PARATHA

Tofu-paneer crisp flatbread

Preparation time: 20 mins; Cooking time: 10 mins

This is an unleavened, innovative flatbread, resembling a simple pizza. It is made with multigrain flour and topped with spicy tofu.

Ingredients for 2 parathas

The topping

4 tsp oil

2 tsp ginger-garlic-green chilli paste

200g tofu, crumbled

1 cup julienned mixed capsicums (red, yellow and green)

1 onion, minced

½ cup green peas, shelled and boiled

½ cup sweet corn kernels, boiled

½ tsp garam masala powder, mixed with water to a paste

A pinch of salt or to taste

The dough

1 cup multigrain flour

To serve

8 tsp tomato chutney (p. 219)

½ cup coriander leaves, chopped

Method

Heat the oil and sauté the ginger-garlic-green chilli paste for a few seconds.

Add the remaining filling ingredients, mix well and sauté for a few mins.

Divide the filling into 2 portions and leave aside, till cool.

Prepare the dough as given for sada chapatti (p. 66) and divide it into 2 portions.

(Method Cont.)

Roll out a portion of the dough on a lightly floured board into a 6" circle.

Put a non-stick pan on medium heat and toast the paratha, till golden brown and crisp on both sides.

Repeat with the remaining portion of dough.

Spread the tomato chutney over the parathas and cover with the filling. Sprinkle with coriander leaves and serve immediately.

Nutritive values for 1 paratha: Calories: 431.0kcal; Carbohydrate: 55.5g; Protein: 17.9g; Fat: 15.9g; Minerals: 1.4g; Fibre: 2.7g.

PARSI BHAKRA

Fried flatbread

Preparation time: 10 mins; Cooking time: 15 mins

Bhakra is a leavened, traditional fried Parsi snack.

Ingredients for 10 bhakras

1 cup wholewheat flour

½ cup semolina

¼ tsp baking powder

½ tsp green cardamom powder

½ tsp nutmeg powder

A pinch of salt or to taste

½ cup sugar, powdered

1 egg, beaten

½ cup curd

1 tbsp ghee

½ tsp vanilla essence

Oil for deep-frying

(Recipe Cont.)

Method

Mix the flour, semolina, baking powder, cardamom powder, nutmeg powder and salt in a bowl.

Add the sugar to the egg and mix in the curd, ghee and vanilla essence.

Stir the egg and the curd mixture into the flour. Mix well.

Knead it for about 10 mins to make a smooth dough.

Cover the dough and leave it aside for about 20 mins.

Knead the dough again for about 5 mins and divide it into 10 portions. Shape them into balls.

Roll out the balls on a lightly floured board into 2"- 3" circles.

Heat the oil in a kadhai or wok and fry the bhakras, till golden brown.

Drain on layers of tissue paper.

When cool, store them in an airtight container.

Serve hot with masala chai.

Nutritive values for 1 bhakra: Calories: 124.0kcal; Carbohydrates: 15.8g; Protein: 2.6g; Fat: 5.6g; Minerals: 0.36g; Fibre: 0.2g.

Healthy modifications: Avoid adding fat to the flour while preparing dough.

Bake the flatbreads in the oven instead of deep-frying.

FLATBREAD SNACKS MADE WITH SEMOLINA AND REFINED WHEAT FLOUR

DAHI BATATA PURI

Small flatbreads with curd and tangy, crunchy toppings

Preparation time: 20 mins; Cooking time: 10 mins

Dahi batata puri is a variation of sev batata puri (p. 198).

Prepare the sev batata puri and spoon 1 cup of thick curd whisked with 2 tsp of sugar over it. Sprinkle chaat masala powder on top and serve.

Nutritive values for 1 serving: Calories: 278.0kcal; Carbohydrates: 42.9g; Protein: 6.2g; Fat: 9.9g; Minerals: 1.4g; Fibre: 1.7g.

Healthy modifications: See sev puri (p. 198).

FLAT PURIS

Preparation time: 20 mins; Cooking time: 10 mins

Flat puris are leavened, traditional flatbreads made with semolina and refined wheat flour. They are used in street foods across the country and are available in the market in packets of 50 or 100 puris.

Ingredients for 28 puris

A pinch of salt or to taste

¾ cup semolina

¼ cup refined wheat flour

¼ tsp baking soda

Oil for deep-frying

Method

Dissolve the salt in 5 tbsp of warm water.

Mix the semolina, flour and the baking soda in a bowl.

Prepare the dough as given for sada chapatti (p. 66).

Divide the dough into 4 portions and shape them into balls.

Roll each ball on a lightly floured board as thin as possible.

Cut out 1" circles using a biscuit cutter or steel cup.

Roll out the remaining dough and cut out more puris.

Prick the puris all over with a fork.

Heat the oil in a kadhai or wok and fry the puris in batches, till crisp and light brown.

Drain them on layers of tissue papers.

Nutritive values for 1 puri: Calories: 29.0kcal; Carbohydrates: 2.7g; Protein: 0.38g; Fat: 1.8g; Minerals: nil; Fibre: nil.

Healthy modifications: Toast the flatbreads in a non-stick pan or bake in an oven preheated to 180°C.

FARSI PURI

Crisp fried flatbread

Preparation time: 20 mins; Cooking time: 10 mins

Farsi puris are unleavened, traditional, Gujarati flatbreads. Farsi means crisp in Gujarati.

Ingredients for 8 puris

A pinch of salt or to taste

1 cup refined wheat flour

2 tbsp semolina

½ tsp cumin seeds

½ tsp carom seeds (ajwain)

Oil for deep-frying

Method

Dissolve the salt in 6 tbsp of water.

Mix the flour, semolina, cumin seeds and carom seeds in a bowl.

Prepare the dough as given for sada chapatti (p. 66).

Divide the dough into 8 portions and roll them out into 3" circles.

Heat the oil in a kadhai or wok and fry the puris, till crisp and golden.

Drain them on layers of tissue paper.

Serve with a sweet and sour mango pickle.

Nutritive values for 1 puri: Calories: 104.0kcal; Carbohydrates: 12.2g; Protein: 1.9g; Fat: 5.3g; Minerals: 0.12g; Fibre: 0.17g.

Healthy modifications: Toast the flatbreads in a non-stick pan or bake in an oven preheated to 180°C.

SEV PURI

Small flatbreads with tangy, crunchy toppings

Preparation time: 5 mins; Cooking time: nil

Sev puri is a popular traditional street food in Indian cuisine.

Mix 1 cup sev (gram flour strings), 1 minced onion, 2 tbsp chopped coriander leaves and a sweet and sour chutney and spoon it over 12 puris to make 4 servings.

Nutritive values for 1 serving: Calories: 206.0kcal; Carbohydrates: 27.8g; Protein: 4.4g; Fat: 8.7g; Minerals: 0.8g; Fibre: 1.4g.

Healthy modifications: Toast the flatbreads in a non-stick pan or bake in an electric oven.

Replace the sev with mixed instant cereals.

SEV BATATA PURI

Small flatbreads with mashed potatoes and tangy, crunchy toppings

Preparation time: 10 mins; Cooking time: 10 mins

Sev batata puri is popular traditional street food in India.

Mix 2 boiled and mashed potatoes with ½ cup sev (gram flour strings), 1 minced onion, 2 tbsp of chopped coriander leaves, a sweet and sour chutney and salt and spoon it over 12 puris to make 4 servings.

Nutritive values for 1 serving: Calories: 220.0kcal; Carbohydrates: 35.4g; Protein: 3.8g; Fat: 7.1g; Minerals: 0.99g; Fibre: 1.5g.

Healthy modifications: See sev puri (above).

PURIS WITH SPROUTS OR SPICY VEGETABLES

Preparation time: 20 mins; Cooking time: 20 mins

Puri with sprouts or spicy vegetables is an innovative snack. The puris are covered with a lettuce and sprout toppings or carrot slices with a spicy vegetable toppings.

Ingredients for 4 servings

The sprouts

1 tsp oil

1 onion, minced

1 tsp ginger-garlic-green chilli paste

2 tomatoes, puréed

1 cup mixed sprouts, boiled

A pinch of salt or to taste

1 lettuce leaf, cut into 6 small circles

The mixed vegetables

1 tsp oil

1 onion, minced

1 tsp ginger-garlic-green chilli paste

¼ tsp red chilli powder

2 tomatoes, puréed

1 cup grated or chopped mixed vegetables (carrot, green pea, cabbage, capsicum, cauliflower), boiled

½ tsp garam masala powder

A pinch of salt or to taste

¼ carrot, cut into 6 slices

The puris

12 flat puris (p. 197), toasted crisp

Method

The sprouts

Heat the oil and sauté the onion and ginger-garlic-green chilli paste for a few mins.

Add the tomatoes and bring to a boil.

Stir in the sprouts and salt and cook on medium heat, till dry.

Place a lettuce leaf circle over the flat puris.

Spoon the sprout topping on top.

Serve immediately.

The vegetables

Heat the oil and sauté the onion and ginger-garlic-green chilli paste for a few mins.

Add the chilli powder and sauté for a second.

Stir in the tomatoes and bring to a boil.

Mix in the vegetables, garam masala powder and salt and cook on medium heat, till dry.

Place carrot slices over the flat puris.

Spoon the spicy mixed vegetable topping on top.

Serve immediately.

Nutritive values for 1 serving: Calories: 103.0kcal; Carbohydrates: 19.8g; Protein: 4.4g; Fat: 0.4g; Minerals: 0.87g; Fibre: 1.5g.

DAHI BATATA PURI

Puffed puris filled with potato, mung and curd

Preparation time: 15 mins; Cooking time: 15 mins

Dahi batata puri is traditional street food in India.

Prepare the dish as given for pani puri (p. 200). Flavour 1 cup of curd with a sweet, sour and hot chutney and pour it into the puris instead of the spiced water

Nutritive values for 1 serving: Calories: 220.0kcal; Carbohydrates: 33.9g; Protein: 6.4g; Fat: 6.7g; Minerals: 1.3g; Fibre: 1.9g.

SMALL PUFFED PURIS

Preparation time: 20 mins; cooking time: 10 mins

These puris are leavened, traditional, puffed biscuits made with semolina and refined wheat flour and used in chaat dishes such as pani puri. They are available in the market in packets of 50 or 100 puris.

Prepare the dough and roll out the puris as given for flat puris (p. 197). Do not prick them. Deep-fry in hot oil and press the puris with a spatula while they are being fried, so that they puff up. Drain and store in airtight containers when cool.

Nutritive values for 1 puri: Calories: 29.0kcal; Carbohydrates: 2.7g; Protein: 0.38g; Fat: 1.8g; Minerals: nil; Fibre: nil.

SPROUT PURI

Puffed puris filled with mixed sprouts and mint-coriander water

Preparation time: 15 mins; Cooking time: nil

Prepare the dish as given for pani puri (alongside). Stuff the puris with 1 cup of mixed boiled sprouts instead of the potatoes and gram. Grind ½ cup mint leaves, ½ cup coriander leaves, a small green chilli, 1 tsp tamarind paste and salt. Mix it with 1 cup of water and use it instead of the spiced water.

Nutritive values for 1 serving: Calories: 116.0 kcal; Carbohydrates: 13.1g; Protein: 3.0g; Fat: 5.6g; Minerals: 0.36g; Fibre: 0.36g.

PANI PURI

Puffed puris filled with potato, mung, spiced water

Preparation time: 10 mins; Cooking time: 15 mins

Pani puri is a traditional street snack, served across the country. The puris are stuffed with boiled potatoes and whole mung and filled with spiced water. The entire puri is put into the mouth.

Ingredients for 4 servings

12 small puffed puris (alongside)

The filling

2 medium-sized potatoes, boiled and mashed

4 tbsp whole mung, boiled

2 tsp pani puri masala

Method

Press the top of the puris with your thumb to make a hole.

Put in 1 tsp of mashed potatoes and 1 tsp of mung.

Mix the pani puri masala powder into 1 cup of water.

Dip each stuffed puri into the spiced water to fill it completely and put it in your mouth immediately.

Nutritive values for 1 serving: Calories: 170.0kcal; Carbohydrates: 23.2g; Protein: 5.6g; Fat: 6.0g; Minerals: 0.85g; Fibre: 1.1g.

FLATBREAD SNACKS MADE WITH RICE FLOUR

KUZHALAPPAM

Rice rolls

Preparation time: 20 mins; Cooking time: 25 mins

Kuzhalappam is an unleavened, traditional fried, flatbread snack made with rice flour, grated fresh coconut and spices in Kerala.

Ingredients for 5 rolls

1 cup rice flour

2 tbsp grated fresh coconut

1 onion, roughly chopped

1 tsp sesame seeds

½ tsp cumin seeds

1 tsp ginger-garlic-green chilli paste

½ cup coconut milk

A pinch of salt or to taste

Coconut oil for deep-frying

(Recipe Cont.)

Method

Tie half the rice flour in a muslin cloth and steam it for 20 mins in a pressure cooker.

Remove, cool and mix it with the remaining flour.

Grind the coconut, onion, sesame seeds and cumin seeds to make a fine paste.

Mix the coconut paste with the ginger-garlic-green chilli paste in a bowl.

Stir in the coconut milk, rice flour and salt and knead it for about 5-10 mins to make a smooth dough.

Cover the dough with a damp cloth and leave it aside for 20-30 mins.

Knead it again for about 5 mins.

Divide the dough into 5 portions and shape them into balls.

Roll the balls on a lightly floured board as thin as possible.

Roll them into cylinders.

Heat the oil in a kadhai or wok and fry the rolls, till crisp and light brown.

Drain them on layers of tissue paper.

When cool, store them in an airtight container.

Nutritive values for 1 kuzhalappam: Calories: 196.0kcal; Carbohydrate: 19.1g; Protein: 2.4g; Fat: 12.2g; Minerals: 0.35g; Fibre: 0.41g.

ODAPPALU

Spicy fried rice flatbread

Preparation time: 20 mins; Cooking time: 6 mins

Odappalu is an unleavened, traditional, fried, Andhra flatbread made with rice flour, Bengal gram, grated fresh coconut and spices.

Ingredients for 12 odappalus

1 cup rice flour

2 tbsp husked, split Bengal gram (chana dal), soaked

2 tbsp grated fresh coconut

4 green chillies, minced

2 onions, minced

2 tsp sesame seeds

2 tsp curry leaves

A pinch of salt or to taste

Oil for deep-frying

Method

Mix all the ingredients, except the oil, in a bowl.

Gradually add 2½-3 tbsp of warm water and knead it for about 5-10 mins to make a smooth dough.

Divide the dough into 12 portions and shape them into balls.

Press the balls on a greased plastic sheet into 2" circles.

Heat the oil in a kadhai or wok and fry the them, till crisp and golden.

Drain them on layers of tissue paper.

When cool, store the odappalus in an airtight container.

Nutritive values for 1 odappalu: Calories: 81.0kcal; Carbohydrate: 9.5g; Protein: 1.5g; Fat: 4.1g; Minerals: 0.24g; Fibre: 0.31g.

Healthy modifications: Toast the flatbreads in a non-stick pan without fat instead of frying them.

FLATBREADS AS FASTING FOODS

Fasting is a common practice in most religions. Fasting can be complete, where a person abstains totally from all food or it could be partial, where a person consumes only fluids in the form of fruit juices. Detoxifying the body with fruits for a day is considered healthy.

Indians usually feast on festivals. However, on some festivals such as Ekadashi, Shivaratri and Navaratri people fast. On Ekadashi and Shivaratri the fasting is for one day only, while for Dusshera, which falls at the beginning of winter, it lasts for nine days. Regular food is only consumed on Vijayadashimi (the tenth day of the festival).

In India, pseudo grains are consumed in the form of flatbreads as fasting foods. These appear to be cereals, but are in fact seeds. Thus amaranth (rajgira) and buckwheat (kuttu) are considered religious foods and are consumed during partial fasting days, when cereals are avoided. They are also staple foods in some rural parts of India. Pseudo grains are rich in proteins, minerals and vitamins. Many restaurants include fasting foods in their menu during Navaratrl. Sago and water chestnut or singhada are also considered fasting foods.

Boiled sweet potatoes and sweet potato halwa are served during Navaratri along with colocasia (arvi), yam (suran), cooking bananas, potatoes and pumpkin, which feature in the home menu during this period as they are available.

Pseudo grains, sago and water chestnuts are often made into high-calorie dishes. Some communities eat only dry chivda and potato chips, while others partake of only fruits and milk during fasting.

FASTING FLATBREADS MADE WITH BUCKWHEAT (KUTTU) FLOUR

Botanically known as Fagopyrum esculentum, of the family Polygoneaceae, buckwheat is a grain-like seed and is not related to wheat. It is a good source of proteins, vitamins, minerals and is rich in the amino acid lysine, which is not found in many cereals. It is also rich in B complex vitamins, macro-minerals such as calcium, magnesium, phosphorus and micro-minerals such as iron, zinc, copper and manganese. It is gluten-free and has a low glycemic index. So it is a good food for diabetics. The phytochemicals in buckwheat have blood pressure and blood cholesterol lowering properties and reduce risks against cardiovascular diseases.

Buckwheat noodles and porridge are popular in Asia, especially China, Japan and Korea. Buckwheat rotis and puris are consumed as fasting foods in north India. Since it is gluten-free, mashed potatoes are usually added to bind the flour.

KUTTU PARATHA

Buckwheat flatbread

Preparation time: 20 mins; Cooking time: 15 mins

Kuttu parathas are an unleavened, traditional flatbread made with a mixture of buckwheat flour and boiled potatoes.

Ingredients for 4 parathas

1 cup buckwheat flour (kuttu)

2 large potatoes, boiled, peeled and mashed

1 tsp garam masala powder

A pinch of salt or to taste

4 tsp ghee

Method

Mix all the ingredients, except the ghee, in a bowl.

Prepare the dough as given for palak paratha (p. 24).

Divide the dough into 4 portions and shape them into balls.

Press a portion of dough on a greased plastic sheet into a 4"- 5" circle.

Put a non-stick pan on medium heat and put a paratha on it. Spoon ½ tsp ghee around the edges.

When the base is golden brown, flip it over, spoon ½ tsp ghee around the edges and cook, till the other side is golden brown.

Repeat with the remaining portions of dough.

Serve hot with curd.

Nutritive values for 1 paratha: Calories: 154.0kcal; Carbohydrate: 22.5g; Protein: 3.0g; Fat: 5.7g; Minerals: 0.79g; Fibre: 2.4g.

Healthy modifications: Replace ghee with oil.

Toast the parathas in a non-stick pan without fat. This will reduce 5g fat and 45 kcal from each paratha.

KUTTU PURI

Fried buckwheat flatbread

Preparation time: 20 mins; Cooking time: 15 mins

Kuttu puri is an unleavened, traditional fried flatbread made with buckwheat flour and boiled potatoes.

Ingredients for 10 puris

1 cup buckwheat flour

2 large potatoes, boiled, peeled and mashed

A pinch of black pepper powder

A pinch of cumin powder

A pinch of salt or to taste

Oil for deep-frying

Method

Mix all the ingredients, except the oil, in a bowl and prepare the dough as given for palak paratha (p. 24).

Divide the dough into 10 portions and shape them into balls.

Press a portion of the dough on a greased plastic sheet into a 2"- 3" circle.

Heat the oil in a kadhai or wok and fry the puris, till light brown.

Drain them on layers of tissue paper.

Serve hot with curd.

Nutritive values for 1 puri: Calories: 87.0kcal; Carbohydrate: 8.8g; Protein: 1.2g; Fat: 5.3g; Minerals: 0.29g; Fibre: 0.9g.

Healthy modifications: Toast the puris in a non-stick pan instead of frying them.

FASTING FLATBREADS MADE WITH AMARANTH (RAJGIRA) FLOUR

Botanically known as Amaranthus caudatus, of the family Amaranthaceae, amaranth seeds are similar to a pseudo grain called quinoa in the West. They are known as rajgira and rajgaro in rural Maharashtra and Gujarat, and in the north as ramdana. Amaranth is a source of high-quality protein, rich in the amino acid lysine which is absent in many cereals. It is a rich source of B vitamins; macro-minerals such as calcium, magnesium, potassium and phosphorus; trace elements such as iron, manganese, zinc and copper; and fibre. The phytochemicals in amaranth have blood cholesterol lowering properties and it is gluten-free.

Popped amaranth seeds are mixed with jaggery to make chikkis (brittle) and ladoos. The flour is used to make rotis and puris. Since it is gluten-free, mashed potatoes are usually added to bind the flour.

RAJGIRA PARATHA

Amaranth flatbread

Preparation time: 20 mins; Cooking time: 15 mins

Rajgira parathas are made in the same way as kuttu paratha (p. 204), replacing the buckwheat flour with amaranth flour.

Nutritive values for 1 paratha: Calories: 177.0 kcal; Carbohydrate: 27.4g; Protein: 4.5g; Fat: 5.6g; Minerals: 1.1g; Fibre: 2.7g.

Healthy modifications: See kuttu paratha (p. 204).

RAJGIRA PURI

Fried amaranth flatbread

Preparation time: 20 mins; Cooking time: 15 mins

Rajgira puri is made in the same way as kuttu puri (p. 205), replacing the buckwheat flour with amaranth flour and omitting the cumin powder.

Nutritive values for 1 puri: Calories: 96.0 kcal; Carbohydrate: 10.6g; Protein: 1.8g; Fat: 5.2g; Minerals: 0.43g; Fibre: 1.0g.

Healthy modifications: See kuttu puri (p. 205).

FASTING FLATBREADS MADE WITH SAGO (SABUDANA) FLOUR

Sago is neither a cereal nor a seed. It comprises the pith cells of the sago palm trunk (cycad species). Sago is a staple food in some rural parts of India and is considered a religious food for fasting, particularly in Maharashtra. Sago is rich in starch and provides the same calories as other cereals. However it has very low nutritive values — proteins, fats, vitamins and minerals. Vegetables, legumes and nuts should be added to increase its nutritive value.

SABUDANA PURI

Fried sago flatbread

Preparation time: 20 mins; Cooking time: 15 mins

Sabudana puri is an unleavened, traditional fried flatbread made with a mixture of soaked sago and boiled green peas or potatoes.

Ingredients for 10 puris

1 cup sago

1 cup shelled green peas

½ tsp garam masala powder

2 green chillies, finely chopped

A pinch of salt or to taste

Oil for deep-frying

Method

Wash the sago, drain it and place it in a bowl. Sprinkle water over it at frequent intervals, till it is soft (3-4 hours).

Boil the green peas and mash well.

Mix the softened sago with the remaining ingredients, except the oil, in a bowl.

Divide it into 10 portions.

Press each portion on a greased plastic sheet into a 2"- 3" circle.

Heat the oil in a kadhai or wok and fry the puris, till light brown and crisp.

Drain them on layers of tissue paper.

Serve hot with curd.

Nutritive values for 1 puri: Calories: 90.0kcal; Carbohydrate: 10.4g; Protein: 0.75g; Fat: 5.1g; Minerals: 0.12g; Fibre: 0.42g.

Healthy modifications: See kuttu puri (p. 205).

SABUDANA THALIPEETH

Sago flatbread

Preparation time: 20 mins; Cooking time: 15 mins

Sabudana thalipeeth is an unleavened, traditional, fried, Marathi flatbread made with a mixture of soaked sago, boiled potatoes and powdered peanuts.

Ingredients for 4 thalipeeths

1 cup sago

2 large potatoes, boiled, peeled and mashed

2 tbsp roasted peanuts, coarsely powdered

2 tbsp coriander leaves, chopped

A pinch of salt or to taste

8 tsp oil

Method

Wash the sago and drain well. Leave it aside overnight. Sprinkle water over it frequently in the morning and mix well, till it is soft.

Mix the softened sago with the remaining ingredients, except the oil, and knead to make a smooth dough.

Divide the dough into 4 portions.

Press a portion of the dough on a greased plastic sheet with your fingertips into a 4"- 5" circle. Prick it on the surface evenly with a fork.

Invert the plastic sheet over the hot pan to slip in the thalipeeth.

Spoon 1 tsp oil around the edges of the thalipeeth.

When the base is crisp and golden, flip it over, spoon 1 tsp oil around the edges again and cook, till the other side is crisp and golden.

Repeat with the remaining portions of dough.

Serve hot with curd.

Nutritive values for 1 thalipeeth: Calories: 246.0kcal; Carbohydrate: 29.6g; Protein: 2.5g; Fat: 13.1g; Minerals: 0.47g; Fibre: 0.36g.

Healthy modifications: See kuttu puri (p. 205).

FASTING FLATBREADS MADE WITH WATER CHESTNUT (SINGHADA) FLOUR

Botanically called Eleocharis dulcis, of the family Cyperaceae, water chestnut or singhada is not a nut, but an aquatic vegetable grown for its edible corms, rich in carbohydrates. The corms are boiled and the edible portion is the white flesh.

SINGHADA ROTI

Water chestnut flatbread

Preparation time: 20 mins; Cooking time: 15 mins

Singhada roti is made in the same way as kuttu paratha (p. 204), replacing the buckwheat flour with water chestnut flour.

Nutritive values for 1 roti: Calories: 180.0 kcal; Carbohydrate: 29.1g; Protein: 4.2g; Fat: 5.4g; Minerals: 1.1g; Fibre: 0.32g.

Healthy modifications: See kuttu paratha (p. 204).

SINGHADA PURI

Fried water chestnut flatbread

Preparation time: 20 mins; Cooking time: 15 mins

Singhada puri is made in the same way as kuttu puri (p. 205), replacing the buckwheat flour with water chestnut flour and omitting the cumin powder.

Nutritive values for 1 puri: Calories: 97.0 kcal; Carbohydrate: 11.4g; Protein: 1.7g; Fat: 5.1g; Minerals: 0.43 g; Fibre: 0.1g;

Healthy modifications: See kuttu puri (p. 205).

PAV (SOFT BREAD)

A pav is a leavened, traditional, soft bread or roll made with refined wheat flour. It is a staple in Maharashtra and Goa, where dishes with pav are popular street foods. Pav made with wholewheat flour is available in high-end shops and is brown. White pav is easy to handle whereas brown pav breaks easily owing to its high fibre content.

PAV

White soft bread

Preparation time: 30 mins; Cooking time: 20 mins

Pav is a leavened, traditional soft bread made with refined wheat flour.

Ingredients for 8 pav

1 tsp dried active yeast

1 tsp sugar

¼ cup warm milk

2 cups refined wheat flour

A pinch of salt or to taste

2 tbsp home-made white butter, melted

Method

Mix the yeast and sugar with the warm milk and leave it aside for 10 mins to froth up.

Mix the flour, salt and butter in a bowl.

Stir in the yeast mixture.

Prepare the dough as given for sada naan (p. 81)

Roll out the entire dough and cut it into 8 pieces.

Shape each piece into an oval.

Place them on a baking sheet and leave for 30 mins to rise.

Bake in an oven preheated to 180°C for 20 mins, till golden brown on top.

Nutritive values for 1 pav: Calories: 120.0 kcal; Carbohydrate: 19.3 g; Protein: 2.9g; Fat: 3.2g; Minerals: 0.27 g; Fibre: 0.1g.

Healthy modifications: Replace half the refined wheat flour with wholewheat flour.

BROWN PAV

Brown soft bread

Preparation time: 30 mins; Cooking time: 20 mins

Brown pav is a leavened, soft bread made with wholewheat flour and refined wheat flour in the ratio of 3:1. Brown pav is now becoming increasingly important. Make it in the same way as white pav (p. 209).

Nutritive values for 1 pav: Calories: 119.0 kcal; Carbohydrate: 18.4 g; Protein: 3.1g; Fat: 3.3g; Minerals: 0.66g; Fibre: 0.37 g.

BUTTERED PAV

Buttered soft bread

Preparation time: 5 mins; Cooking time: 2 mins

Slice a pav (p. 209) horizontally, without separating the pieces. Toast it inside and outside under a hot grill with 1 tsp of home-made white butter and close the 2 sides.

Nutritive values for 1 pav: Calories: 157.0kcal; Carbohydrate: 19.3g; Protein: 2.9g; Fat: 7.2g; Minerals: 0.27g; Fibre: 0.1g.

Healthy modifications: Use brown pav instead of white pav.

Use oil instead of butter for toasting the soft bread.

Toast the pav in a non-stick pan without fat. This will reduce 4g fat and 37kcal from each soft bread.

CHEESE PAV

Soft bread with cheese

Preparation time: 5 mins; Cooking time: 2 mins

Toast the pav as given for buttered pav (alongside) and put a slice of cheese inside.

Nutritive values for 1 pav: Calories: 208.0kcal; Carbohydrate: 20.6g; Protein: 7.7g; Fat: 10.2g; Minerals: 1.2g; Fibre: 0.1g.

Healthy modifications: Use low-fat cheese.

See buttered pav (alongside) for further modifications.

PANEER PAV

Soft bread with paneer

Preparation time: 5 mins; Cooking time: 5 mins

Toast the pav as given for buttered pav (alongside). Stuff them with a mix of 1 minced onion sautéed in ½ tsp ghee, 2 tbsp grated paneer, ¼ tsp garam masala powder and salt.

Nutritive values for 1 pav: Calories: 203.0 kcal; Carbohydrate: 22.2g; Protein: 6.0g; Fat: 9.4g; Minerals: 0.82g; Fibre: 0.25g.

Healthy modifications: Use paneer made from skimmed milk.

See buttered pav (alongside) for further modifications.

PAV BHAJI

Soft bread with spicy mixed vegetables

Preparation time: 20 mins; Cooking time: 20 mins

Toasted pav is served with spicy mixed vegetables and is famous in Mumbai.

Ingredients for 2 servings

The gravy

5 tomatoes, roughly chopped

2 onions, roughly chopped

3 cloves garlic, roughly chopped

1" piece ginger, roughly chopped

2 green chillies, roughly chopped

The bhaji

2 green capsicums, chopped

2 carrots, grated

1 cup shelled green peas

2 potatoes, peeled and cubed

1 tsp ghee

1 tsp pav bhaji masala

A pinch of salt or to taste

The topping

2 tbsp coriander leaves

1 onion, minced

Juice of ½ a lime

1 tsp home-made white butter

The pav

4 pavs (p. 209)

2 tsp home-made white butter

(Recipe Cont.)

Method

Grind the gravy ingredients to make a paste.

Boil the vegetables for the bhaji, till just tender.

Heat the ghee in a pan. Add the ground gravy paste and bring to a boil. Continue to boil for a few mins.

Mix in the boiled vegetables, pav bhaji masala powder and salt and simmer for 5-10 mins, till the contents are thick.

Spoon the bhaji into a serving dish.

Sprinkle all the topping ingredients, except the butter, over it and mix well.

Dot the top with the butter.

Prepare the pav as given for buttered pav (p. 210) and serve with the bhaji.

Alternatively, spread the bhaji inside the pavs and eat.

Nutritive values for 1 serving: Calories: 536.0kcal; Carbohydrate: 82.4g; Protein: 14.3g; Fat: 15.5g; Minerals: 3.7 g; Fibre: 5.9g.

Healthy modifications: Avoid dotting the dish with the butter. This will reduce 4g fat and 37kcal in the dish.

See buttered pav (p. 210) for further modifications.

PANEER PAV BHAJI

Soft bread with spicy mixed vegetables and paneer

Preparation time: 25 mins; Cooking time: 20 mins

Prepare pav bhaji as given on p. 211. Sprinkle 4 tbsp of grated paneer over the bhaji before serving.

Nutritive values for 1 serving: Calories: 616.0kcal; Carbohydrate: 82.8g; Protein: 19.8g; Fat: 21.7g; Minerals: 3.8 g; Fibre: 5.9g.

Healthy modifications: Use paneer made from skimmed milk.

See pav bhaji (p. 211) for further modifications.

CHEESE PAV BHAJI

Soft bread with spicy mixed vegetables and cheese

Preparation time: 25 mins; Cooking time: 10 mins

Substitute cheese for paneer and make it as given for paneer pav bhaji (above).

Nutritive values for 1 servings: Calories: 641.0kcal; Carbohydrate: 84.3g; Protein: 21.6g; Fat: 23.1g; Minerals: 5.0g; Fibre: 5.9g.

Healthy modifications: Use low-fat cheese.

See pav bhaji (p. 211) for further modifications.

PAV WITH MIXED SPROUTS

Preparation time: 15 mins; Cooking time: 20 mins

Make pav bhaji as given on p. 211, using brown pav and substituting 2 cups of boiled mixed sprouts in place of the vegetables. Toast the pav without butter.

Nutritive values for 1 serving: Calories: 443.0kcal; Carbohydrate: 69.3g; Protein: 15.1g; Fat: 10.9g; Minerals: 3.4 g; Fibre: 3.9g.

USAL PAV

Soft bread with a spicy moth bean curry

Preparation time: 20 mins; Cooking time: 25 mins

Usal pav is a breakfast dish and street food in Maharashtra. Usal is a spicy curry made with moth beans (matki) and even with sprouted moth beans. In the coastal regions of Maharashtra, grated fresh coconut is added to usal. Prepare the dish as given for pav bhaji (p. 211), substituting usal (p. 230) for the bhaji.

Nutritive values for 1 serving: Calories: 637.0 kcal; Carbohydrate: 76.8 g; Protein: 17.4g; Fat: 27.8g; Minerals: 4.2 g; Fibre: 6.9g.

Healthy modifications: See pav bhaji (p. 211).

VADA PAV

Soft bread with potato patty filling

Preparation time: 15 mins; Cooking time: 10 mins

Vada pav is a traditional street food from Maharashtra. Butter-toasted pav is smeared with garlic-chilli paste and stuffed with a vada — a spicy potato patty dipped in gram flour batter.

Ingredients for 2 vada pavs

The vada

2 potatoes, boiled, peeled and mashed,

½ tsp garam masala powder

1 tsp ginger-garlic-green chilli paste

½ cup gram flour (besan)

A pinch of red chilli powder

A pinch of salt or to taste

Oil for deep-frying

The pav

2 pavs (p. 209)

8 cloves garlic, puréed

A pinch of red chilli powder

A pinch of salt or to taste

1 tsp home-made white butter

Method

The vada

Mix the mashed potatoes, garam masala powder and ginger-garlic-green chilli paste in a bowl.

Mix the gram flour, chilli powder and salt in a bowl. Add a little water and mix to make a thick, coating batter.

(Method Cont.)

Divide the potato mixture into 2 portions. Shape them into balls.

Heat the oil in a kadhai or wok.

Dip the potato balls in the batter and fry them in the hot oil, till golden brown.

Drain them on layers of tissue paper.

The pav

Slice each pav horizontally, without separating the pieces.

Mix the garlic paste, chilli powder and salt in a bowl.

Heat the butter in a pan and sauté the garlic-chilli paste for a minute.

Open each pav and invert it over the paste, so that the paste spreads on the inside.

Place a vada inside the pav.

Serve immediately.

Nutritive values for 1 vada pav: Calories: 308 kcal; Carbohydrate: 53.6g; Protein: 8.0g; Fat: 11.0g; Minerals: 1.5g; Fibre: 0.88g.

Healthy modifications: Bake the vadas in an electric oven or flatten them and toast in a non-stick pan instead of deep-frying.

Use a pan-toasted mixed vegetable patty insted of a fried potato vada.

See pav bhaji (p. 211) for further modifications.

MISAL PAV

Soft bread with a spicy moth bean curry and crisp toppings

Preparation time: 25 mins; Cooking time: 25 mins

Make usal pav (p. 212) and sprinkle the curry with 2 tbsp sev (gram flour strings), 2 tbsp chivda (rice flake snack), 1 minced onion, 1 chopped tomato, 2 tbsp chopped coriander leaves and the juice of 1 lime.

Nutritive values for 1 serving: Calories: 753.0 kcal; Carbohydrate: 97.2g; Protein: 21.2 g; Fat: 33.8g; Minerals: 5.2 g; Fibre: 7.7g.

Healthy modifications: Sev and chivda are rich in fat, sodium and calories. Replace them with chopped nuts and lightly crushed oats, corn and wheat flakes.

See pav bhaji (p. 211) for further modifications.

VEGETABLE PATTY PAV

Soft bread with vegetable patty filling

Preparation time: 20 mins; Cooking time: 10 mins

This is an innovative dish, where the potato vada is replaced with a vegetable patty. Boil 1 cup of chopped mixed vegetables (carrot, green pea, capsicum) and mash them with ½ tsp garam masala powder and 2 tsp ginger-garlic-green chilli paste to make the filling for the patty. Proceed as given for vada pav (p. 213).

Nutritive values for 1 pav: Calories: 274.0 kcal; Carbohydrate: 36.9g; Protein: 9.1g; Fat: 9.7g; Minerals: 2.0g; Fibre: 2.1g .

CHEESE VADA PAV

Soft bread with cheese and potato patty filling

Preparation time: 15 mins; Cooking time: 10 mins

Make vada pav as given on p. 213, but spread 1 grated cheese cube on both sides of the pav before putting the potato vada inside.

Nutritive values for 1 cheese vada pav: Calories: 378 kcal; Carbohydrate: 54.9g; Protein: 12.8g; Fat: 16.0g; Minerals: 2.3g; Fibre: 0.88g.

Healthy modifications: Use low-fat cheese.

See vada pav (p. 213) for further modifications.

BATATA BHAJJIA PAV

Soft bread with batter-fried potato filling

Preparation time: 25 mins; Cooking time: 10 mins

This is made in the same way as pyaz bhajjia pav (p. 216). Use 2 sliced potatoes instead of the onions and make the green chutney with mint leaves instead of coriander leaves.

Nutritive values for 1 pav: Calories: 381.0kcal; Carbohydrate: 47.1g; Protein: 9.4g

Fat: 16.8g; Minerals: 1.8g; Fibre: 0.9g.

Healthy modifications: See pyaz bhajjia pav (p. 216).

SAMOSA PAV

Soft bread stuffed with fried potato triangle

Preparation time: 20 mins; Cooking time: 10 mins

Buttered pav is smeared with garlic-chilli paste and stuffed with a samosa, a fried potato triangle.

Ingredients for 2 pavs

The samosa filling

1 tsp ghee

1 tsp garlic-ginger-green chilli paste

2 potatoes, boiled, peeled and mashed

½ tsp garam masala powder

A pinch of salt or to taste

The samosa dough

A pinch of salt or to taste

¼ cup refined wheat flour

To fry the samosa

Oil for deep-frying

Coriander chutney

100g coriander leaves

1 green chilli

A pinch of salt or to taste

The pav

2 pavs (p. 209)

1 tsp home-made white butter

8 cloves garlic

A pinch of red chilli powder

(Recipe Cont.)

Method

The samosas

Heat the ghee and sauté the ginger-garlic-green chilli paste for a minute.

Mix in the remaining filling ingredients and divide it into 2 portions.

Leave aside, till cool

Dissolve the salt for the samosa dough in 50 ml of water.

Prepare the dough as given for sada chapatti (p. 66).

Roll out the dough on a lightly floured board into a 6" circle and cut it into half.

Fold each half into a cone and place a portion of the potato filling inside. Cover the filling with the dough and gently seal the edges with moist fingertips.

Heat the oil in a kadhai or wok and fry the samosas, till golden brown.

Drain them on layers of tissue paper.

The coriander chutney

Cut off and discard the roots of the coriander leaves.

Grind all the chutney ingredients together.

The samosa pav

Prepare the pavs as given for vada pav (p. 213).

Spread the coriander chutney on each slice of the pav.

Place a samosa inside each pav and serve immediately.

Nutritive values for 1 pav: Calories: 299.0kcal; Carbohydrate: 43.4g; Protein: 6.7g; Fat: 10.8g; Minerals: 1.6g; Fibre: 1.0g.

Healthy modifications: Bake the samosa in an electric oven instead of deep-frying them in oil.

Use wholewheat flour to prepare the samosa dough.

See vada pav (p. 213) for further modifications.

PYAZ BHAJJIA PAV

Soft bread with batter-fried onion filling

Preparation time: 25 mins; Cooking time: 10 mins

Pav is smeared with chutney and stuffed with batter-fried onion slices. It is a popular street food in Mumbai.

Ingredients for 2 pavs

The green chutney

2 cups coriander leaves

1 small green chilli

A pinch of salt or to taste

The onion bhajjias

½ cup gram flour (besan)

A pinch of red chilli powder

A pinch of salt or to taste

Oil for deep-frying

2 onions, sliced

The pav

2 pavs (p. 209)

1 tsp home-made white butter

Method

Grind the chutney ingredients to make a smooth paste. Add some water, if required.

The onion bhajjias

Mix the gram flour, chilli powder and salt in a bowl.

Add a little water and mix to form a thick batter of coating consistency.

Heat the oil in a kadhai or wok.

Dip the onion slices in the batter and fry in the hot oil, till golden brown.

Drain them on layers of tissue paper.

(Method Cont.)

Divide them into 2 portions.

The onion bhajjia pav

Prepare buttered pavs (p. 209) and smear the slices with the chutney.

Place a portion of onion bhajjias inside each pav and serve immediately.

Nutritive values for 1 pav: Calories: 358.0kcal; Carbohydrate: 41.3g; Protein: 9.2g; Fat: 16.8g; Minerals: 1.7g; Fibre: 1.0g.

Healthy modifications: Bake or toast the bhajjias instead of frying them in oil.

See vada pav (p. 213) for further modifications.

PAV SANDWICH

Soft bread sandwich

Preparation time: 15 mins; Cooking time: 2 mins

These sandwiches are made in the same way as the other pav preparations. The chutney is made by grinding 50g each of coriander and mint leaves, 2 green chillies and salt. The filling comprises onion, capsicum and tomato slices.

Nutritive values for 1 pav: Calories: 185.0kcal; Carbohydrate: 27.0g; Protein: 5.5g; Fat: 5.7g; Minerals: 1.7g; Fibre: 1.6g .

Healthy modifications: See buttered pav (p. 209).

DABELI WITH POTATO PATTY

Soft bread with potato patty filling

Preparation time: 20 mins; Cooking time: 15 mins

Buttered pavs are stuffed with a potato patty, covered with crisp toppings and a sweet and sour chutney. This is a traditional street food in Mumbai and Gujarat.

Ingredients for 2 dabelis

The vadas

1 tsp ghee

1 tsp garlic paste

2 potatoes, boiled, peeled and mashed

½ tsp garam masala powder

The date and tamarind chutney

1 tbsp date paste

2 tbsp tamarind pulp

1 small green chilli

A pinch of red chilli powder

A pinch of salt or to taste

The pavs

2 white pavs

1 tsp home-made white butter

The toppings

1 onion, minced

2 tbsp peanuts, roasted

2 tbsp pomegranate seeds

2 tbsp sev (gram flour strings)

2 tbsp coriander leaves, chopped

Method

Heat ½ tsp ghee and sauté the garlic paste for a minute.

Mix in the mashed potatoes and garam masala powder.

(Method Cont.)

Divide it into 2 portions and shape them into patties.

Heat the remaining ghee in a fresh pan and fry the potato patties, till crisp and golden.

Keep them aside.

Grind the chutney ingredients to make a smooth paste. Divide it into 2 portions

Prepare buttered pav as given on p. 209.

Place a potato patty on one half of a pav, sprinkle half the topping ingredients on top.

Spoon a portion of the chutney over the toppings and cover it with the other half of the pav.

Repeat with the remaining ingredients.

Serve immediately.

Nutritive values for 1 dabeli: Calories: 393.0kcal; Carbohydrate: 55.0g; Protein: 10.1g; Fat: 14.3g; Minerals: 1.9g; Fibre: 3.4g.
Healthy modifications: See vada pav (p. 213).

DABELI WITH VEGETABLE PATTY

Soft bread with mixed vegetable patty filling

Preparation time: 20 mins; Cooking time: 15 mins

This is made in the same way as dabeli with potato patty. Substitute the potato patty with a mixed vegetable one made with 1 cup of boiled, mashed mixed vegetables instead of potatoes.

Nutritive values for 1 dabeli: Calories: 347.0kcal; Carbohydrate: 47.0g; Protein: 11.0g; Fat: 12.3g; Minerals: 2.4g; Fibre: 4.6g.

DISHES SERVED WITH INDIAN BREADS

SOOJI HALWA

Sweet semolina porridge

Preparation time: 15 mins Cooking time: 20 mins

Sooji halwa is a popular sweet preparation in most Indian cuisines, especially in the north. It is served with sada paratha (p. 22), bedmi puri (p. 76) and luchi (p. 93) in the north and is used as a filling for sooji halwa poli (p. 156) in Andhra Pradesh.

Ingredients for 2 servings

1 cup semolina

1 tsp + 2 tsp ghee

1 tbsp seedless raisins

2 tbsp mixed nuts, chopped and roasted

½ cup sugar

¼ tsp saffron strands

¼ tsp green cardamom powder

Method

Roast the semolina in a pan on low heat, till light brown.

Heat 1 tsp ghee and fry the raisins and nuts, till golden. Leave aside.

Boil 2½ cups of water in a heavy-bottomed pan. Add the sugar, 2 tsp ghee, saffron and cardamom powder.

Add the roasted semolina, stirring vigorously to avoid lumps. Cook on medium heat, till it thickens.

Add the fried raisins and nuts and mix well.

Serve hot with any of the dishes mentioned above.

Nutritive values for 1 serving: Calories: 462.0kcal; Carbohydrate: 70.1g; Protein: 8.3g; Fat: 16.5g; Minerals: 0.53g; Fibre: 0.46g

Healthy modifications: Replace ghee with oil.

Avoid fat in the dish.

Replace refined sugar with jaggery or brown sugar.

TAVA BHAJI

Pan-fried vegetables

Preparation time: 15 mins; Cooking time: 10 mins

Tava bhaji is another dry vegetable dish that is consumed with flatbreads. It is served at buffets where partially stir-fried vegetables are arranged along the edges of a large griddle and the spice mix in placed in the centre. The vegetables chosen by a guest are stir-fried in a small portion of the spice mix and served.

Ingredients for 2 servings

2 tbsp oil

2 cups vegetable chunks (aubergine, okra, capsicum, bitter gourd, potato, cauliflower, button mushroom, carrot)

¼ tsp turmeric powder

¼ tsp red chilli powder

½ tsp coriander powder

½ tsp cumin-pepper powder

½ tsp garam masala powder (clove, cinnamon, black cardamom, caraway seeds, bay leaf)

A pinch of salt or to taste

Method

Put the oil in a large griddle on high heat. Add the vegetables and sauté for a few mins, till just tender.

Drain and shift the vegetables to the edges of the griddle.

Add all the spice powders to the oil in the centre of the griddle and sauté for a second.

Bring the vegetables to the centre of the griddle, sprinkle salt over them and sauté, till well coated with the spices.

Serve hot with any paratha.

Nutritive values for 1 serving: Calories: 201.0kcal; Carbohydrates: 10.6g; Protein: 3.7g; Fat: 15.9g; Minerals: 1.0g; Fibre: 2.6g

Healthy modifications: Limit the use of fat in the dish.

SWEET, SOUR AND PUNGENT CHUTNEY

Preparation time: 10 mins; Cooking time: nil

This sweet, sour and pungent chutney is used in chat dishes (street food).

Ingredients for 2 servings

2 tbsp tamarind pulp

2 tbsp puréed dates

¼ tsp red chilli powder

A pinch of salt or to taste

Method

Mix all the ingredients in a bowl.

Store it in the refrigerator till ready to use.

Nutritive values for 1 serving: Calories: 87.0kcal; Carbohydrates: 21.8g; Protein: 0.94g; Fat: 0.14g; Minerals: 0.78g; Fibre: 2.2g.

TOMATO CHUTNEY

Ingredients

4 medium size tomatoes, chopped

¼ tsp chilli powder

A pinch of asafoetida

Salt to taste

Method

Heat oil and sauté the seasoning ingredients.

Add the chopped tomatoes, chilli powder, asafoetida and salt. Mix the contents till well combined.

Simmer and cook on slow fire till the contents are tender and thick.

When cool, blend it in the mixer.

MUGHLAI BAINGAN MASALA

Spicy mughlai aubergine

Preparation time: 15 mins; Cooking time: 20 mins

Baingan masala is a popular dish served with flatbreads in Mughlai cuisine.

Ingredients for 2 servings

250g small aubergines

The filling

2 tsp oil

4 medium-sized onions, finely sliced

2" piece ginger, chopped

5 cloves garlic, chopped

2 dried red chillies

2 tbsp peanuts

1 tbsp sesame seeds

1 tbsp poppy seeds

½ tsp red chilli powder

¼ tsp turmeric powder

¼ tsp aniseed powder

¼ tsp dried mango powder

¼ tsp black pepper powder

½ tsp cumin powder

½ tsp coriander powder

A pinch of mace and nutmeg

½ tsp garam masala powder (clove, cinnamon, black cardamom, caraway seeds, bay leaf)

A pinch of green cardamom powder

A pinch of salt or to taste

The seasoning

1 tbsp oil

½ tsp mustard seeds

½ tsp cumin seeds

The garnish

2 tbsp coriander leaves, chopped

(Recipe Cont.)

Method

Wash the aubergines and pat dry. Using a sharp knife, cut the aubergines at the stem end to make a cross that comes three-quarters of the way down.

Heat the oil for the filling in a pan and sauté the onions, ginger, garlic and red chillies for a minute. When cool, grind them into a paste.

Roast the peanuts, sesame seeds and the poppy seeds on a dry griddle on low to medium heat, till fragrant.

Leave aside, till cool. Grind to make a fine powder.

Mix the ground paste, powder and remaining filling ingredients in a bowl.

Stuff the aubergines with the filling

Heat the oil for the seasoning in a shallow pan and sauté the cumin and mustard seeds on medium heat, till they splutter.

Add the stuffed aubergines and toss gently. Spoon any remaining filling over them.

Cover the pan with a lid and simmer on low heat, turning the aubergines occasionally, till tender.

Garnish with coriander leaves.

Serve hot with any Mughlai flatbread.

Nutritive values for 1 serving: Calories: 398.0kcal; Carbohydrates: 27.6g; Protein: 10.9g; Fat: 26.9g; Minerals: 2.5g; Fibre: 4.3g

Healthy modifications: Limit the use of peanuts, sesame seeds and poppy seeds.

Limit the use of fat in the dish.

NAVRATAN KORMA

Nine vegetable curry

Preparation time: 30 mins; Cooking time: 30 mins

Navratan korma is a Mughlai dish served with flatbreads such as lachha parathas. It is also popular in north Indian cuisine. Navratan means 'nine gems'. The dish has nine vegetables, fruits and dried fruits in the gravy.

Ingredients for 2 servings

The spice paste

2 tbsp mixed nuts (cashew nuts, almonds, walnuts)

2 tsp poppy seeds

2 tsp ginger-garlic-green chilli paste

The gravy

1 tbsp home-made white butter or ghee

2 medium-sized onions, minced

¼ tsp turmeric powder

½ tsp red chilli powder

½ tsp cumin powder

½ tsp coriander powder

¼ tsp aniseed powder

¼ tsp dried mango powder

¼ tsp black pepper powder

A pinch of nutmeg and mace

4 tomatoes, puréed

½ cup curd

A pinch of salt or to taste

½ tsp garam masala powder (clove, cinnamon, black cardamom, caraway seeds, bay leaf)

A pinch of green cardamom powder

2 tbsp cream

The vegetables

2 tbsp seedless raisins, chopped

100g paneer, cubed

(Recipe Cont.)

2 cups chopped mixed vegetables (potato, green pea, corn, French bean, carrot, cauliflower, capsicum)

½ cup pineapple, chopped

The garnish

2 tbsp coriander leaves, chopped

Method

Soak the nuts in water for 1 hour. Drain. Peel the almonds.

Grind all the nuts with the poppy seeds to make a fine paste.

Mix in the ginger-garlic-green chilli paste.

Put the butter or ghee in a pan on medium heat and sauté the onions, till light brown.

Stir in the spice paste and sauté for a minute.

Add all the spice powders, except the garam masala powder and cardamom powder, and sauté for a second.

Add the tomato purée and cook on high heat, till the mixture leaves the sides of the pan and the butter or ghee floats to the surface.

Add the raisins and paneer. Mix well and sauté again for a minute.

Stir in the curd, salt and 1½ cups of water. Mix well and bring to a boil, stirring all the while.

Add the garam masala powder, cardamom powder chopped vegetables, and pineapple. Mix well and boil on high heat for a few mins.

Cover the pan with a lid, reduce heat and simmer, till the vegetables are tender and the gravy is thick.

Add cream, mix well and remove from heat.

Garnish with coriander leaves and serve hot with any Mughlai flatbread.

Nutritive values for 1 serving: Calories: 522.0kcal; Carbohydrates: 40.2g; Protein: 20.1g; Fat: 31.1g; Minerals: 4.5g; Fibre: 4.8g

Healthy modifications: Use low-fat paneer. • Replace paneer with tofu. • Limit the use of dried fruits and nuts in the dish. • Use light instead of heavy cream. • Replace cream with curd. • Replace ghee or butter with oil. • Limit the use of fat in the dish.

SHIMLA MIRCH KA SALAN

Spicy capsicum curry

Preparation time: 20 mins; Cooking time: 20 mins

Shimla mirch ka salan is a traditional dish in Mughlai cuisine, particularly in Hyderabad. This dish is served with biryanis as well as with flatbreads. Salan means curry in Urdu.

Ingredients for 2 servings

The spice powder

1 tbsp peanuts or cashew nuts

1 tbsp sesame seeds

1 tbsp desiccated coconut

2 tsp cumin seeds

2 tsp coriander seeds

The curry

4 green capsicums

2 tbsp oil

2 medium-sized onions, puréed

2 tsp ginger-garlic paste

¼ tsp turmeric powder

½ tsp red chilli powder

¼ tsp black pepper powder

¼ tsp aniseed powder

1 tomato, puréed

2 tbsp tamarind pulp

½ tsp garam masala powder (clove, cinnamon, black cardamom, caraway seeds, bay leaf)

A pinch of salt or to taste

1 tsp sugar

1 tbsp cream

The seasoning

¼ tsp mustard seeds

¼ tsp cumin seeds

¼ tsp nigella seeds

(Recipe Cont.)

¼ tsp fenugreek seeds

A few curry leaves

The garnish

2 tbsp coriander leaves, chopped

Method

Roast the spice powder ingredients on a dry griddle on low heat, till fragrant.

Leave aside, till cool. Grind to make a fine powder.

Wash the capsicums, cut them into halves and scoop out and discard the seeds. Cut into chunks.

Heat the oil in a pan. Sauté the capsicum on medium heat for a few mins. Drain and keep aside.

Add the seasoning ingredients to the same oil and fry, till they splutter.

Mix in the onion purée and sauté, till light brown.

Stir in the ginger-garlic paste and sauté for a minute.

Add all the spice powders, except the garam masala powder, and sauté for a second.

Pour in the tomato purée and cook, till the mixture leaves the sides of the pan and the oil floats to the surface.

Add the roasted spice powder and stir, till well blended.

Pour in 1 cup of water and mix in the tamarind pulp. Bring to a boil.

Add the sautéed capsicum, garam masala powder and salt and cook, till the gravy thickens.

Stir in the sugar and cream and remove from heat.

Garnish with coriander leaves and serve hot with any kulcha.

Nutritive values for 1 serving: Calories: 448.0kcal; Carbohydrates: 34.8g; Protein: 9.3g; Fat: 30.1g; Minerals: 3.1g; Fibre: 6.4g

Healthy modifications: Limit the use of peanuts, sesame seeds and coconut in the dish. • Use light cream instead of heavy cream. • Replace cream with curd. • Limit the use of fat in the dish .

KADHAI SABJI

Sautéed vegetables

Preparation time: 20 mins; Cooking time: 15 mins

Kadhai sabji is a dry vegetable dish ideal to serve with flatbreads. The vegetable juliennes are sautéed on high heat for a few mins, till tender but crisp.

Ingredients for 2 servings

1 medium-sized aubergine

1 medium-sized bitter gourd

1 medium-sized potato

10 okra

2 medium-sized green capsicums

2 tbsp oil

½ tsp garam masala powder (clove, cinnamon, black cardamom, caraway seeds, bay leaf)

¼ tsp turmeric powder

½ tsp red chilli powder

½ tsp cumin powder

½ tsp coriander powder

¼ tsp aniseed powder

¼ tsp black pepper powder

A pinch of salt or to taste

The garnish

2 tbsp chopped coriander leaves

(Recipe Cont.)

Method

Wash the vegetables and cut them into juliennes.

Heat the oil in a pan and sauté the vegetables on high heat for a few mins.

Reduce the heat and add the spice powders and salt.

Mix, till the vegetables are evenly coated with the spices.

Cook, till the vegetables are tender, but still crisp.

Garnish with coriander leaves and serve hot with any naan.

Nutritive values for 1 serving: Calories: 210kcal; Carbohydrates: 13.3g; Protein: 3.2g; Fat: 16.1g; Minerals: 1.1g; Fibre: 2.2g

BHINDI MASALA

Spice-filled okra

Preparation time: 15 mins; Cooking time: 15 mins

Bhindi masala is served with flatbreads in Rajasthan.

Ingredients for 2 servings

250g okra

The filling

4 tbsp gram flour (besan)

2 tbsp coriander powder

2 tbsp cumin powder

1 tsp red chilli powder

1 tsp garam masala powder (clove, cinnamon, black cardamom, caraway seeds, bay leaf)

½ tsp aniseed powder

½ tsp dried mango powder

¼ tsp turmeric powder

¼ tsp black pepper powder

A pinch of salt or to taste

The seasoning

2 tbsp oil

½ tsp cumin seeds

½ tsp mustard or nigella seeds

(Recipe Cont.)

Method

Wash the okra and wipe them immediately. Top and tail them.

Slit the okra lengthwise from the tail end to come three-quarters of the way up.

Mix all the filling ingredients in a bowl.

Stuff the okra with the filling.

Heat the oil in a pan and add the seasoning ingredients. Fry on medium heat, till they splutter.

Add the stuffed okra and cover the pan. Stir occasionally and turn them around to cook on all sides, till tender.

Serve hot with any roti.

Nutritive values for 1 serving: Calories: 423.0kcal; Carbohydrates: 37.7g; Protein: 15.4g; Fat: 23.2g; Minerals: 3.8g; Fibre: 9.8g

Healthy modifications: Limit the use of fat in the dish.

KOLHAPURI SABJI

Kolhapuri mixed vegetables

Preparation time: 20 mins; Cooking time: 25 mins

This dish originates from the town of Kolhapur in Maharashtra. It is cooked with a special mix of spices, Kolhapuri masala, which is available commercially and is very pungent.

Ingredients for 2 servings

Spice powder

2 tbsp desiccated coconut

1 tsp coriander seeds

2 dried red chillies

2 tsp poppy seeds

2 tsp sesame seeds

The vegetables

2 tbsp oil

2 medium-sized onions, puréed

2 tsp ginger-garlic-green chilli paste

¼ tsp turmeric powder

4 tomatoes, puréed

A pinch of salt or to taste

2 cups julienned mixed vegetables (carrot, green pea, capsicum, French bean)

2 tsp Kolhapuri masala

The garnish

2 tsp coriander leaves, chopped

(Recipe Cont.)

Method

Put a griddle on low heat and roast the spice powder ingredients, till fragrant.

Leave aside, till cool. Grind to make a fine powder.

Heat the oil in a pan and sauté the onions on medium heat, till light brown.

Add the ginger-garlic-green chilli paste and sauté for a minute.

Add the turmeric powder and sauté for a second.

Pour in the tomato purée and bring to a boil on high heat. Continue to boil, till the contents leave the sides of the pan and the oil rises to the surface.

Mix in the roasted spice powder.

Add 2 cups of water and the salt and bring to a boil.

Add the vegetables, mix well and cook on high heat for a few mins.

Lower heat and simmer, till the vegetables are tender.

Sprinkle in the Kolhapuri masala, mix well and simmer for a few mins.

Garnish with the coriander leaves.

Serve hot with chapattis.

Nutritive values for 1 serving: Calories: 416.0kcal; Carbohydrates: 28.0g; Protein: 9.3g; Fat: 29.4g; Minerals: 3.1g; Fibre: 6.0g

Healthy modifications: 2 cups of mixed vegetables provides about 100 kcal. Using excess fat for the seasoning, desiccated coconut, sesame seeds and poppy seeds increase the calories of the final dish four times over. • Kolhapuri masala already contains poppy seeds, sesame seeds and dried coconut. Omit these. • Limit the use of fat in the dish.

HARA SOYA-PANEER MASALA

Green tofu curry

Preparation time: 15 mins; Cooking time: 20 mins

Hara soya-paneer masala is a simple dish that can be eaten with flatbreads.

Ingredients for 2 servings

2 cups mixed herbs (parsley, celery, sweet basil, thyme, rosemary, mint, coriander leaves)

1 tsp oil

2 onions, puréed

2 tsp ginger-garlic-green chilli paste

100g tofu, cubed

¼ tsp turmeric powder

½ red chilli powder

½ tsp cumin powder

½ tsp coriander powder

¼ tsp black pepper powder

¼ tsp aniseed powder

¼ tsp dried mango powder

2 tomatoes, puréed

A pinch of salt or to taste

½ tsp garam masala powder (clove, cinnamon, black cardamom, caraway seeds, bay leaf)

(Recipe Cont.)

Method

Wash the herbs and grind to make a paste.

Heat the oil and sauté the onions, till light brown.

Add the ginger-garlic-green chilli paste and tofu. Sauté for a few seconds.

Add all the spice powders, except the garam masala powder, and sauté for a second.

Pour in the puréed tomatoes and bring to a boil on high heat. Continue to boil for a few mins, till it thickens.

Mix in the herb paste, salt and garam masala powder and simmer on medium heat for a few mins.

Serve hot with parathas.

Nutritive values for 1 serving: Calories: 151.0kcal; Carbohydrate: 15.4g; Protein: 8.8g; Fat: 6.3g; Minerals: 2.2g; Fibre: 3.4g

MIXED SPROUTS

Preparation time: 10 mins; Cooking time: 20 mins

Mixed sprouts is a simple side dish for flatbreads.

Ingredients for 2 servings

The spice paste

2 tbsp grated fresh coconut

2 green chillies

1" piece ginger

The sprouts

2 cups mixed sprouts

A pinch of salt or to taste

The seasoning

2 tsp oil

½ tsp mustard seeds

½ tsp cumin seeds

1 tsp husked, split black gram (urad dal)

2 tsp curry leaves

The garnish

2 tsp coriander leaves, chopped

(Recipe Cont.)

Method

Grind the spice paste ingredients to a fine consistency.

Wash the sprouts and drain.

Boil the sprouts in salted water, till just tender, but crisp.

Put the oil in a pan on medium heat and sauté the seasoning ingredients, till the mustard seeds splutter.

Add the spice paste and sauté for a minute.

Stir in the cooked sprouts.

Simmer for a few mins.

Garnish with coriander leaves and serve with parathas.

Nutritive values for 1 serving: Calories: 235.0kcal; Carbohydrate: 22.3g; Protein: 8.5g; Fat: 12.4g; Minerals: 1.3g; Fibre: 2.1g

Healthy modifications: Limit the use of coconut in the dish. Replace the coconut with tofu.

GAHAT KI DAL

HORSE GRAM CURRY

Preparation time: 10 mins; Cooking time: 10 mins

Gahat ki dal is a famous dish of Uttarakhand and is even used to stuff rotis (p. 112).

Ingredients for 2 servings

4 tbsp horse gram

2 onions, chopped

2 tsp ginger-garlic-green chilli paste

¼ tsp turmeric powder

½ tsp red chilli powder

¼ tsp asafoetida powder

1 tsp cumin powder

1 tsp coriander powder

A pinch of salt or to taste

The seasoning

2 tsp oil

1 tsp cumin seeds

The garnish

2 tbsp coriander leaves, chopped

(Recipe Cont.)

Method

Wash the gram and soak it in water for a few hours. Drain and rinse.

Pressure-cook the gram with 1 cup of water on low heat for 15 mins after the cooker reaches full pressure.

Open the cooker after it returns to normal pressure.

Put the oil for the seasoning in a pan on medium heat and sauté the cumin seeds, till they splutter.

Add the onions and sauté for a few mins.

Add the ginger-garlic-green chilli paste and the spice powders. Sauté for a second.

Mix in the cooked gram and salt.

Simmer for 5 mins and remove from heat.

Garnish with coriander leaves.

Serve hot with any ragi/mandua roti (p. 111) or cook till dry and use to stuff them (p. 112).

Nutritive values for 1 serving: Calories: 205.0 kcal; Carbohydrate: 26.5g; Protein: 8.9g; Fat: 6.6g; Minerals: 1.8g; Fibre: 3.9g

SINDHI DAL TO SERVE WITH PAKWAN

Preparation time: 10 mins; Cooking time: 20 mins

Crisp pakwan are dipped into this dal and served as dal pakwan in Sindhi cuisine.

Ingredients for 2 servings

4 tbsp husked split Bengal gram (chana dal)

2 tsp ghee

1 tsp aniseed

1 onion, chopped

2 green chillies, chopped

¼ tsp turmeric powder

¼ tsp black pepper powder

½ tsp coriander powder

½ tsp cumin powder

½ tsp red chilli powder

1 tomato, chopped

½ tsp garam masala powder (clove, cinnamon, black cardamom, caraway seeds, bay leaf)

A pinch of salt or to taste

The garnish

2 tsp coriander leaves, chopped

(Recipe Cont.)

Method

Soak the dal in water for 1 hour and drain.

Put the ghee in a pressure cooker on medium heat and sauté the aniseed, onion and green chillies for a minute.

Add all the spice powders except the garam masala powder, and sauté for a second.

Mix in the tomato and sauté for a minute.

Add the soaked and drained dal and 1 cup of water.

Pressure-cook the dal on low heat for 10 mins after the cooker reaches full pressure.

Open the cooker after it returns to normal pressure. Mix in the salt.

Garnish with coriander leaves.

To serve

Dip the pakwans in the dal and serve immediately.

Nutritive values for 1 serving: Calories: 201.0kcal; Carbohydrates: 24.4g; Protein: 8.2g; Fat: 7.9g; Minerals: 1.5g; Fibre: 1.6g

Healthy modifications: Replace ghee with oil.

USAL

MOTH BEAN CURRY

Preparation time: 20 mins; Cooking time: 25 mins

This curry is used to make usal pav (p. 212) and missal pav (p. 214).

Ingredients for 2 servings

4 tbsp moth beans (matki)

The spice paste

2 onions, roughly chopped

4 cloves garlic, roughly chopped

2" piece ginger, roughly chopped

3 green chillies, roughly chopped

The gravy

2 tbsp oil

½ tsp red chilli powder

¼ tsp turmeric powder

½ tsp cumin powder

½ tsp coriander powder

¼ tsp pepper powder

½ tsp aniseed powder

5 tomatoes, puréed

1 tsp garam masala powder (clove, cinnamon, black cardamom, caraway seeds, bay leaf)

A pinch of salt or to taste

The garnish

2 tbsp coriander leaves, chopped

4 lime wedges

(Recipe Cont.)

Method

Wash the beans and soak them in water overnight. Rinse well and drain.

Put the beans in a pressure cooker with 2 cups of water. Pressure-cook the beans on low heat for 10 mins after the cooker reaches full pressure.

Open the cooker after it returns to normal pressure.

Grind the spice paste ingredients to a fine consistency.

Put the oil in a pan on medium heat. Add the spice paste and sauté for a few mins.

Add all the spice powders, except the garam masala powder, and sauté for a second.

Pour in the tomato purée and bring to a boil on high heat. Continue to boil for a few mins.

Mix in the beans, garam masala powder and the salt and simmer on medium heat, till it thickens.

Garnish with coriander leaves and squeeze lime juice over it.

Serve with pav as usal pav or missal pav.

Nutritive values for 1 serving: Calories: 389.0kcal; Carbohydrates: 42.3g; Protein: 13.1g; Fat: 18.4g; Minerals: 3.7g; Fibre: 6.5g

DAL MAKHANI
Creamy mixed dal

Preparation time: 25 mins; Cooking time: 25 mins

Dal makhani, is a popular dish in Punjabi cuisine.

Ingredients for 2 servings

2 tbsp whole black gram (sabut urad)

1 tbsp small red kidney beans (rajma)

1 tbsp any other mixed dals

The spice paste

1 tbsp cashew nuts, soaked in water for 1 hour

2 medium-sized onions, puréed

2 tsp ginger-garlic-green chilli paste

The gravy

1 tbsp home-made white butter

½ tsp red chilli powder

¼ tsp black pepper powder

¼ tsp aniseed powder

¼ tsp turmeric powder

½ tsp coriander powder

½ tsp cumin powder

3 tomatoes, puréed

½ tsp garam masala powder (clove, cinnamon, black cardamom, caraway seeds, bay leaf)

A pinch of green cardamom powder

1 tsp sugar

A pinch of salt or to taste

2 tbsp cream

(Recipe Cont.)

Method

Wash the dals and soak them in water overnight.

Drain and rinse thoroughly.

Put the dals in a pressure cooker with 2 cups of water. Pressure-cook the dal on low heat for 10 mins after the cooker reaches full pressure.

Open the cooker after it returns to normal pressure.

Drain the cashew nuts and grind to make a paste.

Mix the cashew nut paste with the other spice paste ingredients in a bowl.

Put the butter in a pan on medium heat. Add the spice paste and sauté for a few mins, till light brown.

Add all the spice powders, except the garam masala powder and cardamom powder. Mix well and sauté for a second.

Pour in the tomatoes and cook on high heat, till the contents leave the sides of the pan and the butter floats to the surface.

Add the cooked dals with the garam masala powder, cardamom powder, sugar and salt. Mix well and cook on high heat for a few mins.

Stir in the cream and remove from heat.

Serve with any Mughlai flatbread.

Nutritive values for 1 serving: Calories: 308.0kcal; Carbohydrates: 33.8g; Protein: 11.6g; Fat: 13.3g; Minerals: 2.1g; Fibre: 2.7g

Healthy modifications: Replace cashew nuts with walnut powder. • Replace butter with oil. • Use light instead of heavy cream • Replace cream with curd.

DAL TADKA

Seasoned red gram

Preparation time: 10 mins; Cooking time: 20 mins

Dal tadka is a light, seasoned dal usually prepared with red gram.

Ingredients for 2 servings

4 tbsp red gram (tuvar/arhar dal)

1 medium-sized onion, chopped

1 tomato, chopped

¼ tsp turmeric powder

A pinch of asafoetida powder

2 tsp dried fenugreek leaves

A pinch of salt or to taste

1 lime

The seasoning

2 tsp ghee

½ tsp mustard seeds

½ tsp cumin seeds

2 dried red chillies, broken

2 green chillies, chopped

1" piece ginger, grated

3 cloves garlic, chopped

The garnish

2 tbsp coriander leaves, chopped

(Recipe Cont.)

Method

Wash the dal and put it into a pressure cooker with 2 cups of water. Pressure-cook the dal on low heat for 10 mins after the cooker reaches full pressure.

Open the cooker after it returns to normal pressure.

Put the ghee for the seasoning in a pan on medium heat. Sauté the seasoning ingredients, till the mustard seeds splutter.

Add the onion and tomato and sauté for a few mins.

Mix in the dal, spice powders, fenugreek leaves and the salt.

Mix well and simmer for a few mins.

Squeeze in lime juice and garnish with coriander leaves.

Serve hot with any paratha.

Nutritive values for 1 serving: Calories: 200.0kcal; Carbohydrates: 25.2g; Protein: 9.1g; Fat: 6.9g; Minerals: 1.9g; Fibre: 2.0g

Healthy modifications: Replace ghee with oil.

PANCHMEL DAL

Five pulses gravy

Preparation time: 20 mins; Cooking time : 20 mins

Panchmel dal is a very popular dish served with flatbreads in Rajasthani cuisine. Five dals are used to prepare this dish: husked, split mung, red gram (tuvar/arhar), Bengal gram (chana dal), Egyptian lentils (masoor dal)and black gram (urad dal). It is served with churma (p. 160) and baati (p. 188) as well as with bafla (p. 189).

Ingredients for 2 servings

4 tbsp mixed dals

1 onion, chopped

1 tsp ginger-green chilli paste

A pinch of asafoetida powder

½ tsp turmeric powder

½ tsp red chilli powder

Salt to taste

1 tbsp lime juice

The seasoning

2 tsp ghee

½ tsp cumin seeds

½ tsp mustard seeds

2 green chillies, chopped

The garnish

2 tsp coriander leaves, chopped

(Recipe Cont.)

Method

Wash the dals and pressure-cook them with 1 cup of water on low heat for 5 mins after the cooker reaches full pressure.

Heat the ghee for the seasoning in a pan and sauté the seasoning ingredients, till the mustard seeds splutter.

Add the onion and ginger-green chilli paste and sauté for a minute.

Mix in the cooked dals, spice powders and salt.

Cook for a minute, sprinkle in the lime juice and mix well.

Garnish with chopped coriander leaves.

Serve it as dal baati churma or dal bafla.

Nutritive values for 1 serving: Calories: 213.0kcal; Carbohydrates: 27.6g; Protein: 10.1g; Fat: 6.8g; Minerals: 1.6g; Fibre: 1.8g.

ANDA CURRY

Egg curry

Preparation time: 10 mins; Cooking time: 25 mins

Anda curry is served with rice or flatbreads and is also used as the base to make egg biryani.

Ingredients for 2 servings

2 tsp oil

1 cup chopped spring onions

2 tsp ginger-garlic-green chilli paste

¼ tsp turmeric powder

¼ tsp red chilli powder

¼ tsp black pepper powder

¼ tsp aniseed powder

½ tsp coriander powder

½ tsp cumin powder

4 tomatoes, puréed

½ tsp garam masala powder (clove, cinnamon, black cardamom, caraway seeds, bay leaf)

A pinch of green cardamom powder

A pinch of salt or to taste

1 tbsp cream

2 eggs, hard-boiled

(Recipe Cont.)

Method

Put the oil in a pan on medium heat. Add the spring onions and sauté, till light brown.

Add the ginger-garlic-green chilli paste and sauté for a minute.

Mix in all the spice powders, except the garam masala powder and cardamom powder, and sauté for a second.

Add the tomato purée, garam masala powder, cardamom powder and salt.

Bring to a boil on high heat. Continue to boil, till the gravy thickens.

Add the cream, mix and remove from heat.

Slice the eggs vertically into 2 halves and place them in a serving dish.

Spoon the gravy over them and serve hot with lachha paratha (p. 56).

Nutritive values for 1 serving: Calories: 197.0kcal; Carbohydrate: 9.7g; Protein: 8.7g; Fat: 13.6g; Minerals: 1.4g; Fibre: 1.5g

Healthy modifications: Replace cream with thick curd.

MAKHANI MURGH

Butter chicken

Preparation time: 30 mins; Cooking time: 30 mins

Makhani murgh or shahi murgh korma, is served in Punjabi and Mughlai cuisines.

Ingredients for 2 servings

8 chicken pieces

The marinade

1 cup thick curd

¼ tsp turmeric powder

½ tsp red chilli powder

½ tsp coriander powder

½ tsp cumin powder

¼ tsp black pepper powder

¼ tsp aniseed powder

1 tsp garam masala powder (clove, cinnamon, black cardamom, caraway seeds, bay leaf)

A pinch of green cardamom powder

The spice paste

2 tbsp mixed nuts

2 tsp ginger-garlic-green chilli paste

The curry

2 tbsp home-made white butter

2 medium-sized onions, minced

4 tomatoes, puréed

A pinch of salt or to taste

2 tbsp cream

The garnish

1 tsp cream

(Recipe Cont.)

Method

Wash the chicken and drain thoroughly.

Combine all the marinade ingredients in a bowl and mix well.

Add the chicken and mix, till well coated. Keep aside to marinate for 1 hour.

Soak the nuts in water for 1 hour.

Drain and grind to make a paste. Mix in the ginger-garlic-green chilli paste.

Put the butter in a pan on medium heat. Add the onions and sauté, till light brown.

Add the spice paste and sauté for a minute.

Pour in the tomato purée and bring to a boil on high heat. Continue to boil, till the contents leave the sides of the pan and the butter floats to the surface.

Add the chicken with the marinade and bring to a boil, stirring continuously.

Mix in ½ cup of water and the salt, cover the pan, and cook on medium heat, till the chicken is tender and the gravy is thick.

Stir in 2 tbsp of cream and remove from heat.

Garnish with 1 tsp cream and serve with tandoori roti.

Nutritive values for 1 serving: Calories: 383.0kcal; Carbohydrates: 17.0g; Protein: 33.6g; Fat: 19.6g; Minerals: 3.2g; Fibre: 2.2g

Healthy modifications: Use chicken breast, which is the leanest meat. • Limit the use of nuts in the dish. • Use light instead of heavy cream. • Replace butter with oil. • Limit the use of fat in the dish.

MUTTON MASALA

Spicy lamb curry

Preparation time: 30 mins; Cooking time: 30 mins

Mutton masala can be used as a base for biryani or served with flatbreads, particularly in Mughlai cuisine.

Ingredients for 2 servings

200g mutton pieces

The marinade

½ cup curd

¼ tsp turmeric powder

½ tsp black pepper powder

½ tsp red chilli powder

½ tsp dried mango powder

A pinch of salt or to taste

The curry

1 tbsp oil

2 onions, puréed

2 tsp ginger-garlic-green chilli paste

¼ tsp red chilli powder

½ tsp cumin powder

½ tsp coriander powder

¼ tsp aniseed powder

A pinch of nutmeg and mace

5 tomatoes, chopped

1 tsp garam masala powder (clove, cinnamon, black cardamom, caraway seeds, bay leaf)

A pinch of green cardamom powder

A pinch of salt or to taste

The garnish

2 tsp coriander leaves, chopped

(Recipe Cont.)

Method

Wash the mutton and drain thoroughly.

Mix the marinade ingredients in a bowl.

Add the mutton and mix, till well coated. Leave aside to marinate for 1 hour.

Put the oil in a pressure cooker on medium heat. Add the onions and sauté, till light brown.

Add the ginger-garlic-green chilli paste and sauté for a minute.

Sprinkle in all the spice powders, except the garam masala powder and cardamom powder, and sauté for a second.

Add the tomatoes and sauté, till the contents leave the sides of the pan.

Mix in the mutton with the marinade and sauté for 5 mins, till light brown.

Pour in 1 cup of water and mix in the garam masala powder, cardamom powder and salt.

Pressure-cook the mutton on low heat for 10 mins after the cooker reaches full pressure.

Open the cooker and continue to cook on low heat, till the gravy thickens.

Garnish with coriander leaves and serve with any Mughlai flatbread.

Nutritive values for 1 serving: Calories: 294.0kcal; Carbohydrates: 15.7g; Protein: 26.1g; Fat: 14.0g; Minerals: 2.8g; Fibre: 2.7g

Healthy modifications: Select lean portions of meat.

GLOSSARY OF INGREDIENTS

ENGLISH	HINDI
CEREALS	
Barley	Jau
Bread	Double roti
Finger millet	Mandua/ragi
Indian barnyard millet	Jhangora
Italian millet or foxtail millet	Kangni
Jowar	Jaur
Kodo millet	Kodra
Little millet	Kutti
Maize	Makkai
Oat meal	Jav
Pearl millet	Bajra
Proso millet	Barri
Rice, parboiled	Usna chawal
Rice, raw	Chawal
Rice bran	Konda
Rice flakes	Chewra
Rice, puffed	Murmurra
Rye	Nachni
Sago	Sabudana
Semolina	Sooji
Vermicelli	Sevian
Wheat	Gehun
Wheat bran	Gehun ka chokar
Wheat flour, refined	Maida
Wheat flour, whole	Gehun ka atta
Wheat germ	Gehun ka tilula
Wheat, bulgur	Dalia

<table>
<tr><th>ENGLISH</th><th>HINDI</th></tr>
</table>

CONDIMENTS AND SPICES

English	Hindi
Aniseed	Saunf
Asafoetida	Hing
Black pepper	Kali mirch
Caraway seeds	Shahi jeera
Cardamom, black	Kala elaichi
Cardamom, green	Hara elaichi
Carom seeds	Ajwain
Chilli, green	Hari mirch
Chilli, red	Lal mirch
Cloves	Lavang
Coriander seeds	Dhania
Cumin seeds	Jeera
Dried fenugreek leaves	Kasoori methi
Dried mango powder	Amchoor
Fenugreek seeds	Methi
Garlic	Lassoon
Ginger	Adrak
Mace	Javitri
Nigella seeds	Kalonji
Nutmeg	Jaiphal
Poppy seeds	Khus-khus
Salt	Namak
Tamarind	Imli
Turmeric	Haldi

FATS AND OILS

English	Hindi
Butter	Makkhan
Coconut oil	Nariyal ka tel
Ghee	Ghee
Groundnut oil	Mungphali ka tel
Hydrogenated oil	Vanaspati
Mustard oil	Rai ka tel
Safflower oil	Kardi tel
Sesame oil	Til ka tel
Sunflower oil	Surya mukhi tel

FRUITS

English	Hindi
Apple	Seb
Apricot	Khoomani
Banana	Kela
Cherries	Gilas
Dates	Khajur
Fig	Anjeer
Grapes	Angoor
Jackfruit	Kathal
Lime	Nimbu
Mango	Aam
Orange	Santra
Papaya	Papita
Peach	Adu
Pear	Nashpati
Pineapple	Ananas
Raisins	Kishmish
Tomato	Tamatar
Water chestnut	Shingada

MILK AND MILK PRODUCTS

English	Hindi
Buttermilk	Lassi
Cheese	Kheer
Cottage cheese	Paneer
Cream	Malai
Curd	Dahi
Milk solids	Mawa/khoya

ENGLISH	HINDI
Milk, buffalo	Bhains ka doodh
Milk, cow	Gai ka doodh

NUTS, AND SEEDS

ENGLISH	HINDI
Almond	Badaam
Amaranth seeds	Rajkheera/ramdana
Cashew nut	Kaju
Coconut	Nariyal
Dried lotus seeds	Makhana
Flax seeds	Alsi
Groundnut/peanut	Moong phalli
Mustard seeds	Rai
Pistachio	Pista
Pumpkin seeds	Kaddu ka beej
Sesame seeds	Til
Walnut	Akhrot
Water melon seeds	Tarbuj ka beej

PULSES AND LEGUMES

ENGLISH	HINDI
Bengal gram, roasted	Bhuna chana
Bengal gram, split	Chana dal
Bengal gram, whole	Sabut chana
Black gram, split	Urad dal
Chickpeas	Kabuli chana
Cow peas	Lobia
Field beans	Sem
Green peas (dry)	Matar
Horse gram	Kulthi
Kidney beans	Rajma
Lentil	Masur dal
Moth beans	Matki
Red gram	Arhar/tuvar dal
Soya bean	Bhat

SEAFOOD, MEAT AND POULTRY

ENGLISH	HINDI
Chicken	Murgh
Egg	Anda
Fish	Machi
Mutton	Bakri ka ghosht
Prawns	Chingri

SWEETENERS

ENGLISH	HINDI
Cane sugar	Cheeni
Jaggery	Gud

VEGETABLES — LEAFY

ENGLISH	HINDI
Amaranth	Chauli saag
Brussels sprouts	Chhoti gobhi
Cabbage	Band gobhi
Celery leaves	Celery patta
Chenopodium	Bathua saag
Colocasia leaves	Arvi ka saag
Coriander leaves	Hara dhania
Curry leaves	Kadipatta
Dill leaves	Sua
Fenugreek leaves	Methi saag
Lettuce	Salad ka patta
Mint	Pudina
Mustard leaves	Sarson ka saag
Radish leaves	Mooli saag
Red spinach	Poi (mayalu)
Sour spinach	Chuka
Spinach	Paalak
Turnip greens	Shalgam ka saag

VEGETABLES — ROOT AND STEM

English	Hindi
Beetroot	Chukandar
Carrot	Gaajar
Colocasia	Arvi
Onion	Pyaaz
Potato	Aloo
Radish	Muli
Sweet potato	Shakarkand
Tapioca	Shimla aloo
Turnip	Shalgam
Water chestnut	Shingara
Yam	Zimikand/suran

VEGETABLES — OTHER

English	Hindi
Ashgourd	Petha
Aubergine/ brinjal	Baingan
Bitter gourd	Karela
Bottle gourd	Lauki/dudhi
Broad beans	Bakla
Capsicum	Shimla mirchi
Cauliflower	Phul gobhi

English	Hindi
Chow-chow marrow	Phuti kakudi
Cluster beans	Guar ki phalli
Cucumber	Khira
Double beans	Chastang
Drumstick	Saijan ki phalli
Field beans	Sem
French beans	French beans
Knoll-khol	Kohl-rabi
Leeks	Vilayiti pyaz
Mango green	Kacha aam
Mushrooms	Tila chhattoo
Okra/ fadies finger	Bhindi
Plantain, cooking	Kachcha kela
Plantain flower	Kele ka phool
Pumpkin	Kaddu
Ridge gourd	Torai
Round gourd	Tinda
Snake gourd	Chachinda
Spring onion	Hara pyaaz

www.ingramcontent.com/pod-product-compliance
Lightning Source LLC
LaVergne TN
LVHW080012150726
843364LV00042B/1519